RULES AND REPRESENTATIONS

WOODBRIDGE LECTURES
DELIVERED AT COLUMBIA UNIVERSITY
IN NOVEMBER OF 1978

NUMBER ELEVEN

RULES AND REPRESENTATIONS

Noam Chomsky

1980
Columbia University Press
New York

Library of Congress Cataloging in Publication Data

Chomsky, Noam.
    Rules and representations.
    (Woodbridge lectures delivered at Columbia University ;
no. 11, 1978)
    Includes bibliographical references and index.
    1. Languages—Philosophy.   2. Psycholinguistics.
I. Title.   II. Series: Woodbridge lectures, Columbia
University ; no. 11, 1978.
P106.C544   301.2′1   79-26145
ISBN 0-231-04826-2

Columbia University Press
New York   Guildford, Surrey
Copyright © 1980 Noam Chomsky
All rights reserved
Printed in the United States of America
10 9 8 7 6 5 4 3 2

Contents

Preface

The first four chapters of this book are based on lectures delivered as the Woodbridge Lectures at Columbia University in November 1978 and, in a somewhat different form, as the Kant Lectures at Stanford University in January 1979. Chapter 5 is a slightly modified version of a lecture delivered at a Cornell University symposium in honor of Eric Lenneberg in April 1976. The final chapter is the text of the Edith Weigert Lecture, sponsored by the Forum on Psychiatry and the Humanities at the Washington School of Psychiatry, November 1976.

I am much indebted to Ned Block, Harry Bracken, Norbert Hornstein, Justin Leiber, Julius Moravcsik and Sidney Morgenbesser for very helpful comments on an earlier draft of this manuscript, and to them as well as Sylvain Bromberger, Roy Edgley, Jerry Fodor, Gilbert Harman, Anthony Kenny, Thomas Nagel and Bernard Rollin, and also many students and colleagues at MIT, Columbia, Stanford and elsewhere for very valuable critical comment and discussion that have frequently caused me to rethink my views on questions considered here. I have left chapters 5 and 6 in virtually their original form instead of eliminating some redundancy. This work was supported in part by a fellowship grant for the year 1978–79 from the National Endowment for the Humanities, to whom I would like to express my gratitude. I am also grateful to Bonnie Wilker for extensive assistance in preparation of the final manuscript.

Noam Chomsky

Cambridge, Mass.
February 1979

Part I

1

Mind and Body

IN THESE LECTURES, I would like to explore a number of issues relating to human cognitive capacities and the mental structures that serve as the vehicles for the exercise of these capacities. Plainly, this formulation of a problem embodies assumptions that are far from clear and are highly controversial insofar as they are clear. I will try to make them clearer, and, I hope more plausible, as I proceed. In the end, the best way to clarify these assumptions and to evaluate them is to construct specific models guided by them in particular domains, then to ask how these models fare when interpreted as explanatory theories. If the leading ideas are appropriate, they will be sharpened and justified by the success of explanatory theories that develop them in a specific way. I will not attempt a systematic presentation of such a model here, but will discuss properties of some that are being investigated, though in technical studies they are not presented in these terms, which, I want to suggest, are the appropriate terms. The cognitive domain that will primarily concern me is human language. The reason for the choice is in part personal, relating to limits of my own understanding. I think it is fair to say, however, that the issues are more easily formulated and better understood in connection with human language than other domains of human cognition—which is not to say that they are clearly formulated or well understood. There are some who would virtually identify the study of language and the study of mind, Quine for example.[1] This is not my own view.

I would like to think of linguistics as that part of psychology that focuses its attention on one specific cognitive domain and one faculty of mind, the language faculty. Psychology, in the sense of this discussion, is concerned, at the very least, with human capacities to act and to interpret experience, and with the mental structures that underlie these capacities and their exercise; and more deeply, with the second-order capacity to construct these mental structures, and the structures that underlie these second-order capacities.[2]

The term "capacity" is used with varying degrees of strictness. When I say that a person has the capacity to do so-and-so at a particular time, I mean that as physically and mentally constituted at that time, he needs no further instruction, training, physical development, etc., to do so-and-so if placed under appropriate external conditions. Thus a person who does not know how to swim lacks the capacity to swim, in this sense. Similarly, the Olympic swimming champion lacks the capacity to swim if his arms and legs are amputated or broken, but not if he is tied to a chair or asleep or absorbed in a book. Having the capacity to do so-and-so is not the same as knowing how to do so-and-so; in particular, there is a crucial intellectual component in "knowing how."[3] We might distinguish further between what one is able to do at will and what falls within one's capacity, though we cannot do it at will. Thus Babe Ruth had the capacity to hit a home run, but not at will, whereas he had the capacity to lift a bat at will.[4]

There is also a second-order sense of "capacity," as when we say that any normal child has the capacity to swim, or to run a mile, or to speak Italian, if only given the appropriate training or opportunities for development. In this sense, the child does not have the capacity to fly and other (terrestrial) organisms do not have the capacity to speak Italian.[5] Sometimes the term is used more loosely, as when we speak of "capacities" in the sense of "mental faculties." The distinctions can be sharpened, but this should be enough for my purposes here.

To begin with, let us assume that it makes sense to say, as we normally do, that each person knows his or her language, that you and I know English for example, that this knowledge is in part shared among us and represented somehow in our minds, ultimately in our brains, in structures that we can hope to characterize abstractly, and in principle quite concretely, in terms of physical mechanisms. When I use such terms as "mind," "mental representation," "mental computation," and the like, I am keeping to the level of abstract characterization of the properties of certain physical mechanisms, as yet almost entirely unknown. There is no further ontological import to such references to mind or mental representations and acts. In the same way, a theory of human vision might be formulated in concrete terms, referring, say, to specific cells in the visual cortex and their properties; or it might be formulated abstractly in terms of certain modes of representation (say, images or stick figure sketches), computations on such representations, organizing principles that determine the nature of such representations and rules, and so on. In the latter case, the inquiry belongs to the study of mind, in the terminology that I will adopt, though it need in no sense imply the existence of entities removed from the physical world.

It is perhaps worth stressing, in this connection, that the no-

tion of "physical world" is open and evolving. No one believes
that bodies are Cartesian automata[6] or that physical systems are
subject to the constraints of Cartesian mechanism, or that physics has come to an end. It may be that contemporary natural
science already provides principles adequate for the understanding of mind. Or perhaps principles now unknown enter
into the functioning of the human or animal minds, in which
case the notion of "physical body" must be extended, as has
often happened in the past, to incorporate entities and principles of hitherto unrecognized character. Then much of the so-
called "mind-body problem" will be solved in something like
the way in which the problem of the motion of the heavenly
bodies was solved, by invoking principles that seemed incomprehensible or even abhorrent to the scientific imagination
of an earlier generation.[7]

It may be that the operative principles are not only unknown
but even humanly unknowable because of limitations on our
own intellectual capacities, a possibility that cannot be ruled out
a priori; our minds are fixed biological systems with their intrinsic scope and limits. We can distinguish in principle between
"problems," which lie within these limits and can be ap-
proached by human science with some hope of success, and
what we might call "mysteries," questions that simply lie
beyond the reach of our minds, structured and organized as
they are, either absolutely beyond those limits or at so far a
remove from anything that we can comprehend with requisite
facility that they will never be incorporated within explanatory
theories intelligible to humans. We may hope that the questions
we pursue fall into the domain of "problems" in this sense, but
there is no guarantee that this is so.

It might be that some of the questions that have resisted any significant insight, for example, questions having to do with will and choice, would be accessible to an intelligence differently organized than ours, though they will forever remain mysteries to a human mind. Descartes apparently took a still stronger position: that we may not "have intelligence enough" to comprehend how free action can be indeterminate though "we are so conscious of the liberty and indifference which exists in us, that there is nothing that we comprehend more clearly and perfectly" and "it would be absurd to doubt that of which we inwardly experience and perceive as existing within ourselves, just because we do not comprehend a matter which from its nature we know to be incomprehensible."[8] His position is stronger because he felt that we *know* the matter to be incomprehensible and that the limits are not those of *human* intelligence, a specific biological system, but rather of undifferentiated mind, not part of the biological world at all.[9]

Descartes's position is explained by his expositor La Forge who observed that "by instinct, and by the actions attributable thereto, be it in man or beast, [Descartes] merely means . . . that secret disposition of the invisible parts of the body of the animal, and principally of its brain, according to which, after being imprinted by an object, man feels incited and inclined—and the animal feels compelled—to make appropriate actions and movements." Man, as distinct from animals, is not "compelled" but only "incited and inclined" because "the Soul, despite the disposition of the body, can prevent these movements when it has the ability to reflect on its actions and when the body is able to obey."[10] But how the Soul allows us to choose to do or to reject that to which we are "incited and inclined" remains an impenetrable mystery, in this view. Rousseau, developing Cartesian ideas in an original way, remarked that "Nature commands every animal, and the beast obeys. Man feels the same impetus, but he realizes that he is free to acquiesce or resist; and it is above all in the consciousness of this freedom that the spirituality of his soul is shown." And "the power of willing, or rather of choosing," as well as "the sentiment of this power," lies beyond the bounds of physical explanation, he believed. This essential capacity of the human to act as a "free agent," able to choose to follow or to disregard "the rule that is prescribed to it" by nature lies at the heart of his libertarian social philosophy.[11]

In Cartesian rationalism or the romanticism of Rousseau, it is not denied that we can profitably study motivation, contingencies that guide action, drives and instinct, control of behavior, and many similar topics, and even take these factors in behavior, thought and feeling to be reducible in principle to biology. But their view is that these factors do not "compel" but only "incite and incline"—the freedom to choose remains, and remains inexplicable in these (or any) terms.

A narrower version of this thesis seems to me not unreasonable.[12] The theoretical physicist Stephen Weinberg recently made a similar point in discussing what Husserl called "the Galilean style" in physics, that is, "making abstract mathematical models of the universe to which at least the physicists give a higher degree of reality than they accord the ordinary world of sensation." He points out that

it is remarkable that physics in this Galilean style should work. The universe does not seem to have been prepared with human beings in mind, and the idea that humans can build mathematical models of the universe and find that they work is remarkable. Of course, one may doubt that the Galilean style will continue to be successful; one may question whether the mathematical ability of human beings

can penetrate to the level of the laws of nature. I recall a statement by
J. B. S. Haldane in which he said, in effect, that the universe is not only
a good deal queerer than we know; it is a good deal queerer than we can
know. Sometimes I believe that is true. But suppose it is not. Suppose
that by pursuing physics in the Galilean style we ultimately come to
an understanding of the laws of nature, of the roots of the chains of
explanation of the natural world. That would truly be the queerest
thing of all. [13]

These remarks seem to me quite apt. It might be that physics
with its various offshoots, developed through inquiry in the
Galilean style, is a remarkable historical accident resulting from
chance convergence of biological properties of the human mind
with some aspect of the real world. [14] Whether this proves true
or not, we have no present alternative to pursuing the "Galilean
style" in the natural sciences at least.

Some might argue, perhaps along Vicoesque lines, that we
can do still better in the "human sciences" by pursuing a different path. I do not mean to disparage such possibilities. It is
not unlikely, for example, that literature will forever give far
deeper insight into what is sometimes called "the full human
person" than any mode of scientific inquiry can hope to do. But
I am interested here in a different question: To what extent and
in what ways can inquiry in something like "the Galilean style"
yield insight and understanding of the roots of human nature in
the cognitive domain? Can we hope to move beyond superfici-
ality by a readiness to undertake perhaps far-reaching idealization and to construct abstract models that are accorded more
significance than the ordinary world of sensation, and correspondingly, by readiness to tolerate unexplained phenomena or
even as yet unexplained counterevidence to theoretical constructions that have achieved a certain degree of explanatory

depth in some limited domain, much as Galileo did not abandon his enterprise because he was unable to give a coherent explanation for the fact that objects do not fly off the earth's surface?[15] Perhaps such an approach will prove to have narrow
limits, either because of the nature of its object or the nature of
those components of human intelligence that underlie what is
sometimes misleadingly called "the scientific method"—there is
no known "method" for inquiry, in any very useful sense of the
term—but there is no reason to be unduly pessimistic on this
score. As for the matter of unexplained apparent counterevidence, if someone were to descend from heaven with the
absolute truth about language or some other cognitive faculty,
this theory would doubtless be confronted at once with all sorts
of problems and "counterexamples," if only because we do not
yet understand the natural bounds of these particular faculties
and because partially understood data are so easily miscon-
strued.

We might tarry for a moment on the reference to Vico, and
the view that the products of our mind are "made by men" and
hence accessible to an approach quite different from that of the
natural sciences, one that perhaps yields a higher degree of certainty. Such a view has often been expressed in one or another
way, for example, by Richard Rorty, who writes that "it is easier
to understand biological or sociological questions about how we
managed to make the particular language we have made, or
how we teach it to our young, than questions about how anything could do what we have made language do."[16] This is part
of an argument that leads him to various conclusions about language and philosophy, in particular, the conclusion that they
have little to do with one another and that philosophy has little
to do at all. There are two crucial factual assumptions here: that

we have "made" our language and that our children come to know our language because we teach it to them. The second is not true in general (if ever), as a matter of fact. The first seems at best quite misleadingly formulated. Have we, as individuals, "made" our language? That is, have you or I "made" English? That seems either senseless or wrong. We had no choice at all as to the language we acquired; it simply developed in our minds by virtue of our internal constitution and environment. Was the language "made" by our remote ancestors? It is difficult to make any sense of such a view. In fact, there is no more reason to think of language as "made" than there is to think of the human visual system and the various forms that it assumes as "made by us," and even if it were true that our language had at one time been "made" in some sense that has yet to be explained, that would not alter the crucial fact that for each of us, it develops as a consequence of the way we are now constituted, when we are placed in the appropriate external environment.

I am interested, then, in pursuing some aspects of the study of mind, in particular, such aspects as lend themselves to inquiry through the construction of abstract explanatory theories that may involve substantial idealization and will be justified, if at all, by success in providing insight and explanations. From this point of view, substantial coverage of data is not a particularly significant result; it can be attained in many ways, and the result is not very informative as to the correctness of the principles employed. It will be more significant if we show that certain fairly far-reaching principles interact to provide an explanation for crucial facts—the crucial nature of these facts deriving from their relation to proposed explanatory theories. It is a mistake to argue, as many do, that by adopting this point of view one is disregarding data. Data that remain unexplained by some coherent theory will continue to be described in whatever descriptive scheme one chooses, but will simply not be considered very important for the moment.

Later on, I want to turn to some arguments that have been raised against proceeding in this way in the particular case of language. Right now I would like to consider certain arguments that bear on psychology in general. These are often presented with regard to the theory of meaning, but the form of argument, if valid at all, would apply far more generally.

Consider, for example, the argument against what is called "the museum myth." Here is a recent version by Jonathan Lear:

> Quine, like Wittgenstein, categorically rejects the notion that meaning can essentially involve anything private to an individual, such as a hidden mental image. This is the myth of the museum—that words name specimen mental objects—which Quine rightly urges us to reject. If we are to explain language-mastery, and thus the meaning our words and sentences have, we must do it on the basis of our experience: the sensory evidence of all types to which we have over time been exposed and our sensitivity to it. Positing interior mental objects that are named by words only gets in the way of an explanation, for it merely papers over the gaps in our understanding of how language-mastery is acquired.[17]

I am not concerned here with the conclusion of the argument—perhaps it is indeed a mistake to posit meanings as mental objects for some other reason—but rather with its force. The argument turns on no specific properties of language-mastery or its acquisition as compared with other aspects of cognitive development.[18] The fact that the interior mental objects in question are "named by words" adds no special force to the argument. If positing such interior mental objects "merely papers over gaps in our understanding" because language-mastery must be "explained . . . on the basis of our experience," then the same should be true of interior mental objects quite generally, whether or not they are named by words. Hence if the argument has any force it should apply as well to all types of rules and representations for language, not simply to meanings; and in fact to psychological theory quite generally. So it seems that we are presented with an argument against mental representations quite generally, and many of those who denounce the museum myth—Quine and Wittgenstein at least—seem happy with this conclusion. But does the argument establish anything at all? Not until something is added to explain why positing interior mental objects gets in the way of explanation and papers over gaps in our understanding of the acquisition of language-mastery, and furthermore why this must be the case. In the absence of such additional steps, what we have is a pseudo-argument against theoretical entities. Suppose that we can find laws and principles stated in terms of interior mental objects and can show that these have explanatory power with regard to the acquisition of language mastery and its exercise. Nothing in the arguments advanced against the museum myth based on the fact that language-mastery must be grounded in experience shows that this is impossible. That meanings of words or other putative mental elements must be "explained" on the basis of experience is indisputable in one sense, namely, the sense in which the positing of theoretical entities in any domain has to be justified in terms of empirical fact. Beyond this, such arguments against the museum myth establish nothing.

It is worth noting that some of those who inveigh against the museum myth in the specific case of the theory of meaning nevertheless accept the existence of other sorts of mental repre-

sentation. For example, there is interesting recent work suggesting that we have images that share fundamental properties with
pictorial representation.[19] These are mental images in the sense
of this discussion; how they are physically represented is unknown and irrelevant in the present context. Hilary Putnam,
who firmly rejects the museum myth, accepts as plausible the
conclusion "that the brain stores *images*" and also insists that
"On any plausible theory" the brain does "something like computation," from which it follows that a theory of mind should
include some notion of mental representation and rule.[20] Similarly, he would surely not dismiss out of hand theories of vision
that involve analysis in terms of abstract mental computations
and elements that enter into them. I will turn to Putnam's own
argument against the "myth" in a moment, merely noting here
that he will have to introduce some special considerations concerning language or other areas of psychological description for
which the "myth" is wrong, if he wishes to maintain the view
that mental images and mental computations can figure in
"plausible theory" for psychology (but see note 20). In any
event, no general argument based on the fact that knowledge of
language arises from experience will carry any weight against
the positing of interior mental objects, unless one is willing to
abandon theory altogether, in every domain.[21]

As the references cited make explicit, all of this is held to
relate to Quine's thesis of "indeterminacy of translation," which
has been widely discussed for the past twenty years. This thesis,
as Quine has emphasized, applies not just to translation between languages but to one's own language, and not just to
problems of meaning but to any theoretical move in linguistics,
for example, the postulation of phrase boundaries, as when
someone tries to show that in the sentence "the man you met

read the book I wrote," the two substrings "the man you met" and "the book I wrote" are phrases, and furthermore phrases of the same category, whereas the substring "met read the" is no phrase at all. According to Quine, there is no fact of the matter in such cases as these, and therefore no sense to the construction of a theory of language and mind that tries to establish that the rules of grammar assign phrases in one or another way in mental representations.[22] Furthermore, as Putnam insists, the thesis holds as well as in any domain of psychological description. His "main point," he writes, is that "indeterminacy of translation is equivalent to indeterminacy of the transition from functional organization (in the sense of machine table, or whatever) *to* psychological description."[23]

I will not review Quine's various formulations of the indeterminacy thesis or his arguments for it. I have done so elsewhere, arguing that nothing follows beyond the observation that theories are underdetermined by evidence, and that Quine's efforts to show otherwise have not only been futile but lead to internal inconsistency.[24] Consider, then, Putnam's more recent formulation, in his 1976 John Locke lectures. First, let me clear up a misunderstanding. Putnam believes, as Quine does too,[25] that I regard the indeterminacy thesis as false; on the contrary, I regard it as true and uninteresting.[26] Putnam believes that what he calls my " 'realism' about psychology," based on alleged rejection of this thesis, "*ignores the existence of . . . pairs of equivalent descriptions*,"[27] but that too is incorrect. Putnam's example is the familiar one: two descriptions of a person's "psychology," one of which holds that he takes a presented stimulation to be a rabbit and another which asserts that he takes it to be an undetached rabbit part. The possibility of such alternatives clearly exists, but—along with the general thesis—is obvious and uninteresting. What is really at stake is only what Donald Hockney has called "the bifurcation thesis," that is, the thesis that theories of meaning, language and much of psychology are faced with a problem of indeterminacy that is qualitatively different in some way from the underdetermination of theory by evidence in the natural sciences.[28] For this conclusion, no argument at all has been presented; and as Hockney shows, the bifurcation thesis leads to contradiction within Quine's system.

One can easily see how the general argument offered against the "museum myth" might be used to support the bifurcation thesis. Suppose, as in Quine's presentation, that we grant a complete knowledge of physics. A person has certain sensory experience, and the psychologist proceeds to attribute to him certain mental structure, including knowledge of the meanings of words, the position of phrase boundaries, and so on. But this will seem illegitimate, if we make the fallacious move just noted, concluding from the fact that meanings, phrase boundaries, etc. must be "explained . . . on the basis of our experience," that "positing interior mental objects . . . only gets in the way of an explanation, for it merely papers over the gaps in our understanding of how language-mastery is acquired." Someone could argue in this way only if he assumed that the presupposed "complete knowledge of physics" does not include an account of how the brain is initially structured so that experience leads to specific knowledge of word meaning, phrase boundaries, or whatever. This assumption is what advocates of "indeterminacy" must establish, if the thesis is to be a significant one.

A version of the bifurcation thesis runs as a common thread through Putnam's discussion of a range of issues. For example, he argues that "the barbarous idea" of " 'scientizing' the social sciences" collapses[29] because of such simple facts as the following: while studying Hebrew, Putnam learned that the word "shemen" means oil. But because of the problems of indeterminacy of translation, "knowledge of such a *simple* fact as '*shemen* means oil' cannot be justified/confirmed by following the paradigms of inductive logic." It involves "*practical* knowledge" which goes beyond scientific inference. "The idea that what we *know* is coextensive with what we can check 'publicly' following well-understood paradigms of scientific testing does not even fit some of the *simplest* facts we know, such as the meaning of the words in a foreign language." Elsewhere he says that such knowledge cannot be " 'verified' by a verification that publicly conforms to the criteria of 'scientific methodology' " and that psychological explanations cannot be given "*anything like* a 'scientific proof'."

All of this might be more convincing if there were any reason to believe that the natural sciences could withstand such criticism. Can the paradigms of inductive logic justify or confirm theoretical statements in the natural sciences in some way that we know to be unavailable in principle in the case of "*shemen* means oil"? Do the criteria of "scientific methodology" offer "scientific proofs" that avoid the problem of underdetermination of theory by evidence in the natural sciences? No reason has been advanced for any such belief. Putnam argues further that we would need a "*huge* psychological theory" to cover all the relevant special circumstances,[30] that "we do *not* have an explicit theory of" interactions that are features of practical knowledge and that such knowledge is "unformalizable"—elsewhere, that it is "hopeless" to seek such theories or that theories of full functional organization "may well be *unintelligible*" to humans when stated in any detail or that psychological theories would have to be so complex that predictions using them could not proceed in real time.[31] These speculations may be correct or not, but it is not at all clear what significance they have, even if correct. We would also need huge theories to deal with the physiology of complex organisms (though the basic theory might turn out to be simple) and predictions from them might not be possible in real time; or such theories might be unintelligible to humans because of their complexity or for other reasons. Do we therefore conclude that assimilating physiology to the natural sciences is a barbarous idea that "collapses"?

In his defense of the indeterminacy thesis, Putnam responds to what he calls "Chomskian 'realism'," arguing that "we *should* be 'realists' in both areas [psychology and physics]—*sophisticated* realists. And a sophisticated realist recognizes the existence of equivalent descriptions . . ."[32] I entirely agree.[33] For moderately sophisticated realists, the underdetermination of theory by evidence, hence the existence of equivalent theories in Putnam's sense, is no surprise in physics or psychology. So far there is no issue, when misreadings are overcome.

But Putnam simultaneously puts forward a very different view. Namely, he proposes what he calls "a substantive metaphysical theory of what 'correctness' *is* in linguistics" (and presumably psychology as well), namely, that the correct theory *is* whatever "best explains the behavior of the speaker."[34] Why is this a different thesis? The reason is that Putnam regards explanation as "interest-relative"; the best explanation depends on our interests and purposes, and will vary as these do. There is no absolute "best explanation." Furthermore he denies that there is any sense to the notion "evidence available at the limit." There is no "ideal limit" of scientific investigation.

Therefore he is offering as a substantive metaphysical thesis that correctness in linguistics (and psychology) *is* what best explains the currently available data about the behavior of the speaker given some current interest; what is correct today will be false tomorrow, and what is correct depends on our current interests and purposes. But this is definitely not the view that he urges upon a sophisticated realist in the natural sciences; quite the contrary. I will not go into his interesting development of the issues in the natural sciences, but merely note that implicit in the remarks just cited is a strong version of a bifurcation thesis as part of the underpinnings for a metaphysical principle, but without any argument that I can detect.

Putnam offers still another version of his position in response to a "vague" argument that he says he often hears "from Chomskians." The argument he hears is that the interest-relativity of explanation is common to all of science, "physics as much as psychology. So you haven't shown that there is any special reason to regard psychology (and translation) as more indeterminate than *physics*." Assume that someone argues in this way against the bifurcation thesis. But Putnam responds, "This seems to be a bad reply to *Quine*, actually, because Quine is arguing that there is 'under-determination' *for the same reasons* in both physics and psychology, *and* the 'under-determination' in psychology *remains* even if we 'fix' the physics." Putnam is confusing the issue somewhat by failing to distinguish interest-relativity from underdetermination, two quite different matters, but let us put that aside and consider his response to such a rejection of the bifurcation thesis.

Consider, then, the thesis that there is underdetermination for the same reasons in both physics and psychology, but underdetermination in psychology remains even if we fix the physics.

The term "physics" in this discussion is used simply as a cover word for the natural sciences. Putnam's response, then, is based on an implicit claim (attributed to Quine) that psychology is not part of the natural sciences. If this claim is correct, then it follows trivially that underdetermination remains in psychology if we fix the physics; and furthermore, if physics is not part of psychology, then it also follows, equally uninterestingly, that underdetermination remains in physics if we fix the psychology. Similar remarks hold of electromagnetic theory and mechanics, or biochemistry and thermodynamics, or the theory of vision and the theory of language. In contrast, if psychology *is* part of the natural sciences, Putnam's version of Quine's thesis is, plainly, false. The crucial question, then, is whether psychology is part of the natural sciences. To answer this question, we must begin with some characterization of the intrinsic properties of these two domains; presumably it is of no interest merely to remark that current psychology does not fall within current physics, so far as we know. For reasons already discussed, it is not very clear what sense there is to the more general question: whether in principle psychology falls within the natural sciences. Perhaps the problems of psychology already fall in principle within contemporary physics, or perhaps we will continue, as in the past, to assimilate to the natural sciences whatever comes to be reasonably well understood, modifying our notion of "physics" if need be in the process. Putnam must have some demarcation in mind, or he could not have formulated this version of his argument. It is his problem, then, to clarify and motivate this demarcation, just as advocates of the bifurcation thesis must bear the burden of establishing it.[35] Others can simply adopt Putnam's quite reasonable advice elsewhere to maintain the same "sophisticated realism" in all realms, thereby rejecting all of these moves.

Putnam asks why Quine's thesis of indeterminacy "seems so implausible" and answers that "we think of the doctrine from the point of view of *our* interests, explanation-spaces, etc." I would put it differently. The thesis of indeterminacy does not seem implausible; rather it seems obvious. Theories are undetermined by evidence, or they would have no interest at all. What seems implausible—at least, quite unargued—is the bifurcation thesis. While the general thesis of indeterminacy seems obvious, it nevertheless *is* implausible to say of another person, or of someone in another culture, that he means *undetached rabbit part* when he uses our term "rabbit" (or another term that we would tend to translate as "rabbit"). The reason seems straightforward enough. We know, of ourselves, that we mean *rabbit* and not *undetached rabbit part*. [36] We assume that the next person is like us in relevant respects, unless we have evidence to the contrary, just as a chemist who analyzes two samples from the same solution assumes, unless there is evidence to the contrary, that they are the same in relevant respects; or just as a geneticist assumes with regard to two fruitflies. When pressed, all would agree that even the fullest evidence could not show definitively that these assumptions are correct, in the natural sciences, or in the case of our neighbor's use of the word "rabbit." Furthermore, if we do not accept Quine's arbitrary limitation of experiment to investigation of assent and dissent and consider other evidence as well, the assumption that the other person is like us in relevant respects would be confirmed, as we would find by investigating his use of the words "part," "undetached," etc., and from evidence of a variety of other sorts. Of course we know, as Quine insists, that there are ways to make all the evidence compatible with innumerable other interpretations no matter how much evidence we accumulate, just as there would be no way to defeat conclusively the claim that two samples from the same solution are differently constituted, no matter how many tests we run. We rely, in such cases, on concepts of simplicity, insight and explanatory power that are not at all understood and that are presumably rooted in our cognitive capacities. The question of interest-relativity of explanation seems to have little to do with it. Nor is the question of any particular relevance to psychology, when we drop the bifurcation thesis.

I think it is worth remarking on the fact that these issues have been so much debated in the past twenty years in the domain of psychology and language, while the comparable questions concerning indeterminacy in the natural sciences have received far less attention; and where they have been investigated, in connection with the question of realism, the framework and conclusions have been entirely different. What has happened, in fact, is that psychology has been asked to confront questions that are simply dismissed in the case of the natural sciences, where no one is much concerned with the fact that two samples might in principle be differently constituted, that theories are undetermined by evidence, and so on. This seems a strange state of affairs. Questions of a fundamental nature should be raised where the hope of gaining illumination is highest; in this case in physics, not psychology. The very successes of physics make it reasonable to raise questions that are simply inappropriate in the domain of psychology or linguistics, not because these subjects should be immune from critical analysis but because their achievements are so much slighter that they offer far less hope of providing insight or even offering sensible examples to consider. It is a fair rule of thumb that questions should not be raised concerning the foundations of psychology if they cannot be answered in some measure at least in the case of physics. This reasonable principle has been drastically violated, with the obvious consequence that nothing much comes of the discussion, even when confusions are eliminated.

Notice that Putnam might be right in supposing that some aspects of psychology really are fundamentally different from the natural sciences, for example, the study of intent, mood, etc. If so, this will not help his argument, which attempts to offer a substantive metaphysical thesis for linguistics (and psychology) in general. He would have to claim in addition that study of psychology requires a uniquely holistic approach rejecting idealization, and that no subdomains can be isolated that are exempt from whatever considerations he believes to be in order for certain aspects of the study of "the natural kind 'human being'." I won't try to pursue the matter further, but merely conclude that I do not see a thesis of any substance or significance here, certainly none that has been shown to bear on the actual pursuit of quite central domains of psychology, including linguistics.

Putnam's "sophisticated realism" is perhaps not very different from that of Descartes, when he writes that

although I have shown how all natural things can be formed, we have no right to conclude on this account that they were produced by these causes. For just as there may be two clocks made by the same workman, which though they indicate the time equally well and are externally in all respects similar, yet in nowise resemble one another in the composition of their wheels, so doubtless there is an infinity of dif-

ferent ways in which all things that we see could be formed by the
great Artificer [without it being possible for the mind of man to be
aware of which of these means he has chosen to employ].³⁷

This "thesis of indeterminacy," which Descartes attributes to
Aristotle, can be formulated in ways that seem straightforward
enough. If there is a fundamentally different version, one that
bears crucially on psychology or linguistics, it has yet to be advanced, to my knowledge.

I do not believe, then, that consideration of museum myths
or indeterminacy sheds any light on the enterprise I have been
discussing, nor does it suggest that the effort to isolate systems of
the mind that can be studied in the manner of the natural
sciences must come to grief. I will therefore continue to pursue
the working hypothesis that there are aspects of the study of
mind that lend themselves to inquiry in "the Galilean style,"
and that there may some day even be a kind of "Galilean revo-
lution" in psychology if such an approach reaches a sufficient
level of explanatory depth. One aspect of the study of mind that
seems particularly susceptible to this approach is the study of
our knowledge of language and the origins of this knowledge,
though the problem of how this knowledge is put to use, and in
particular what I have called elsewhere "the creative aspect of
language use," seems to resist such endeavors, perhaps for reasons expressed in the narrowed version of Descartes's thesis of
incomprehensibility noted earlier.

I once presented what I thought was an innocent and uncontroversial statement of an idealization that seems to me of critical importance if linguistic theory is to be pursued along these
lines: namely, that "Linguistic theory is concerned primarily
with an ideal speaker-listener, in a completely homogeneous

speech-community, who knows its language perfectly and is unaffected by" memory limitations, distractions, etc.[38] The formulation seems to me innocent, but it is obviously far from uncontroversial. It has aroused quite a storm of protest, focusing primarily on the notion "homogeneous speech community." As we will see, rejection of the idealization is also implicit in some contemporary work in philosophy.

Exactly what is the source of the objection? Obviously, it cannot be that real speech communities are not homogeneous. That is as obvious as it is irrelevant. Nor can the objection be that this idealization necessarily impedes the study of matters that do not fall within it, say, linguistic variation, or what Putnam calls "the social division of linguistic labor." On the contrary, what is implicitly claimed by someone who adopts the idealization is that these further questions are properly studied within a framework that makes use of the results obtained by inquiring into the idealization. If the idealization does make it possible to unearth real and significant properties of the language faculty, this conclusion would seem to be justified, indeed inescapable.

So we are left with what must be the crucial question: does the idealization so falsify the real world that it will lead to no significant insight into the nature of the language faculty, or does it, on the contrary, open the possibility for discovering fundamental properties of the language faculty? In short, is the idealization legitimate?

Suppose that someone takes the negative stand on this question. Such a person is committed to one of the following two beliefs:

1. People are so constituted that they would be incapable of learning language in a homogeneous speech community;

variability or inconsistency of presented evidence is a necessary condition for language learning.

2. Though people could learn language in a homogeneous speech community, the properties of the mind that make this achievement possible do not enter into normal language acquisition in the real world of diversity, conflict of dialects, etc.

I cannot believe that anyone who thinks the matter through would really maintain either of these beliefs. In fact, each seems hopelessly implausible. Suppose, then, that we reject them. Thus we accept that humans have some property of mind which would enable them to learn the language of a homogeneous speech community were they to be placed in one, and that this property of mind plays a role in language acquisition. But then the idealization is legitimate; it opens the way to the study of a fundamental property of mind, namely, the one in question. Furthermore, one who rejects the idealization and the results obtained by pursuing it to the point where we discover this fundamental property of mind is impeding the study of other aspects of language, say, the acquisition and use of language under conditions of diversity, the division of linguistic labor, the questions of sociolinguistics, and so on.

Once the issues are clarified, it is hard to see how anyone could reject the idealization, and, to my knowledge no one in fact does, including its most vocal opponents, as we see when we look in detail at their actual work on such topics as dialect variation. This is unfortunately typical of the kind of debate that beclouds the issue of idealization all too often. I will assume that this idealization is a legitimate one, considering, as we proceed, further steps that should, I think, be taken to isolate coherent subsystems of the mind for special study.

Suppose that an inquiry of the sort so far outlined achieves some success. How might such success contribute to the more general study of mind? It has been argued that knowledge of language is not a "central case" or characteristic kind of knowledge: that "the situation of the child learning his first language is anyway far from being a normal case of the acquisition of knowledge."[39] This view seems to me more or less plausible, depending on how we interpret it. What is currently understood even in a limited way seems to me to indicate that the mind is a highly differentiated structure, with quite distinct subsystems. If so, an understanding of the properties of one of these systems should not be expected to provide the principles by which others are organized and function. Even an account of knowledge of language that is overflowing with insights is unlikely to contribute directly to the study of factors that enter into our understanding of the nature of the visual world, or conversely. This is not to deny, of course, that these systems interact and may share some general properties. But we should remain open to the possibility—even the strong likelihood—that they are organized in quite different ways. In this respect, knowledge of language may not be a central case; nor knowledge of or about anything else.[40] There are other peculiarities of knowledge of language. The question of truth, conformity to an external reality, does not enter in the way it does in connection with our knowledge of the properties of objects. Granting all of this, I still can think of no way to undertake the study of mind except by investigating the specific character of particular systems, such as the language faculty. The principles cannot be expected to carry over, but the results attained and the mode of successful inquiry may prove suggestive elsewhere, much as the study of vision has proven suggestive for the study of language. And any results attained are direct contributions to the theory of mind.

Throughout the discussion I have been referring to *human* language and *human* cognition. I have in mind certain biological properties, the most significant of these being properties that are genetically-determined and characteristic of the human species, which I will assume for the purposes of this discussion to be genetically uniform, a further idealization. These properties determine the kinds of cognitive systems, language among them, that can develop in the human mind. In the case of language, I will use the term "universal grammar" to refer to these properties of human biological endowment. Thus the properties of universal grammar are "biologically necessary," but in the interesting cases not logically necessary elements of what someone might choose to call a language. If, indeed, the mind is modular in character, a system of distinct though interacting systems, then language-like systems might be acquired through the exercise of other faculties of mind, though we should expect to find empirical differences in the manner of acquisition and use in this case. The actual systems called "languages" in ordinary discourse are undoubtedly not "languages" in the sense of our idealizations, if only because of the nonhomogeneity of actual speech communities, and might also be "impure" in the sense that they incorporate elements derived by faculties other than the language faculty and hence depart in certain respects from principles of universal grammar. These again are possibilities that are neither particularly surprising nor unique to this inquiry.

It is important to distinguish this usage from a different one, which takes "universal grammar" to be a characterization not of human language but of "language as such." In this sense, universal grammar attempts to capture those properties of language that are logically or conceptually necessary, properties such that if a system failed to have them we would simply not call it a language at all: perhaps the property of having sentences and words, for example. The study of biologically necessary properties of language is a part of natural science: its concern is to determine one aspect of human genetics, namely, the nature of the language faculty. Perhaps the effort is misguided. We might discover that there is no language faculty, but only some general modes of learning applied to language or anything else. If so, then universal grammar in my sense is vacuous, in that its questions will find no answers apart from general cognitive principles. But still, universal grammar conceived as a study of the biologically necessary properties of human language (if such exist) is strictly a part of science. The criteria of success or failure are those of the sciences. In contrast, the study of logically necessary properties of language is an inquiry into the concept "language." I should add at once that I am skeptical about the enterprise. It seems to me unlikely to prove more interesting than an inquiry into the concept of "vision" or "locomotion." But in any event, it is not an empirical investigation, except insofar as lexicography is an empirical investigation, and must be judged by quite different standards.

Richmond Thomason, who edited Montague's papers, has written rather disparagingly about the study of properties of language that he describes as "merely psychologically universal"[41]—these would be the biologically necessary properties that constitute universal grammar in my sense. He advocates instead the development of universal grammar as a part of mathematics, and he argues that so-called "Montague grammar" is such a theory. It is, he suggests, analogous to topology regarded as a general theory of geometry. The enterprise he outlines, then, will be evaluated not by "merely empirical" criteria but by the standards of mathematics—the depth of its theorems and the like; an evaluation that is quickly concluded, in this case. I would, incidentally, be a little surprised to learn that a person working in a somewhat richer branch of mathematics, say David Hilbert, had disparaged the study of physics in similar terms as concerned with the "merely physical" properties of the universe.

An inquiry into universal grammar in the sense of the term that I am adopting here falls within what Hume called "moral philosophy," that is, "the science of human nature," which is concerned with "the secret springs and principles, by which the human mind is actuated in its operations," and most importantly, those "parts of [our] knowledge" that are derived "from the original hand of nature." Descartes took this to be the most useful inquiry in which we can engage: "to determine the nature and the scope of human knowledge."[42] The problem has run through the history of human thought from the earliest times. Some have argued that the frame of reference I am assuming is so different that it is improper to regard the current inquiry as concerned with the traditional problems. For Descartes, mind is not a part of the biological world. Furthermore, he appears to regard the mind as uniform and undifferentiated: "there is within us but one soul, and this soul has not in itself any diversity of parts"; "the mind is entirely indivisible."[43] One might then argue that we are not studying Descartes's problem when we consider the human mind as a specific biological system, one with components and elements of varied kinds, to be explored as we would study any other aspect of the physical world. This conclusion holds, however, only if we regard Descartes as an irrational dogmatist, that is, as putting forth doctrines that define the domain of inquiry, rather than as arguing for principles that he believed he had established within an inquiry more broadly construed. That seems to me a questionable move.

As for Hume, I think he was wrong in his empirical assumptions about the principles by which the mind is actuated, innate and acquired, but right in the way he formulated the question, particularly, in taking his inquiry to be analogous to physics. I do not mean to suggest that other concerns and other questions are illegitimate, but rather that these central concerns of the philosophical tradition are legitimate and important, whatever current terminology one may choose to clothe them in.

From this point of view, we can proceed to approach the study of the human mind much in the way that we study the physical structure of the body. In fact, we may think of the study of mental faculties as actually being a study of the body—specifically the brain—conducted at a certain level of abstraction. It may be useful, as a point of departure, to consider for a moment how we do proceed to study the human body.

We assume, no doubt correctly, that the human species is characterized by a certain biological endowment. The embryo grows ultimately to the adult as its genetic program unfolds under the triggering and shaping effect of the environment. These effects are worth distinguishing. Take the standard conditioning paradigm, in which a course of behavior is constructed in a step-by-step process by manipulation of reinforcement contingencies, that is, contingencies that for some reason or another change the probability of behavior. This is an example of a shaping effect of the environment. Or suppose that there is some domain, however narrow, in which traditional empiricist psychology is valid; say that a child receives simultaneously a visual and an auditory impression and associates them, the residue of the auditory impression serving as the name of the object taken to have caused the visual impression. There are notorious problems in working any of this out, crucially, the problem of how we can have sensory experience uninformed by conceptual judgment.[44] That this is possible has often been denied, by seventeenth-century Cartesians for example. Schopenhauer, who develops a post-Kantian version, attributes this view to "the ancients," citing for example "the famous verse of the philosopher Epicharmus": "Only the mind can see and hear; everything else is deaf and blind."[45] But suppose that we put these problems aside. Then the empiricist paradigm can serve as an example of the shaping effect of the environment on knowledge, furthermore a case in which there is some sort of "resemblance" between what is in the mind and what it perceives.

Suppose, in contrast, that certain environmental conditions are required to set in operation an intrinsically determined process, as nutrition is required for cellular growth to take place in predetermined ways. It has been reported, for example, that handling of rats induces lateralization for spatial and affective processes.[46] In such cases, the processes that take place are not shaped by the environment; they do not reflect the course of interchange with it or somehow "resemble" the stimulus, any more than a child is a reflection of the food he eats. When external conditions are necessary for, or facilitate the unfolding of, an internally controlled process, we can speak of their "triggering" effect. If institutionalized children do not learn a language, the reason may be that a crucial triggering factor, appropriate social interchange, is lacking, as in the case of Harlow's deprived monkeys; but we would not therefore say that attention, care and love shape the growth of language in the sense that a schedule of reinforcement shapes the behavior of a pigeon. The distinction between the two kinds of effects of the environment is not sharp, but it is conceptually useful. My own suspicion is that a central part of what we call "learning" is actually better understood as the growth of cognitive structures along an internally directed course under the triggering and partially shaping effect of the environment. In the case of human language, there evidently is a shaping effect; people speak different languages which reflect differences in their verbal environment.[47] But it remains to be seen in what respects the system that develops is actually shaped by experience, or rather reflects intrinsic processes and structures triggered by experience.

Returning to the analogy to the physical body, we take for granted that the organism does not learn to grow arms or to reach puberty—to mention an example of genetically-determined maturation that takes place long after birth. Rather, these developments are determined by the genetic endowment, though the precise manner in which the genetic plan is realized depends in part on external factors, both triggering and shaping. For example, nutritional level can apparently affect the time of onset of puberty over a considerable range. As the biological plan unfolds, a system of interacting organs and structures matures—the heart, the visual system, and so on, each with its specific structures and functions, interacting in largely predetermined ways.

Our biological endowment determines both the scope and limits of physical growth. On the one hand, it permits the growth of a complex system of highly articulated physical organs, intrinsically determined in their essential properties. Were it not for this highly specific innate endowment, each individual would grow into some kind of an amoeboid creature, merely reflecting external contingencies, one individual quite unlike another, each utterly impoverished and lacking the intricate special structures that make possible a human existence and that differentiate one species from another. Our biological endowment permits a vast potential for development, roughly uniform for the species. At the same time, it in fact narrowly limits what each individual can become; the human embryo presumably cannot become a bird by modification of the external environment. Scope and limits of development are intimately related. Innate factors permit the organism to transcend experience, reaching a high level of complexity that does not reflect the limited and degenerate environment. These very same factors rule out many possible courses of development and limit drastically the final states that can be attained in physical growth.

Now all of this should be transparent and hardly controversial. Apparently very little is known about how any of it happens, but no one really doubts that something of this sort is roughly true. If it were proposed that we "make" our physical constitution, or are "taught" to pass through puberty, or "learn" to have arms rather than wings, no one would take the suggestion very seriously, even in the present state of ignorance concerning the mechanisms involved. Why is this so? Presumably, the reason derives from the vast qualitative difference between the impoverished and unstructured environment, on the one hand, and the highly specific and intricate structures that uniformly develop, on the other. In essence, this is a variant of a classical argument in the theory of knowledge, what we might call "the argument from poverty of the stimulus." Socrates' success in eliciting knowledge from the slave boy is a classical example. To take a variant of this argument that seems to me quite relevant to contemporary concerns, consider Descartes's argument for innate ideas in the perceptual domain. Descartes argues in the *Dioptrics* that

> there is no need to suppose that anything material passes from objects to our eyes to make us see colors and light, nor that there is anything in these objects that is similar to the ideas or the sensations that we have of them: just as nothing moves from the objects that a blind man senses that must pass along his stick to his hand, and the resistance or the movement of these bodies which is the only cause of the sensations that he has of them, is in no way similar to the ideas that he conceives of them. And in this way, your mind will be freed of all those little images flying through the air, called *intentional species*, which so exercise the imagination of the philosophers.[48]

Experience conforms to our mode of cognition, as his immediate successors, and later Kant, were to say. This mode of cognition must, Descartes argued, involve such innate ideas as geometrical figures, as well as all the "common notions," since the stimulus does not resemble what the mind produces on the occasion of stimulation. As he suggested elsewhere, we take a presented figure to be a distorted triangle, not a perfect example of what it is, presumably because the mind is organized in terms of principles of geometry.[49] Hume, in contrast held that we have no concept at all of regular geometrical figures, indeed that it is absurd to imagine that we have any such concept beyond what the senses convey,[50] a conclusion that should be interpreted, I think, as a *reductio ad absurdum* argument against empiricist beliefs as to the shaping effect of stimulation on the mental structures they evoke. Descartes's argument, in effect, relies on the observation that the stimulus does not contain the elements that constitute our knowledge, though it may serve as the occasion for the mind to produce an interpretation of experience in terms of conceptual structures drawn from its own inner

resources. "The book of nature is legible only to an intellectual
eye," as Cudworth wrote.[51]

While the argument is controversial in the case of the mind,
more so than I think it should be, it is not discussed at all in the
case of the physical body, but rather assumed without notice as
the basis for scientific inquiry. There have, however, been intriguing discussions of similar issues in other domains of biology. I will return to some of these later, in discussing the question of learning and growth. Note that the argument is of course
nondemonstrative. It is what is sometimes called an inference to
the best explanation, in this case, that what the stimulus lacks is
produced by the organism from its inner resources; in other
words, organisms endowed with different modes of cognition
might interpret the stimulus quite differently, so that our attention is directed to these modes of cognition and their origin, if
we are concerned to understand the organism-environment interaction and the essential nature of the organism involved.

Descartes's arguments for innate ideas, when they are considered at all, are generally regarded as somehow missing the point
or as "a ludicrous failure" if understood as offering "a general
causal principle."[52] But I think the objections miss the point. It
is quite true, as Roy Edgley says in an interesting discussion of
the issues, that "An idea in the mind would be attributable entirely to an external object only, so to speak, if there were no
mind there at all." This is, in effect, Hume's position, as expressed, for example, in his image of the mind as "a kind of
theatre, where several perceptions successively make their appearance; pass, repass, glide away, and mingle in an infinite variety of postures and situations," though "The comparison of
the theatre must not mislead us" since there is no stage: "They
are the successive perceptions only, that constitute the mind."[53]

It would be quite wrong, then, to suggest that no empiricist would deny that ideas "must be in part attributable to the nature of experience and the mind, and the external item is at most a necessary condition of having the idea," except in a very special sense: namely, the limiting case, in which the contribution of the mind is null, since the mind is simply constituted of a succession of impressions and faded impressions.[54] As for Hume's "instincts," which compel us to expect the future to be like the past, there is a very serious empirical question as to whether these are characterized in a way that is anywhere near correct. The import of these questions comes out clearly in the contrary positions held by Descartes and Hume with regard to geometrical objects. I think it is reasonable to interpret the issue as at its core an empirical one, and to conclude that Descartes's use of the argument from poverty of the stimulus is not at all "ludicrous" or "trivial," but rather a substantive (though we would say, nondemonstrative)[55] argument with regard to the actual character of the mind. Similarly, when Edgley says that "not even the meagre framework of explanation proposed in stimulus-response theory violates [the] principle" that the nature of the mind in part determines the effects produced by a stimulus, he is not wrong, but is again missing an important point: nontrivial stimulus-response theories do have something to say about the structure of the mind, or can be so construed, but what they say is wrong, in that they do not postulate specific structures adequate to the task of explanation. Descartes, furthermore, went well beyond the "general causal principle" that Edgley dismisses as "a ludicrous failure."

It may turn out in fact that a variant of Descartes's conclusion is not only not ludicrous but in fact correct, when understood essentially in his terms rather than those of contemporary philosophical discussion. That is, it may be true that the mind is so constituted that it constructs regular geometrical figures as "exemplars" for the interpretation of experience; it is even possible that recent work in neurophysiology offers the bare beginnings of an account as to how this happens, though one that is not within Descartes's specific framework, any more than contemporary physics is within Galileo's framework.[56]

When we turn to the mind and its products, the situation is not qualitatively different from what we find in the case of the body. Here too we find structures of considerable intricacy, developing quite uniformly, far transcending the limited environmental factors that trigger and partially shape their growth. Language is a case in point, though not the only one. Think for example of the capacity to deal with the number system, common to humans apart from pathology and as far as we know, unique to humans, surely a major factor in the remarkable success of the "Galilean style" in physics. Russell once wrote that we would not have developed the concept of number had we lived on the sun. Perhaps the opportunity to employ those faculties of mind that present us with a world of individual objects provides a triggering effect for the growth of the "number faculty," but beyond that, it seems reasonable to suppose that this faculty is an intrinsic component of the human mind. One should not be misled by the fact that some birds, for example, can be taught to pick n elements from an array for small n—about up to seven.[57] The very essence of the number system is the concept of adding one, indefinitely. The concept of infinity is not just "more" than seven, just as human language, with its discrete infinity of meaningful expressions, is not just "more" than some finite system of symbols that can laboriously be imposed on other organisms (nor, by the same token, just "less" than an essentially continuous system of communication, like the dance of bees). The capacity to deal with the number system or with abstract properties of space is surely unlearned in its essentials. Furthermore it is not specifically "selected" through evolution, one must assume—even the existence of the number faculty could not have been known or the capacity exercised until human evolution had essentially reached its current stage.

We may usefully think of the language faculty, the number faculty, and others, as "mental organs," analogous to the heart or the visual system or the system of motor coordination and planning. There appears to be no clear demarcation line between physical organs, perceptual and motor systems, and cognitive faculties in the respects in question. In short, there seems little reason to insist that the brain is unique in the biological world in that it is unstructured and undifferentiated, developing on the basis of uniform principles of growth or learning—say those of some learning theory, or of some yet-to-be conceived general multipurpose learning strategy—that are common to all domains.

David Hubel, who has pioneered some of the most exciting work of recent years on the physical basis for mammalian vision, concludes that

we are led to expect that each region of the central nervous system has its own special problems that require different solutions. In vision we are concerned with contours and directions and depth. With the auditory system, on the other hand, we can anticipate a galaxy of problems relating to temporal interactions of sounds of different frequencies, and it is difficult to imagine that the same neural apparatus deals with all of these phenomena . . . for the major aspects of the brain's operation no master solution is likely.[58]

There may well be properties common to diverse systems. For example, experience is necessary for "fine tuning" in the case of the visual and auditory systems as in other systems that develop in accordance with fixed genetic instructions. Recent work on motor coordination in monkeys seems to show "that many motor programs are part of a primate's genetic endowment. No sensory feedback or spinal reflex loops are necessary for learning the repertoire of movements . . . [though] . . . sensory feedback is necessary for 'fine tuning' . . ."[59] Perceptual and motor systems are no doubt in part "set" by the shaping effect of some aspects of the environment,[60] but the systems that emerge seem to be highly specialized, intrinsically programmed in quite different ways. In short, what is taken for granted without direct evidence in the case of physical growth on the basis of an implicit argument from poverty of the stimulus is also being found in the study of the brain and nervous system; unsurprisingly, one would think.

In the case of cognitive faculties, it is widely assumed that development is uniform across domains and that the intrinsic properties of the initial state are homogeneous and undifferentiated, an assumption found across a spectrum of opinion reaching from Skinner to Piaget, who differ on much else, and common in contemporary philosophy as well. Notice that there are two issues here: the issue of innate structure and of modularity. One might hold that there is rich innate structure, but little or no modularity. But there is a relation between the views, in part conceptual. Insofar as there is little in the way of innate structure, what develops in the mind of an individual will be a homogeneous system derived by the application to experience of common principles that constitute the innate endowment. Such differentiation as there may be will reflect differentiation in the environment. Correspondingly, the belief that various systems of mind are organized along quite different principles leads to the natural conclusion that these systems are intrinsically determined, not simply the result of common mechanisms of learning or growth. It is not surprising, then, to find that opinions "cluster." Those who tend toward the assumption of modularity tend also to assume rich innate structure, while those who assume limited innate structure tend to deny modularity.

Once we begin to take seriously the actual states attained in particular cases, we are, I believe, led to the conclusion that intrinsic structure is rich (by the argument from poverty of the stimulus) and diverse (by virtue of the apparent diversity in fundamental principles of capacities and mental structures attained). These conclusions are, I think, to be expected in the case of systems that have any significant function in the life of an organism. As noted, they are taken for granted without much thought or evidence in the study of physical development; no one doubts that the instructions for a liver and a visual system will be quite different. Insofar as anything is known about cognitive systems—which is not very far—the related assumptions of poverty of initial structure and homogeneity do not seem tenable, and the general line of argument that keeps analogous assumptions from being considered at all in the case of physical growth seems applicable. The more we learn about specific systems, the more applicable it becomes, and I would hazard a guess that this will continue to be so. In the case of human conceptual systems, for example, intrinsic even to such apparently elementary notions as "thing" or "object" there is a subtle interaction between conditions of spatio-temporal contiguity, the willed acts of an agent responsible for the object, and other factors.[61] It is difficult to interpret this except in terms of our intrinsic modes of cognition. When we turn to language, many examples have been studied of shared knowledge that appears to have no shaping stimulation—knowledge without grounds, from another point of view—and that seems to be based on principles with only the most superficial resemblance to those operative in other cognitive domains.

Let me give some simple examples, in part to illustrate the point and in part for later reference. Consider, for example, the process of forming questions. We select some Noun Phrase in a sentence, replace it by an appropriate question-word, place the latter at the beginning of the sentence, and with other mechanical operations, form a question. Thus, on the model of the sentence "John saw a man" we can form "who did John see?" Or to take a more complex case, on the model of the sentence "the teacher thought that his assistant had told the class to study the lesson," we can question "the class" and ask: "Which class did the teacher think that his assistant had told to study the lesson?" But consider the following example, of roughly comparable complexity: "the lesson was harder than the teacher had told the class that it would be." Here, if we question "the class," we derive: "which class was the lesson harder than the teacher had told that it would be?" Evidently, this is not a well-formed question, though its intended sense is clear enough and perfectly intelligible, with a little thought. It is difficult to imagine that people capable of these judgments have all had relevant training or experience to block the obvious inductive generalization to the ill-formed example. Rather, it seems that some specific property of the human language faculty—hence a general property of language—leads to these consequences, a property that derives from our modes of cognition.

To take a second case, consider the rule forming reciprocal expressions such as "the men saw each other." A child learning English, or someone learning English as a second language, must learn that "each other" is a reciprocal expression; that is an idiosyncratic fact about English. Given that it is a reciprocal expression, it must have an antecedent: for example, "the men" in "the men saw each other," which has the meaning, roughly: "each of the man saw the other(s)." The antecedent can be in a different clause, as in "the candidates wanted [each other to win]," where "each other" appears in a subordinate clause as the subject of "win" whereas its antecedent, "the candidates," appears in the main clause. Sometimes, however, the reciprocal cannot find its antecedent outside of its clause, as in "the candidates wanted me to vote for each other," which is not well-formed with the perfectly sensible meaning: "each of the candidates wanted me to vote for the other." One might assume that the antecedent must be the "nearest Noun Phrase." But this is false; this condition is neither sufficient nor necessary. It is not sufficient, as we can see from such examples as "the candidates thought each other would win," which is not well-formed with the meaning: "each of the candidates thought the other would win." It is not necessary, as we can see from such examples as "the candidates hurled insults at each other." While this sentence could mean that the candidates hurled each insult at the other insults, plainly that is not the way we normally interpret it.

In this case too, it can hardly be maintained that children learning English receive specific instruction about these matters or even that they are provided with relevant experience that informs them that they should not make the obvious inductive generalization, say, that "each other" takes some plural antecedent that precedes it. Children make many errors in language learning, but they do not assume, until corrected, that "the candidates wanted me to vote for each other" is a well-formed sentence meaning that each candidate wanted me to vote for the other. Relevant experience is never presented for most speakers of English, just as no pedagogic or traditional grammar, however compendious, would point out these facts. Somehow, this is information that children themselves bring to the process of language acquisition, as part of their mode of cognition.

Some general principle of language applies to permit the proper choice of antecedent, not an entirely trivial matter, as these examples suggest. Similarly, some general principle of language determines which phrases can be questioned. These principles, which have many ramifications, are among those that provide a basic framework within which knowledge of language develops as the child progresses to the mature state of knowledge; they are on a par with the factors that determine that the child will have binocular vision. As we consider such principles and their interaction, we begin to approach the richness of the language faculty, one element of our biological endowment, and, it appears, a distinctive element.

It would be surprising indeed if we were to find that the principles governing these phenomena are operative in other cognitive systems, although there may be certain loose analogies, perhaps in terms of figure and ground, or properties of memory, as we see when the relevant principles are made explicit.[62] Such examples illustrate two points, in the present connection: first, that there is good reason to suppose that the functioning of the language faculty is guided by special principles specific to this domain; second, that the argument from poverty of the stimulus provides a useful device for inquiry into these principles, indeed, at the moment the most useful device, I think, for inquiring into universal grammar.

It seems reasonable to assume that the language faculty—and, I would guess, other mental organs—develops in the individual along an intrinsically determined course under the triggering effect of appropriate social interaction and partially shaped by the environment—English is not Japanese, just as the distribution of horizontal and vertical receptors in the visual cortex can be modified by early visual experience. The environment provides the information that questions are formed by movement of a question word and that "each other" is a reciprocal expression; in other languages this is not the case, so that these cannot be properties of biological endowment in specific detail. Beyond such information, much of our knowledge reflects our modes of cognition, and is therefore not limited to inductive generalization from experience, let alone any training that we may have received. And just as the visual system of a cat, though modified by experience, will never be that of a bee or a frog, so the human language faculty will develop only one of the human languages, a narrowly constrained set.

A familiar argument against a modular approach to the study of mind is that it "reduces the possibility of viewing language as an aspect of the total corpus of behavior" and "obscures the connections between language and other aspects of cognition."[63] By parity of argument, we should conclude that the belief that the eye and the ear work on different principles reduces the possibility of viewing vision as an aspect of behavior and obscures the relations between vision and hearing. It is a sad commentary on the field that such arguments can even be advanced.

Consider again the question whether cognitive functions are both diverse, and determined in considerable detail by a rich innate endowment. If the answer is positive, for some organism, that organism is fortunate indeed. It can then live in a rich and complex world of understanding shared with others similarly endowed, extending far beyond limited and varying experience. Were it not for this endowment, individuals would grow into mental amoeboids, unlike one another, each merely reflecting the limited and impoverished environment in which he or she develops, lacking entirely the finely articulated, diverse and refined cognitive organs that make possible the rich and creative mental life that is characteristic of all individuals not seriously impaired by individual or social pathology—though once again we must bear in mind that the very same intrinsic factors that permit these achievements also impose severe limits on the states that can be attained; to put it differently, that there is an inseparable connection between the scope and limits of human knowledge.

Finally, let me emphasize the limits on the enterprise I have been outlining. Two individuals with the same genetic endowment and common experience will attain the same state, specifically, the same state of knowledge of language (random elements aside). But this does not preclude the possibility of diversity in the exercise of this knowledge, in thought or action. The study of acquisition of knowledge or of interpretation of experience through the use of acquired knowledge still leaves open the question of the causation of behavior, and more broadly, our ability to choose and decide what we will do.

2

Structures, Capacities, and Conventions

I BEGAN THE first lecture by speaking of human cognitive capacities and mental structures that serve as their vehicles, and then went on to consider the legitimacy of studying such mental structures in the manner of the natural sciences and the prospects for this study, ending by expressing some skepticism as to whether the mind is uniform and undifferentiated in the sense of much of modern psychology and philosophy. Numerous questions arise at every point along the way. The questions of initial structure and modularity are relatively straightforward empirical questions, if we accept the presuppositions they embody: is the mind organized into distinct cognitive faculties with their specific structures and principles, or are there uniform principles of learning, accommodation, assimilation, abstraction, induction, strategy, or whatever that simply apply to different stimulus materials to provide our knowledge of the behavior of objects in physical space, our knowledge that certain strings of words do or do not have certain meanings, and so on. It is reasonably clear how to proceed to settle these issues. As I have already indicated, the available evidence seems to me to favor a modular approach. The other questions, while they have an empirical component, are nevertheless of a very different order.

To know a language, I am assuming, is to be in a certain mental state, which persists as a relatively steady component of transitory mental states. What kind of mental state? I assume further that to be in such a mental state is to have a certain mental structure consisting of a system of rules and principles that generate and relate mental representations of various types. Alternatively, one might attempt to characterize knowledge of language—perhaps knowledge more generally—as a capacity or ability to do something, as a system of dispositions of some kind, in which case one might be led (misled, I think) to conclude that behavior provides a criterion for the possession of knowledge. In contrast, if such knowledge is characterized in terms of mental state and structure, behavior simply provides evidence for possession of knowledge, as might facts of an entirely different order—electrical activity of the brain, for example.

The choice between these alternatives cannot be settled by *a priori* argument, but only by trying to refine each of them to the point where we can ask how they fare as theories that explain some significant range of facts; for example, that certain sentences do or do not mean such-and-such and that we know this to be the case. For the moment, at least, there is no substantive issue. There has been a fair amount of work sketching theories of rules and representations that have at least a degree of descriptive and explanatory success. The proposal that particular items of our knowledge such as those given for illustration in the last lecture can be explained on the assumption that "the speaker has a number of abilities" or "has acquired a number of psychological dispositions"[1] remains merely a promissory note.

I won't attempt to explore the possibilities of fulfilling the promise. I suspect that the attraction will dim when it is recognized
how little can be said in terms of "sets of dispositions." Generally the dispositional analysis is put forth on the grounds that
the facts do not compel us to adopt the alternative, which is
true, but hardly relevant.[2] Surely it suffices that the alternative
stands as the "best explanation," if that much is correct. In the
absence of a coherent alternative, and with at least partial successes to show from the study of theories of rules and representations, I will continue to assume that it is correct to analyze
knowledge of language, and to offer explanations for particular
instances, in terms of mental structures of rules and representations; to assume, in short, that our linguistic abilities are based
on such mental structures.

As already noted, the concept of mental capacities as lacking
structured vehicles is a traditional one. It survives in much contemporary criticism of what is alleged to be the traditional
theory. One version of such a view is found in Wittgenstein, as
for example, when he denies that there are processes in the
brain "correlated with associating or with thinking":

I mean this: if I talk or write there is, I assume, a system of impulses
going out from my brain and correlated with my spoken or written
thoughts. But why should the *system* continue further in the direction
of the centre? Why should this order not proceed, so to speak, out of
chaos? The case would be like the following—certain kinds of plants
multiply by seed, so that a seed always produces a plant of the same
kind as that from which it was produced—but *nothing* in the seed corresponds to the plant which comes from it; so that it is impossible to
infer the properties or structure of the plant from those of the seed that
comes out of it—this can only be done from the *history* of the seed. So
an organism might come into being even out of something quite
amorphous, as it were causelessly; and there is no reason why this

should not really hold for our thoughts, and hence for our talking and writing.

"It is thus perfectly possible that certain psychological phenomena *cannot* be investigated physiologically, because physiologically nothing corresponds to them."[3] It would also follow that these phenomena cannot be investigated within the framework of a theory of mind of the sort I have been discussing. Since physiologically nothing corresponds to our talking, writing and thinking, on this view, there can be no theory of mental structures and processes that attempts to formulate the properties of the nonexistent physiological mechanisms and their operation. We are left with a descriptive study of behavior, potential behavior, dispositions to behave, and so on, a study that in my opinion cannot, in the end, be pursued in a coherent way, for reasons that I have discussed elsewhere.[4]

The two terms of Wittgenstein's analogy—the seed and plant, on the one hand; the brain (or mind) and thoughts (etc.) on the other—have fared very differently in current thinking. We would certainly not want to say that the properties and structure of the plant can in principle only be inferred from the history of the seed, not from its properties and structure. In contrast, Wittgenstein's view of the mind and brain has been influential. It therefore should be considered on its own, without reference to the analogy he proposes, which if anything, counts against his view.

The issue here is not a straightforward empirical one, but it does have an empirical component. In particular, success in developing a structural theory of mind, knowledge and belief would count against the picture of cognition in terms of capacities without structured vehicles, and would indicate that the prevailing concern with organization of and potential for behavior misconceives a certain category of evidence as criterial.

If, as I am now assuming, to know a language is to be in a certain mental state comprised of a structure of rules and principles (comparably, for certain other aspects of cognition), then in theory one could know a language without having the capacity to use it, a possibility that would be denied on the contrary view just mentioned. Let's begin by considering this issue.

Imagine a person who knows English and suffers cerebral damage that does not affect the language centers at all but prevents their use in speech, comprehension, or let us suppose, even in thought.[5] Suppose that the effects of the injury recede and with no further experience or exposure the person recovers the original capacity to use the language. In the intervening period, he had no capacity to speak or understand English, even in thought, though the mental (ultimately physical) structures that underlie that capacity were undamaged. Did the person know English during the intervening period?

This is reminiscent of the question whether a person who is in a dreamless sleep can properly be said to know English, or to know his name. The cognitive property that concerns me holds of the person who possesses the mental structure, thus of the aphasic throughout, as we learn from the fact of his recovery. In this case, the fact of his recovery provides evidence that he had knowledge of English, though none of his behavior (even his thought) at the time provided any evidence for possession of this knowledge.

Suppose that there is a second aphasic like the first, but because of some other and irrelevant problem (say, a circulatory disorder) he never recovers speech. Should we say in this case that the knowledge of English was lost? That would seem perverse. The first aphasic recovered because he had retained a certain mental (ultimately physical) state, a certain state of knowledge, namely, knowledge of English. His recovery provides evidence for the fact. One can imagine all sorts of evidence that might indicate that the aphasic who did not recover was in exactly the same (relevant) state; say, electrical activity of the brain or evidence from autopsy. The conclusion that the second aphasic retained his knowledge of English would have to be based on evidence, of course, but not necessarily evidence from behavior. To deny that the aphasic who did not recover had knowledge of his language would seem as odd a move as to deny that the one who did recover knew his language when he was unable to use this knowledge.

Both of these aphasics remained in a certain cognitive state throughout. "Knowing English" seems to me the appropriate term for designating this state. Were we to identify capacity and knowledge, we would presumably be led to say that the aphasic does not know English when the capacity is lacking, and hence would be committed to the belief that full knowledge of English can arise in a mind totally lacking this knowledge without any relevant experience whatsoever, as the case of recovery shows, something that is plainly not true of the child's mind and seems an exotic claim. I do not want to argue terminology, but will use the term "knows English" with reference to the person with the appropriate mental structure, quite apart from his capacity to use the internally represented knowledge (even in thought) or even to gain access to it. In these terms, which do not seem to me to strain normal usage, two individuals might share exactly the same knowledge (e.g., of English, of music, of calculus, of geography, etc.) but differ greatly in their capacity to use it, which also seems a commonplace; and a person might increase his capacities while gaining no new knowledge. In the same usage, behavior is no criterion for knowledge, though it provides evidence for possession of knowledge, along with much else, in principle. Similar remarks apply in the case of "knowing how," which also involves a crucial intellectual component, often ignored.[6]

Consider now a different case, a child learning English. Suppose that the child is at the stage in which he produces so-called "telegraphic speech," that is, a series of content words without grammatical elements. Imagine the following (not entirely hypothetical) sequence of events. At one point the child produces only telegraphic speech. Shortly after, he makes correct use of grammatical particles such as "do" and, let us say, the whole auxiliary system of English, and does so across the board, that is, in questions, assertions, negations, etc. At the earlier stage, the child did not have the capacity to use such items, so his behavior indicates. Did he have the knowledge of the appropriate rules and forms? In the framework that I am suggesting, the answer might be that he did. That is, it might be that he had fully internalized the requisite mental structure, but for some reason lacked the capacity to use it; perhaps he spoke through a filter that passed only content words, perhaps because of limits on memory. There is evidence in other domains that changes in memory or attention can lead to what appears to be change in the stage of cognitive development.[7] I am assuming this to be a question of fact, for which we might find varied sorts of evidence. One kind of evidence that the child did have the knowledge though without any capacity to use it would be that the whole system appeared, full-blown, in all constructions. This could be explained on the assumption that the knowledge was already internalized though not exhibited because of a filtering effect, a conclusion that might be supported, for example, if we found evidence for the lifting of the memory restriction in other domains. Or, experiment might show that at the earlier stage, the child understood normal speech better than speech with noncontent words randomly interspersed, a finding which would again provide evidence that he possessed the knowledge.[8] Or in principle more exotic means might be devised, say, study of electrical activity of the brain. We cannot enumerate the kinds of evidence that might bear on the truth of the hypothesis that the child had the knowledge, any more than we can in the case of investigation of some other complex system, the internal elements and working of which we are trying to determine. But I see no reason to deny that there is a fact of the matter, however difficult it may be to establish, or that behavior is only one kind of evidence, sometimes not the best, and surely no criterion for knowledge.

Suppose that in contrast to the above sketch, our tests indicated that the child did not have knowledge of the full system of relevant rules when he was in the stage of telegraphic speech. We might then propose a very different account of his state of knowledge at the time. Here is one possibility, again not entirely fanciful. Suppose that what we call "knowing a language" is not a unitary phenomenon, but must be resolved into several interacting but distinct components. One involves the "computational" aspects of language—that is, the rules that form syntactic constructions or phonological or semantic patterns of varied sorts, and that provide the rich expressive power of human language. A second component involves the system of object-reference and also such relations as "agent," "goal," "instrument," and the like; what are sometimes called "thematic relations" or (misleadingly) "case relations." For want of a better term, let us call the latter a "conceptual system." We might discover that the computational aspect of language and the conceptual system are quite differently represented in the mind and brain, and perhaps that the latter should not strictly speaking be assigned to the language faculty at all but rather considered as part of some other faculty that provides "common sense understanding" of the world in which we live. Involved in this system might be what Julius Moravcsik, in a series of very interesting papers, has called the "aitiational" structure of our concepts,[9] that is, their analysis, more or less along Aristotelian lines, in terms of such "generative factors" as origin, function, material constitution, and the like, notions that have reentered recent discussion in the misleading framework of "essences of things" and "identity across possible worlds."[10] Supposing all of this, let us distinguish a system of "computational" rules and representations that constitute the language faculty, strictly speaking, and a system of conceptual structure organized along the lines just indicated. The two systems interact. Thus certain expressions of the linguistic system are linked to elements of the conceptual system and perhaps rules of the linguistic system refer to thematic relations. But it nevertheless might be correct, in a fuller theory of the mind, to distinguish these systems much as we distinguish the visual and circulatory system, though of course they interact. The conceptual system, for example, might have a central role in all sorts of mental acts and processes in which language plays no significant part, might have a different physical basis and different evolutionary history and so on.

Tentatively assuming such a framework as this, let us return to the child in the telegraphic speech stage. Suppose that his conceptual system in the sense of the preceding remarks has partly matured, but his linguistic system has not, apart perhaps from peripheral components that provide sounds and words. The transition from the telegraphic stage to the later stage might be behaviorally identical to the first case we considered, but markedly different in actual character. In the first case, a peripheral change, say in memory, led to the capacity to use an already represented system of knowledge; in the second case, the system of knowledge changed from one state to a different state. Again, the two distinct processes could in principle be distinguished by evidence of varied sorts, but the child's behavior occupies no privileged place and may in fact tell us little or nothing.

Pursuing the matter further, consider again the child in the second example, with a partially developed conceptual system and a minimally functioning language system—which we might think of on the analogy of incipient fluttering motions of a bird before the system of flight has matured.[11] This child might be able to make sense of much of the adult speech around him, as we can often make out what is said in a foreign language when we can identify some of the words, impose a thematic and aitiational structure and use contextual cues, even without much knowledge of the grammar. Actually, normal comprehension under noisy conditions in our own language is in some ways a similar task. But the child's success would not lie in his possession of knowledge of the language that he hears, apart from peripheral aspects.

To evaluate a picture such as this, we might, again, turn to evidence of varied sorts. For example, there might be clinical evidence. It seems that individuals whose left hemispheres were surgically removed in infancy do not, as had been thought previously, develop fully normal language. They show surprising abnormalities in handling very simple structures that involve a degree of computational facility, simple passive sentences for example, though general understanding in normal life is so good that these abnormalities may go unnoticed.[12] Conceivably, further research might show that while the conceptual system is intact, certain elements of the language system are not, and that language use, while superficially normal, involves rather different mechanisms.

Or, to mention another possible example, consider a recent study of a child deprived of language experience until age 13 who showed a degree of apparent language development in subsequent years under therapy and training, with a fair degree of comprehension attained. There is some reason to believe that her knowledge of language does not involve the normal computational system of language, but rather may involve the use of a conceptual system of the type just outlined, a system that is quite distinct from language (though it interacts with it) and perhaps is in a sense more "primitive."[13] One might speculate that higher apes, which apparently lack the capacity to develop even the rudiments of the computational structure of human language, nevertheless may command parts of the conceptual structure just discussed and thus be capable of elementary forms of symbolic function or symbolic communication[14] while entirely lacking the human language faculty. Possible support for such a view derives from work indicating that humans with severe language deficit—perhaps literal destruction of the language faculty—can acquire systems similar to those that have been taught to apes,[15] as if, to put it very loosely, apes were in this regard like humans without the language faculty.

These speculations are not to be confused with a traditional view that *reason* is a distinctly human possession, with normal use of human language an indication of possession of reason as in Descartes's Gedankenexperiments, or that "the express manifestation or work of reason . . . is evidently reduced to what is possible only to abstract, discursive, reflective, and mediate knowledge that is tied to words," that is, that *ratio* is reduced to *oratio*, and thus distinctly human.[16] While the two views are different, they are extensionally similar, insofar as *ratio* devoid of the projective mechanisms of the computational system of human language is severely impaired, almost mute.

These speculations are directed to two points. First, the approach to the study of mind and language that I have been outlining leaves open a variety of avenues of inquiry into the nature and organization of mental structures and the ways in which they develop. While evidence is meager and research is barely beginning, there is enough promise, I think, to suggest that the approach is well worth pursuing, quite apart from what has been achieved within the narrower frame of linguistic inquiry under the idealizations already mentioned. Second, we should not exclude the possibility that what we normally think of as knowledge of language might consist of quite disparate cognitive systems that interweave in normal cognitive development. The system of conceptual structures that involves object-reference with all of its subtleties and complexities, thematic structures, aitiational factors, and the like, might be distinct from the langage faculty, though related to it. The latter possibility relates in obvious ways to recent debate in the philosophical literature about the theory of meaning and belief systems, in part an outgrowth of Quine's important and influential critique of empiricist semantics and in part influenced by Wittgenstein's insights into use of language against the background of belief, intent, and so on, among other sources.

How these issues will be resolved, we can only guess. My own guess is that something along the lines I have just described may be correct. Let us tentatively assume so and continue to inquire into the unitary or modular character of the faculty of language itself. It makes sense, I think, to analyze the mental state of knowing a language into further components, in particular, to distinguish what is sometimes called "grammatical competence" from "pragmatic competence." The term "competence" entered the technical literature in an effort to avoid entanglement with the slew of problems relating to "knowledge," but it is misleading in that it suggests "ability" an association that I would like to sever, for reasons just discussed. By "grammatical competence" I mean the cognitive state that encompasses all those aspects of form and meaning and their relation, including underlying structures that enter into that relation, which are properly assigned to the specific subsystem of the human mind that relates representations of form and meaning. A bit misleadingly perhaps, I will continue to call this subsystem "the language faculty." Pragmatic competence underlies the ability to use such knowledge along with the conceptual system to achieve certain ends or purposes. It might be that pragmatic competence is characterized by a certain system of constitutive rules represented in the mind, as has been suggested in a number of studies.

Again, there are empirical assumptions embedded in the conceptual distinction. For example, I assume that it is possible in principle for a person to have full grammatical competence and no pragmatic competence, hence no ability to use a language appropriately, though its syntax and semantics are intact. To adopt an analogy of Asa Kasher's,[17] this would be something like the case of a policeman who knows the syntax of traffic signals (red and green lights and their sequence, etc.) and their semantics (red means *stop*, etc.) but lacks the knowledge of how to use them to direct traffic. There have, in fact, been some clinical descriptions of language disability that might reflect such a situation, in part at least.[18] The assumptions involved are by no means innocent. They bear directly on questions about "the essence of language" that have figured significantly in contemporary philosophy.[19]

Keeping to grammatical competence, what is to be included under aspects of form and meaning properly assigned to the language faculty? If one rejects the modular approach outlined earlier, the question is meaningless, or rather, the decision is arbitrary, since there is no language faculty and the mental state of knowing a language is some arbitrarily selected subpart of one's total mental state. By "arbitrary" I do not mean "selected on no basis at all," but rather selected on no basis having to do with the structure of the mind. But if one believes the modular approach to have merit, as I do, the question is a reasonable one. It is on a par with the question: what is the human visual system, or the heart, or the circulatory system? Such systems are not physically isolable. As in the case of a "mental organ," which I am taking to be an integrated system of rules and principles generating representations of various sorts, the question is one of appropriate idealization at a certain level of theoretical discussion, a question with empirical content no doubt, but one that can be fully resolved only in the context of broader study of a system that incorporates the given idealized "organ" as a part. It seems to me that no problem of principle arises in the case of the language faculty that does not arise in the case of the visual system or some other system conventionally isolated for special study. We abstract away from connections that obviously exist, hoping to be able to reconstruct ultimately a full picture of the structure and functioning of the total system—recognizing, at the same time, that even the "total system," in this case the individual organism, is itself an idealization reflecting a particular way of looking at things and processes in the world, which does not come ontologically prepackaged as a set of individuals with properties (essential or other) apart from our mode of conception.

In the case of the language faculty, there is a fair consensus on some of the elements that should be incorporated within it, along with considerable dispute about others, in particular those on what might be called "the periphery," to use a metaphor that I hope will not be too misleading. It is conventional, at least since Aristotle, to think of language as form with a meaning. If so, among the representations provided by the system of grammatical competence—henceforth, the grammar—will be representations of form and representations of meaning. These representations are "peripheral" in the sense that they may be regarded as the point of contact between the language faculty and other systems of the mind—again not a necessary assumption, but a reasonable one, I think. We may think of these representations as the ones that enter directly into the use of language. What are the elements of these representations? What is their character? On the modular assumptions outlined, these are obscure empirical questions, to be clarified and answered by empirical inquiry.

To what extent, for example, does the organization of sound properly belong to the system of language rather than to other systems? Here there are real and significant empirical questions concerning perceptual categorization and its possible special relation to language.[20] Studying the interaction between the perceptual system and the system of language, with particular attention to possible specialization for language, we can hope to refine our understanding of the representation of form provided by grammar, and thus of the rules that enter into determining this representation.

Still more debated, perhaps more intractable problems arise in considering representations of meaning. Do the "semantic rules" of natural language that are alleged to give the meanings of words belong to the language faculty strictly speaking, or should they be regarded perhaps as centrally-embedded parts of a conceptual or belief system, or do they subdivide in some way? Much of the debate about these matters has been inconclusive. It turns on dubious intuitions as to whether we would still call our pets "cats" if we learned that they are descended from robots controlled by Martians, or whether we would call the stuff in the Ganges "water" were we to discover that it differs in chemical composition from what flows in the Mississippi. It is harder, I think, to make up a story compatible with the assumption that I persuaded you to leave but at no point did you intend to leave; quite generally, arguments for analytic connections of some sort involving properties of the verbal system, with its network of thematic relations, are more compelling than those devised for common nouns. Even assuming there to be certain analytic connections, as I believe to be the case, the question remains whether these are to be assigned to the language faculty, hence to appear in some form in its representations of meaning, or to a conceptual system of a sort perhaps organized along the lines already discussed. Similarly, suppose that our notion of a "thing" involves considerations of spatio-temporal contiguity as well as human action, as discussed in the references noted earlier (see chapter 1, note 61). If so, have we isolated a "semantic universal" or a fact about our conceptual systems? Similar questions arise in connection with more complex semantic properties, for example, certain possible universals relating to abstract and concrete interpretation of common nouns.[21]

Or consider another question that has been much debated. Certain discourses are appropriate in a sense in which others are not. For example, if I say "it was DICKENS who wrote *Moby Dick*,"[22] you can appropriately respond: "No, it was MELVILLE," but not: "No, it was DAVID COPPERFIELD." If you were to give the latter response, I would understand you to be asserting that David Copperfield wrote *Moby Dick*. The point can be expressed in terms of focus and presupposition, in one of the senses of these terms, and relates to the position of main stress. In this a matter of semantics or pragmatics? Is it to receive expression in terms of the representations provided by the grammar or not?

Or to take a last case, suppose that we agree that some sort of representation of quantificational structure is to be given by the grammar at the level of representation of meaning. Does the notation matter? Should the representation involve quantifiers or variables, or be in a variable-free notation, or is the question without empirical import?

There are innumerable questions of this sort. How we proceed to deal with them depends on the point of view we adopt towards what we are doing. Suppose, for example, that someone rejects the approach outlined here or is just not interested in it, and is pursuing some other aim, let us say, to codify logical inference using natural language sentences.[23] Then all properties entering into such inference and only these will appear in his "representations of meaning." For example, suppose it can be shown that pragmatic rather than logical presupposition is involved in the case of "it is DICKENS who wrote *Moby Dick*." Then the relevant properties of this sentence will not be encoded in "representations of meaning," for the study of logical entailment, no matter what the character of the rules that govern the phenomenon may be. Suppose it turns out that presupposition in the sense required to account for these cases is governed by rules that fall within grammar in a narrow sense, perhaps rules that enter into determining representations involved in logical inference in other cases. Then the person who is concerned to map out the properties of the language faculty will include these properties in his "representations of meaning," whatever the status of the presupposition. There has been much empty discussion of these questions, though perhaps deeper issues are masked in it, for example, questions of psychological realism and modularity.

If one adopts the point of view that I have been discussing here, then it is clear how to proceed to answer these questions, at least in principle. We will try to construct coherent and integrated systems with explanatory power and see where the examples fall. If the idealization to the language faculty and its subcomponents is legitimate, that is, if it corresponds to some significant aspect of reality, we may be able to find an answer to these questions. My impression is that at the moment we often cannot; the available evidence is inadequate and the theories not sound enough to bear the weight. In some cases, I think there are possibilities for an answer. For example, in the matter of stress and presupposition, there is reason to believe that the rules fall within grammatical competence, so that the properties appear in the representations of meaning it provides.[24] Were it to be shown that these matters do not bear on logical inference but only, say, on conversational implicature, we would then conclude that representations of meaning generated by the rules of grammar provide materials for conversational implicature, not that they must exclude these elements. And if some attribute of a sentence that enters into logical inference turns out not to be provided by the best theory of grammar that we can devise, we will conclude that this is not an element of the representations of meaning provided by grammatical competence. Proceeding in this way, we will try to identify just what it is that we have loosely been calling "representations of meaning," much in the way that we will try to determine the properties of linguistic representations of sound. The fact that the conclusions may not conform to some a priori scheme or satisfy some specific need such as codifying inference is, plainly, irrelevant to this empirical inquiry. I am assuming, in short, that we are trying to answer a difficult empirical question, only partially clear, which can become more precise only in the course of finding some answers to it: namely, what are the real components of mental states.

Taking a grammar to be a system of rules that provides representations of sound and meaning (among others), their specific character to be determined as research progresses, our task is to discover the representations that appear and the rules operating on them and relating them; and more important, to discover the system of universal grammar that provides the basis on which they develop. One may think of the genotype as a function that maps a course of experience into the phenotype. In these terms, universal grammar is an element of the genotype that maps a course of experience into a particular grammar that constitutes the system of mature knowledge of a language, a relatively steady state achieved at a certain point in normal life.

Thinking about the question we now face in rather general and qualitative terms, we can make a fair guess as to what we should discover, if this inquiry succeeds. An investigation of the final states attained, that is, the grammars, reveals that the knowledge acquired and to a large extent shared involves judgments of extraordinary delicacy and detail. The argument from poverty of the stimulus leaves us no reasonable alternative but to suppose that these properties are somehow determined in universal grammar, as part of the genotype. There is simply no evidence available to the language learner to fix them, in many crucial cases that have been studied. Nevertheless, people obviously speak different languages depending on their limited individual experience. As translators are well aware, there need be no point-by-point comparison between languages, and linguistic work reveals considerable variety. Given these properties of language, what we should expect to discover is a system of universal grammar with highly restrictive principles that narrowly constrain the category of attainable grammars, but with parameters that remain open to be fixed by experience. If the system of universal grammar is sufficiently rich, then limited evidence will suffice for the development of rich and complex systems in the mind, and a small change in parameters may lead to what appears to be a radical change in the resulting system. What we should be seeking, then, is a system of unifying principles that is fairly rich in deductive structure but with parameters to be fixed by experience. Endowed with this system and exposed to limited experience, the mind develops a grammar that consists of a rich and highly articulated system of rules, not grounded in experience in the sense of inductive justification, but only in that experience has fixed the parameters of a complex schematism with a number of options. The resulting systems, then, may vastly transcend experience in their specific properties but yet be radically different from one another, at least on superficial examination; and they may not be comparable point-by-point in general.

Keeping to the rather vague level of these qualitative remarks, which I will try to make a bit more precise in the fourth lecture, the problem of accounting for the growth of different languages, each of which lacks an inductive grounding in experience,[25] is not unlike the general problem of growth, or for that matter, speciation. It appears that the biochemistry of life is rather similar across all living organisms and that, as François Jacob puts it:

it was not biochemical innovation that caused diversification of organisms. . . . What accounts for the difference between a butterfly and a lion, a chicken and a fly, or a worm and a whale is not their chemical components, but varying distributions of these components . . . specialization and diversification called only for different utilization of the same structural information. . . . It is thanks to complex regulatory circuits, which either unleash or restrain the various biochemical activities of the organism, that the genetic program is implemented. [In related organisms, mammals for example], the diversification and specialization . . . are the result of mutations which altered the organism's regulatory circuits more than its chemical structures. The minor modification of redistributing the structures in time and space is enough to profoundly change the shape, performance, and behavior of the final product.[26]

The logic is rather similar to what I have outlined in the case of acquisition of knowledge of language. In a system that is sufficiently intricate in structure, small changes at particular points can lead to substantial differences in outcome. In the case of growth of organs, mental organs in our case, small changes in parameters left open in the general schematism can lead to what appear to be very different systems.

I think we may now be at the stage where, for the first time really, we can propose systems of universal grammar that at least have the right properties. I have no doubt that they are incorrect, at least in detail, perhaps in general conception. But they do have the right properties, and that seems to me of some importance. That is, the systems that are now being investigated by a number of linguists do have a deductive structure that permits a range of empirical phenomena to be derived from some simple and I think rather natural principles, and they also have the property that small changes in the parameters in some of the general principles lead to quite different languages. These are the kinds of systems we hope to find, whether or not the systems of universal grammar currently being investigated will prove to be on the right track.

Steven Stich has pointed out that even if we entirely abandon the empiricist framework that both he and I regard as inadequate for the study of cognition,[27] it does not follow logically that one must postulate that there are certain "linguistic universals," by which he means certain features common to all languages.[28] He is quite correct, for several reasons. In the first place, no theory of what underlies language acquisition follows logically from a rejection of the empiricist framework. It might turn out, for example, that it takes place by black magic. What is at stake, again, is "argument to the best explanation."[29] But he goes further and argues that no evidence at all has been provided for specific theories of language universals that I (and others) have advanced. Here he is just wrong; some evidence has certainly been provided, for example, by application of the argument from poverty of the stimulus already discussed, though the argument is certainly inconclusive—as it must be—and perhaps, one might argue, not strong enough to ground the hypotheses put forth as the "best explanation," an entirely different matter. A second point has to do with his interpretation of the term "linguistic universals," which is quite different from the usage of the work he criticizes, in which "universal grammar" is taken to be the set of properties, conditions, or whatever that constitute the "initial state" of the language learner, hence the basis on which knowledge of language develops. It by no means follows from such an account that there must be specific elements or rules common to all languages, or what he calls "features" common to all languages, unless we take these "features" in a suitably abstract manner, in which case, the controversy dissolves.

I have been speaking of "knowing English" as a mental state (or a stable component of mental states), or a property of a person in a certain mental state, but we may want to analyze this property in relational terms. What is it that is known? Ordinary usage would say: a language—and I have so far been keeping to this usage, speaking of knowing and learning a *language*, e.g., English. But it is implicit in what I have said that this way of talking can be misleading. I think it has been, and would now like to explain why. To avoid terminological confusion, let me introduce a technical term devised for the purpose, namely "cognize," with the following properties. The particular things we know, we also cognize. In the case of English, presented with the examples "the candidates wanted each other to win" and "the candidates wanted me to vote for each other," we know that the former means that each wanted the other to win, and that the latter is not well-formed with the meaning that each wanted me to vote for the other. We therefore cognize these facts. Furthermore, we cognize the system of mentally-represented rules from which the facts follow. That is, we cognize the grammar that constitutes the current state of our language faculty and the rules of this system as well as the principles that govern their operation. And finally we cognize the innate schematism, along with its rules, principles and conditions.

In fact, I don't think that "cognize" is very far from "know" where the latter term is moderately clear, but this seems to me a relatively minor issue, similar to the question whether the terms "force" and "mass" in physics depart from their conventional sense (as they obviously do). If the person who cognized the grammar and its rules could miraculously became conscious of them, we would not hesitate to say that he knows the grammar and its rules, and that this conscious knowledge is what constitutes his knowledge of his language. Thus "cognizing" is tacit or implicit knowledge, a concept that seems to me unobjectionable. Putting aside until the next lecture the case of "innate knowledge," cognizing has the structure and character of knowledge, but may be and in the interesting cases is inaccessible to consciousness. Concluding this terminological disgression, I will return to the terms "know" and "knowledge," but now using them in the sense of "cognize"—that is, admitting both conscious and tacit knowledge—and hoping that possible confusion will have been allayed.[30] The fundamental cognitive relation is knowing a grammar; knowing the language determined by it is derivative. Correspondingly, it raises additional problems, to which I will return.

This way of formulating the issues is commonly thought to involve difficulties that do not arise under some other way of construing the notion "knowledge of a language." Once again, the matter is often discussed in the context of the theory of meaning, but the general difficulty holds, if at all, in the case of other parts of the theory of language as well. J. A. Foster, for example, urges that "Instead of demanding a statement of those metalinguistic facts which the mastery of a language implicitly recognizes, let us demand a statement of those facts explicit recognition of which gives mastery."[31] In our case, this amounts to the injunction that we should not try to formulate the grammar that a person implicitly knows (so we claim), but rather to state the facts that he explicitly knows, e.g., the facts about reciprocals just mentioned. There is, however, a problem in understanding Foster's term "statement of the facts," since the facts are infinite in number. We can therefore state them only by giving something like a grammar. His point, I take it, is that we should not regard the grammar we postulate as a component of the mind, then seeking to test this hypothesis in whatever way we can; we should not take the normal "realist" stance towards our theoretical constructions. By parity of argument, a scientist studying vision might develop a theory involving certain types of computation and representation for identification of objects in motion, but he should not attribute the mechanisms he postulates to the organism he is studying, nor, presumably, go on to investigate the correctness of his theory by bringing other kinds of evidence to bear on it; nor should he search for mechanisms with the properties he has specified. If his theory "states the facts" about the identification of objects in motion, that is where he should stop. I doubt that Foster would take this position with regard to the theory of vision, still less the theory of the atom or solar physics. Why then does the study of language fall under these strictures? Why should we adopt this version of the bifurcation thesis?[32]

The reason Foster adduces is this: "What we are then demanding is still a theory of meaning, but without the questionable assumption that one who has mastered the language has, at some deep level, absorbed the information which it supplies. The theory reveals the semantic machinery which competence works, but leaves undetermined the psychological form in which competence exists." Note again that there is nothing special here about the theory of meaning; the same considerations hold, if at all, for phonology, syntax, pragmatic competence, and so on.

I do not find this very compelling. Suppose we have a theory which reveals the machinery that enters into competence, whether semantic, phonological, syntactic, or pragmatic. In what sense does that theory "leave undetermined the psychological form in which competence exists?" Or to put it differently, what does the theory lack that some further theory might provide that would not leave the psychological form undetermined? I can't imagine what the answer to this question might be. To find "the psychological form in which competence exists," just as to find the answers to the questions of the theory of vision or solar physics, all that we can do is try to construct the best theories possible to explain interesting evidence, then assuming that our theories are true accounts so that we can proceed to confront them with further empirical tasks of explanation. It is not that I object to Foster's qualifications; I simply do not see in what respects his proposal differs from some other one that he wants to reject as perhaps too audacious or metaphysically unsound.

Furthermore, in what respect is it a "questionable assumption" to say that someone who has mastered a language has absorbed the information that the best theory we can devise supplies? Certainly such an assumption is questionable in one respect: the theory might be incorrect, and in practice probably is.

But this is the general condition of all empirical work. So if this is the reason, it ought to be an equally questionable assumption that the light emitted from the sun is caused by hydrogen turning into helium, and so on.[33] I do not believe that a case has been made for these strictures, or even that they are particularly intelligible.

Sometimes arguments against the approach I have been outlining are cast in a Wittgensteinian mode, which seeks to cure us of the idea that there is anything puzzling to explain at all. A case in point is a critical essay by J. F. M. Hunter called "On How We Talk."[34] Hunter believes that proposals of the sort I have been outlining are so wrong as to be "incredible." Specifically, it is "incredible" to propose that there could be some explanatory power to a theory that attributes tacit knowledge of principles of universal grammar to a child, and then accounts for his resulting state of knowledge of language by deriving the grammar that expresses this knowledge from the interplay of tacit knowledge and experience.

Let us assume that more is at stake here than a debate about the term "knowledge." If that were the issue, then we could shift to "cognize" and recast the discussion in these terms, noting, however, that we are concerned to account for examples of what anyone would call "knowledge."[35] It is clear that that is not what Hunter has in mind. Rather, he is concerned to show that there can be no explanatory power to an account given in these terms, that at most such theories might be "useful" for such purposes as programming a computer to do translation or for code-breaking.

Hunter's argument is not that theories actually developed along these lines have various inadequacies, but rather that even if they were completely successful in their own terms, they would in no sense be explanatory in the sense in which a theory of the internal workings of the sun explains the character of the light emitted from its periphery, but would only be useful for this or that purpose. To use his own analogy, they would be like the discovery that a planet follows a certain path, but in principle not like Newtonian physics, which proposes an explanation for the fact. Furthermore, we would have no warrant to regard anything discovered in this quest as characterizing a state or property of a person or an element of his mental state. In his words, it does not "follow, if our linguistic output can be shown to have just the shape that would be generated by following a certain set of rules, that it is by our following those rules that it comes to have that shape." Therefore a theory of grammar cannot be "explanatory," nor can a theory of universal grammar serve as part of a still deeper explanation for specific facts. If there are any explanations at all for "how we talk," they will be of a very different order; exactly what, he does not say, nor does he suppose that there is or need be any explanation for this ability.

Before turning to Hunter's argument, let us consider more carefully its conclusion. Consider again a specific set of facts, say, those already used for illustration: the sentence "the candidates wanted each other to win" has roughly the meaning that each wanted the other to win, whereas "the candidates wanted me to vote for each other" is not a well-formed sentence meaning that each wanted me to vote for the other. These are things that we know, in anyone's sense of "know." These instances of our knowledge are on a par with some fact about the light emitted by the sun. The facts don't have to come out this way on any logical grounds; these are empirical facts, if anything is. It is difficult to see any reason, then, for denying that it makes sense to seek an explanation as to why the facts come out this way rather than some other way.

Suppose that someone proposes a system of rules that yields these consequences, with all other meritorious qualities that one would like the "best theory" to have. According to Hunter, this might be useful for code-breaking but however meritorious, it could not be said to explain the facts but only to describe them, as distinct from a physical theory about the interior of the sun, which offers an explanation for the character of the emitted light, right or wrong. His reason is that it does not "follow" from their success in dealing with the facts that these rules give the correct account of what we actually do, or by the same token, of the neural processes involved. So far he is surely correct. Similarly, it does not "follow" from any degree of success, however spectacular, that a theory of the solar interior is correct.[36] It might be, to adapt Hunter's comments about the mind and brain, that little men within the sun are turning gears and cranks. Do we then deny any explanatory power even in principle to a theory of solar physics? We should, on Hunter's grounds.

Suppose that someone proposes an even deeper theory to account for the facts just cited; namely, a theory of universal grammar from which we can, let us say, literally deduce the grammar that gives a first-order account of the facts, given boundary conditions set by experience. Not only would this achievement carry no explanatory power, according to Hunter, but it is "incredible" to propose otherwise. He considers this sufficiently obvious to pass without comment. This is a stance which really does merit the term "incredible."

Note again that Hunter is not merely making terminological points. He thinks he is establishing something about explanatory theories, in particular, theories about "how we talk." He suggests that our ability to speak does not really "*need* an explanation," as we see when we cure ourselves of some misleading ideas, such as those I have been discussing. After all, we already know how to talk. In fact, "if one does not know how to talk, one can not ask how it is done, or understand the answer." Notice that a serious confusion underlies these remarks, even in Hunter's own framework. There is a vast difference between knowing how to do so-and-so and knowing how we do so-and-so; the latter is not a case of "knowing how" at all.

Hunter's basic argument against the approach I have outlined with its aspirations to potential descriptive and explanatory power is the one just mentioned; it does not "follow" from descriptive or predictive (or any other kind of) success that the principles postulated actually are the correct ones, which is certainly true, but irrelevant. He offers other arguments, but they really are terminological. Thus he has in mind a notion of "rule" as in "the rules of golf," and argues that we cannot say that the nervous system follows rules in his sense, which again is true but completely uninteresting; the relevant question, surely, is whether the nervous system can be said to follow rules in the sense of "rule" advanced in the theories he regards as incredible, and on this matter he says nothing.

It is worth inquiring a bit further into the source of these strange conclusions, which are in fact not uncommon ones. Hunter's actual arguments are actually not directed specifically against proposed explanations of the sort I have been discussing, though his conclusions are so sweeping as to count against such explanations, were these conclusions valid. Rather, his argument is directed against proposed explanations for how we talk, that is, for what I have called "the creative aspect of language," the ability of all normal persons to produce speech that is appropriate to situations though perhaps quite novel, and to understand when others do so. He believes that "linguistic theorists are making a fundamental mistake if they suppose that generative grammar explains how we actually talk," and therefore concludes that such linguistic theories are at best useful for some such purpose as code-breaking but can in principle have no psychological import. Note that he completely excludes from consideration the problem of explaining such facts as the ones I have just mentioned; even the best and deepest explanation of these and any number of similar facts would not provide an explanation for how we talk. While rejecting as "incredible" any claim to explanatory power put forward with regard to universal grammar, he entirely overlooks the class of facts that such theories hope to explain.

This omission alone suffices to undermine Hunter's argument. He is quite correct when he says that "linguistic theorists are making a fundamental mistake if they suppose that generative grammar explains how we actually talk," or further, if they were to suppose that universal grammar provides a still deeper explanation, by accounting (if successful) for the development of grammar in the mind. But surely no one whose work Hunter is discussing has ever supposed this. The question of how we talk remains in the domain of mysteries, in the sense of the first lecture.

It has been emphasized ad nauseum in the literature that a generative grammar is not a "talking machine," in Hunter's sense. Virtually the whole of his argument is directed against input-output theories that purport to explain how we talk. This part of the argument is in part reasonable enough but offers no support at all for his general conclusions, unless we accept his tacit premise that there are only two possibilities for linguistic theory: either it explains how we talk, that is, explains the creative aspect of language use, or it explains nothing, even in principle. But this dilemma merely reflects a serious failure of imagination.

As soon as we recognize that there is much else to be explained apart from the creative aspect of language use, we can proceed to construct theories of grammar and universal grammar, disregarding Hunter's qualms about theories that purport to explain how we talk. The sole consideration that remains is the contention that in this domain (though presumably not in others) we must reject the normal realist stance of other branches of empirical inquiry and must be brought to a halt by the fact that theories do not follow from evidence. This attitude appears throughout Hunter's discussion, for example, when he says that even if we had some account of how we talk (as we surely do not) in terms of some hypothetical "talking machine," we would still "need evidence, not only that the task can be performed in the way the machine does it, but that it is in fact so performed." He mentions some possible kinds of evidence, e.g., conscious awareness of the processes proposed, correctly dismissing them (though there are, in fact, innumerable types of potential evidence that are not so easily dismissed, as already noted in other connections). But what is odd is his belief that we "need" such additional evidence. Surely no evidence we could obtain would suffice to prove that the task is performed in the way the hypothetical machine does it, but by the same token every empirical theory must be rejected, and will be rejected for all time. We might "need evidence" because what we have so far is simply not compelling, but that again is the familiar condition of empirical inquiry, hardly noteworthy in this connection. Apart from the impossible demands it places on empirical inquiry, Hunter's discussion involves a clear violation of the reasonable rule that I mentioned earlier: that it is absurd to pose requirements for psychology that the "hard" sciences cannot meet, and that if we do want to consider the nontrivial questions of realism (broadly understood), it is pointless to consider the weak and emerging sciences, with the very limited insight they provide; rather, we should raise these questions in connection with scientific work that has achieved incomparably more firm and significant results, at least, if our aim is to gain some understanding of the issues.

If confusions of the sort just noted are eliminated, Hunter would perhaps want to fall back on another position that he puts forth; namely, that when a "question can be asked and answered outside of philosophy, it is philosophically uninteresting." Perhaps the questions I have been discussing, or the answers that have been suggested or might in principle be provided, are "outside of philosophy," though in this case his attempt to show why any such approach is deeply misguided in principle is entirely beside the point. This too is a familiar move. There is no doubt that one can progressively limit "philosophy" so that it approaches the null set of interesting questions, or perhaps limit it to questions that while extraordinarily interesting seem to lie beyond the domains of inquiry as we can currently conceive them (or perhaps ever conceive them, given the nature of our intelligence), for example, the problem of accounting for the creative aspect of language use or other similar questions that arise when we consider Descartes's "indeterminate" action, questions of will and choice that will remain shrouded in mystery even if we achieve the fullest imaginable success in a study of the mind of the sort I have been discussing. Recall again that even the most amazing success in this endeavor, while it might identify the mechanisms of mind, would not answer the question of how they are used. Delimiting philosophy in this way, it is necessary to conclude that major philosophers of the past and present—Hume, Descartes, Quine and others—have seriously misidentified what they are doing, and such conclusions have in fact commonly been drawn within the philosophical tradition in which Hunter works.

Perhaps Hunter's insistence that a theory of language must explain "how we talk" if it is to explain anything at all derives from the belief that in some sense yet to be explained, the "essence of language" is communication. Therefore unless one talks about a "talking machine," one is really not talking about language at all in any serious way. It is true enough that views of this nature are sometimes expressed. I have yet to see a formulation that makes any sense of the position that "the essence of language is communication."[37] People who feel that they understand it, and who believe further that it is true, should still be able to recognize that facts of the sort I have been discussing still demand explanation, whatever may be "the essence of language." Even were we to grant their claim, we could still search for explanatory theories that are concerned with the state of knowledge attained by someone who knows a language and the basis in the human genetic constitution for the acquisition of such knowledge, recognizing that even full success will still not have answered all questions, for example, the question "how we talk," just as an account of our knowledge would still leave open the question of "how we act." It would be quite correct to say that something very important is left out, in both cases; I not only agree, but insist on that. Those who claim further that "the essence" is left out have yet to explain themselves, at least to my satisfaction.

Let us return to Foster's argument that we should limit ourselves to stating the facts "explicit recognition of which gives mastery" of a language, rather than try to construct a theory with truth claims concerning mastery of language. A more extended argument with somewhat similar import appears in an interesting and lucid paper by David Lewis that deals with questions similar to those I have been discussing, but reaches very different conclusions.[38] Lewis puts forth two theses concerning "language and languages," one having to do with conventions in language and the other with the pairing of sound and meaning. The first thesis offers an analysis of the phrase "the language L is *used* by a population P"; this is so if and only if "there prevails in P a convention of truthfulness and trust in L, sustained by an interest in communication." A "convention," in Lewis's sense, is a regularity "in action or in action and belief" sustained by the belief that others conform to the regularity. Note that this is a rather restricted sense of the term "convention." There are, no doubt, conventional aspects of language: for example, the fact that one says "hello" in answering a telephone or calls a chair "a chair." But it is questionable that people have reasons in anything like Lewis's sense for acting in accordance with these conventions. Furthermore, regularities in action and belief are quite restricted, at least if we insist that "regularities" have detectable probabilities; there is little reason to suppose that aspects of language that are commonly called "conventional" involve detectable regularities. Other questions can be raised about the first thesis, but I am concerned only with one, namely, how a population or a person can observe conventions or have beliefs concerning a language L. This leads us to the second thesis, which offers a characterization of the object L that is "used by a population" and concerning which individuals observe conventions.

Lewis defines a language as a function associating sound and meaning. Putting aside his definition of "meaning" in terms of possible worlds, which seems to me wrong if only because of familiar problems concerning propositional attitudes,[39] his characterization of a "language" as a pairing of sound and meaning over an infinite domain is traditional and reasonable as a point of departure. It brings us back to questions already noted: namely, what are the proper representations of sound and meaning, what are the rules of grammar relating them, and what is the relation between the person and these rules and representations?

Lewis objects to what I have just been saying about these questions: basically that universal grammar is part of the genotype specifying one aspect of the initial state of the human mind and brain, and that the language faculty assumes the character of a particular grammar under the triggering and shaping effect of experience, where the grammar is a system of rules and principles that determines a pairing of sound and meaning (or better, a pairing of conditions on sound and meaning given by appropriate representations). The grammar is a function in intension, though this remark is misleading, since the grammar has many important properties beyond specifying a language in extension and in fact may not even specify such a language, though it will be none the worse for that, a matter to which I will return in the next lecture. From the point of view I have adopted, universal grammar and the steady state grammar are real. We expect to find them physically represented in the genetic code and the adult brain, respectively, with the properties discovered in our theory of the mind. But the language is epiphenomenal. Its ontological status is the same as that of a set of pairs of expressions that rhyme—a set that may also be determined by the grammar—or the set of responses in some idealized psycholinguistic experiment in which extralinguistic factors are eliminated.

Lewis explicitly rejects this point of view. He is "much less certain that there are internally represented grammars than . . . that languages are used by populations," and he "know[s] of no promising way to make objective sense of the assertion that a grammar Γ is used by a population P whereas another grammar, Γ', which generates the same language as Γ, is not." He believes that "there are facts about [the population] P which objectively select the languages used by P" but he is "not sure there are facts about P which objectively select privileged grammars for those languages." He believes that a problem of inductive uncertainty arises in the case of grammars but not, or not in the same pernicious way, in the case of the notion "language used by the population P." He might be interpreted as offering a version of the thesis that the capacity to use language has no structured vehicle, but from a different intellectual tradition than the ones I have mentioned.

I think he is wrong on all counts. Conventions in his sense, that is regularities in action and belief, even putting aside the crucial question of "reasons," will cover only some finite and in fact extremely small set of phenomena; again, if we insist that "regularities" have detectable probabilities. There is, for example, no "regularity" that relates to the fact that "the candidates wanted each other to win" is paired with roughly the same meaning as "each candidate wanted the other to win," whereas "the candidates wanted me to vote for each other" is paired with no meaning. Outside of the surely finite and in fact extremely small domain of conventional pairings, the language remains to be somehow fixed. Since the language is infinite, it makes no sense to speak of it as "given," except insofar as some finite characterization—a function in intension—is given. The inductive problem is to determine this function in intension, the grammar, given some finite amount of data. That is the problem both for the language-learner and for the linguist. A person can neither follow conventions for an infinite language nor have expectations with regard to observance of conventions by others, without some finite characterization of the language that is somehow under his control. We can perhaps make sense of Lewis's notion, "the language L is used by a population P," but only indirectly, through the medium of a specific character- ization of L, a grammar (or perhaps even more indirectly, through a class of weakly equivalent grammars).[40] This notion unpacks into something like: each person in P has a grammar determining L in his mind/brain. Contrary to what Lewis as- serts, any fact that "objectively selects" the language also "objec- tively selects" the grammar—that is, the fact provides evidence for the grammar, hence indirectly for the infinite set L (the lan- guage) determined by the grammar, or the set of rhyming pairs, etc. Without reference to the grammar, and to a theory of ac- cessible grammars, the given facts tell us nothing at all about the language, except that these facts pertain to it somehow. In fact, the language-learner and (rational) linguist may reject cer- tain alleged facts on grounds provided by the theory of gram- mar. Contrary to what Lewis maintains, the inductive problem arises in a far more serious form for "language" than for "gram- mar," in fact, in an insuperable form, since there are no constraints at all on how the "induction" is to proceed (in fact, I think there is no "induction" in any meaningful sense of the term, but that is still another problem). Furthermore, the range of facts relevant to choosing a grammar goes far beyond sound-meaning pairings, since the grammar has consequences far beyond this pairing that it determines. In fact, one can go further still and hold, correctly, that we have no clear sense of the notions "sound" and "meaning" that enter into Lewis's data except in terms of a theory of grammar, for reasons already discussed.

Lewis's belief that it is easier to make sense of the notion "language L is used by population P" than of the notion "language L is determined by internally represented grammar G" seems quite wrong. Certainly he presents no way to make sense of his notion, and I can imagine no reasonable way except derivatively, in terms of shared internal representation. His problem is to explain how a person can use an infinite language, or have an infinite set of expectations about sound-meaning pairings and much else, without any internal representation of that infinite object, and further, how that infinite object—a language—can be "shared" by a population without any internal representations in the minds of members of this population. I concede that it is not a logical impossibility; for example, all members of the population might be controlled by some demon. But I don't see any basis for his belief that it is easier to make sense of his notion than of the notion "internal representation of a grammar." At least, if current natural science is anywhere near the mark, a very different conclusion seems warranted. Lewis has rejected an approach that at least might be correct in favor of one that makes no sense at all. Both of his theses seem to me fundamentally flawed.

There are many other versions of the same position. One extreme version is Quine's claim that it is senseless to say that if two grammars generate the same language (are "extensionally equivalent," in his terminology)[41] then one might be right and the other wrong. Perhaps the source of these positions, apart from the heavy hand of empiricist doctrine, lies in the fact that for a given language there may be many (in fact, infinitely many) grammars,[42] which may lead one to believe, erroneously, that the inductive problem of selecting a grammar is harder than that of selecting a language (perhaps infinitely harder, i.e., impossible). But attention to the empirical conditions of the task of acquiring mastery of an infinite system shows that this is an error.

Notice that it might be a reasonable move to abstract away from grammars and consider only the languages that they generate. Most of the work in mathematical linguistics does just that, and results have been attained that even have some empirical significance. It might turn out that there are significant properties of a class of grammars—say, those provided by universal grammar—that are best expressed and studied in terms of the languages they generate, just as on so-called "functionalist" grounds, it is argued that certain properties of nervous systems may best be studied by abstracting away from the physical realization and considering them in the context of a theory of mind. But it is important to recognize that when we move from grammar to language we are moving a step further away from the mechanisms; we are moving to a higher stage of abstraction, and perhaps illegitimately so, for reasons to which I will return in the next lecture. The common conception that the opposite is true is seriously in error.

I see no reasonable alternative to the position that grammars are internally represented in the mind, and that the basic reason why knowledge of language comes to be shared in a suitably idealized population (and partially shared in actual populations) is that its members share a rich initial state, hence develop similar steady states of knowledge. There are, obviously, many reasons for skepticism about specific proposals that are put forth in the effort to characterize these grammars and the universal grammar from which they allegedly develop, and about the various idealizations that enter into them. In the next two lectures, I want to consider some further questions about knowledge of grammar and to sketch what seem to me to be some promising ideas about grammars and universal grammar.

3

Knowledge of Grammar

IN THE PRECEDING lectures, I have been discussing elements of a theory of human knowledge that is concerned with
such traditional questions as "What is human knowledge?"
"How does it arise in the individual?" "In what respects is it
shared?" Comparable questions arise concerning other cognitive
systems, for example, systems of individual and shared belief.
The discussion has been "mentalistic," but I think in an innocuous sense. It takes no stand on issues of materialism (in fact, I
have expressed some skepticism about the content of these issues, given that "body" is an open and evolving concept), but
rather proceeds as an inquiry at a certain level of abstraction
into the nature of certain mechanisms, presumably neural
mechanisms, now largely unknown. The level of abstraction is
appropriate insofar as it enables fundamental properties of these
systems to be isolated, analyzed, and explained; and insofar as
results obtained at this level provide a guide for the study of
mechanisms, much as study of chemical properties provides a
guide for inquiry into atomic theory or as a theory of feature detectors of the auditory system might lay a basis for research into
the neurophysiology of hearing. I am tentatively assuming the
mind to be modular in structure, a system of interacting subsystems that have their own special properties. What little is known

supports this view. The only reasonable research strategy, so far as I can see, is to study particular systems and their interaction. If the modular approach is incorrect, such study will reveal, contrary to what I expect, that these systems involve the same principles and develop in the same way from a common basis.[1] I have been attempting to isolate for special study one of these systems, the faculty of human language. I have suggested that what we loosely call "knowledge of language" involves in the first place knowledge of grammar—indeed, that language is a derivative and perhaps not very interesting concept—and beyond that other cognitive systems that interact with grammar: conceptual systems with their specific properties and organizing principles may be quite different in character from the "computational" language faculty; pragmatic competence might be a cognitive system distinct and differently structured from grammatical competence; these systems may furthermore be composed of distinct though interacting components. If so, we should not expect a unitary answer to the question "What is knowledge of human language and how does it arise?" Rather, we will find that the question was wrongly put; it does not identify a natural kind. If this turns out to be correct, it should occasion no surprise. There is little reason to suppose that ordinary common sense notions will prove any more appropriate for the theory of knowledge than they are for the study of the physical world (or I should say, other aspects of the physical world).

I am assuming grammatical competence to be a system of rules that generate and relate certain mental representations, including in particular representations of form and meaning, the exact character of which is to be discovered, though a fair amount is known about them. These rules, furthermore, operate in accordance with certain general principles. I have informally discussed rules of grammar which, for example, move a question-word to the front of a sentence or associate an antecedent with an anaphoric expression such as "each other." Such rules can be formulated quite precisely within an explicit theory of rules and representations, along lines to which I will return in the final lecture. I offered a few linguistic examples to illustrate certain principles that govern the application of these rules. For the moment, I will simply give names to these principles, leaving further characterization to later discussion: the movement rule is governed by a principle of "locality"—elements of mental representation can't be moved "too far"—and the choice of antecedent by a principle of "opacity"—variable-like elements can't be free in certain opaque domains, in a sense specific to the language faculty.

Certain factors that govern or enter into the adult system of rules, representations and principles belong to universal grammar; that is, they are somehow represented in the genotype, along with the instructions that determine that we will grow arms instead of wings, or have a mammalian eye instead of an insect eye. Among the elements of the genotype, I am tentatively assuming, are the principles of locality and opacity, the option of moving question-words and relating a variable-like expression such as *each other* (an anaphor) to an antecedent, and in general, certain basic properties of the mental representations and the rule systems that generate and relate them. These will become empirical hypotheses, once stated in more explicit form.

One basic element in what is loosely called "knowledge of a language," then, is knowledge of grammar, now analyzed in terms of a certain structure of rules, principles and representations in the mind. This grammar generates paired represen-

tations of sound and meaning, along with much else. It thus
provides at least partial knowledge of sound-meaning relations.
A fuller account of knowledge of language will consider the interactions of grammar and other systems, specifically, the system of conceptual structures and pragmatic competence, and
perhaps others, for example, systems of knowledge and belief
that enter into what we might call "common sense understanding" of the world. These systems and their interactions also
arise from a primitive basis, part of an innate endowment that
defines "the human essence."

Keeping to knowledge of grammar, I have also been speaking
of knowledge of the rules and principles of grammar, and also
knowledge of the innate elements that enter into this mature
knowledge. It is, I feel, a relatively uninteresting question
whether "knowledge" in the sense of this discussion is the same
concept as is expressed by the English word "knowledge." If one
disagrees, he can replace "know" wherever I am using it by the
technical term "cognize," which has just the properties I am assigning to it. In fact, it is not at all clear that the ordinary concept of "knowledge" is even coherent, nor would it be particularly important if it were shown not to be. Thus, the Gettier
problems seem to show that justified true belief may not yet
constitute knowledge; something more than justification is
needed. But it has also occasionally been argued that justification is not even a necessary requirement for possession of
knowledge.[2] Arthur Danto once pointed out that in principle
there might be a "Spanish pill" with the property that by taking
it, "we should have been caused (adventitiously) to be masters of
Spanish without having learned the language."[3] I am not sure
how seriously he meant the observation, but I think that it is
important, and that there would be no reason to withhold the

characterization "knows Spanish" from such a "master of Spanish." Presumably, the possibility Danto describes would be denied by someone who insists that language is "made by us" or taught or learned, or who analyzes "knowledge of rules" as "the state of one who has *learned* to follow the rule or rules in question".[4] Suppose, however, that Danto is right, as I think he is; in fact, the analogy may be more revealing with regard to the actual fact of the matter than is commonly assumed. If so, then knowledge of language need not be justified knowledge; it may simply be caused.

We cannot rule out in principle the possibility that taking a pill might bring about the mental state that constitutes knowledge of Spanish. By the same token, then, we cannot rule out the possibility that mutation or genetic engineering might create an organism that would know Spanish without any experience at all, that is, would have this mental state as an innate property. Similar remarks carry over to the system of pragmatic competence, hence the capacity to use a language appropriately. If this is correct, then "justification" or even "grounding in experience" in some looser sense may be neither necessary nor sufficient for an analysis of knowledge.

Note that knowledge of language is quite different in character from the kinds of knowledge discussed in the Gettier cases; we do not "believe" rules of grammar or other cognitive systems, as John Fisher properly emphasizes.[5] But knowledge of grammar does involve propositional knowledge and belief. A person who knows English knows that "the candidates want me to vote for each other" is not a well-formed sentence meaning that each wants me to vote for the other, and also believes this. If his knowledge of English derived from taking a pill or genetic engineering, then such examples of *knowing that* are not justified by any evidence or grounded in experience. Would one want to speak of "a priori knowledge" in such cases? Putting that possibility aside, let us turn to what may in fact be the real world situation: presented with evidence that the phrase "each other" is a reciprocal expression (a category presumably belonging to universal grammar, i.e., innately given), the mind develops a grammar that uses the innate principle of opacity to yield this particular case of knowledge. In this case, surely, we do not want to say that the resulting knowledge is a priori, but I think it would be stretching the terms "grounding" or "justification" or "having reasons" beyond any point where they might serve the epistemological function demanded of them to say that the knowledge is grounded or justified or supportable by good reasons; rather it is, in significant respects, caused.

These remarks carry over, I believe, to other kinds of knowledge and belief, for example, our knowledge of the properties and behavior of objects.[6] Suppose that for certain types of motion, say, along a parabola, we can extrapolate and determine where a moving object will hit a target; in such cases, we know that the object will hit the target at such-and-such a point (unless stopped, etc.). Similarly, we know that if the moving object passes behind a screen it will emerge at such-and-such a point. We also know that if we step off a cliff we will fall. And so on. In all such cases it is at least possible that such things are known without experience, and in fact it is quite possibly true that they are known with only triggering experience, which is irrelevant in this context. To return to Roy Edgley's interesting paper,[7] the fact that knowledge of language may not be a "central" or "typical" case of knowledge does not seem to me crucial in the present connection, contrary to his view. Rather, it seems that the concepts of "grounding," "justification," and "reasons" may be inappropriate in many instances to an analysis of the nature and origin of knowledge—or to deflect the terminological question, to the analysis of the nature and origin of the cognitive structures that in fact enter into what is called "knowledge" in ordinary discourse and the tradition of epistemology.[8] Much of the knowledge that enters into our "common sense understanding" appears to lack grounds, justification or good reasons, just as in the case of knowledge that linguistic expressions have certain properties. In principle similar considerations might hold still more broadly. If a student says "I wish I could take a pill that would cause me to understand quantum mechanics," I don't think that he is talking nonsense; he might, on taking the pill, be in exactly the same state as someone who learned physics in the usual way (for which the notions "grounding," etc., may also be inappropriate). It would seem appropriate in this case to say that the student who took the pill knows quantum mechanics as well as the one who learned physics in the usual way. One can think of more complex cases in which such an attribution of knowledge would be unwarranted without some form of justification, but that is another matter entirely.

A standard argument against "innate knowledge," offered in this case by Roy Edgley, is that to qualify as knowledge, a person's belief, e.g., that it will snow tomorrow must be justified "by his having good reasons for being certain" that it will (not merely "by there being good reasons for thinking that it will snow"); and "If we had any innate knowledge it would necessarily fail this . . . condition, for this condition entails that the knowledge in this paradigm case is learned or discovered or inferred."[9] This condition would exclude all the cases of knowledge just discussed. The child need not have (in fact may not have) learned, discovered, or inferred that an object in parabolic motion passing behind a screen will emerge at a specific point, nor need he have good reasons for his certainty, though he may very well know that it will, if he can be said to know anything about the world at all. The same is true of the other examples, purely hypothetical or possibly real. Even where there is triggering experience, this does not supply "good reasons" in any useful sense of the term.

Edgley argues that the child who learns language could, were he a scientist, cite the evidence to which he has been exposed "in justification of his claim to knowledge.[10] But if this relation between evidence and knowledge is to count as justification, the concept will bear none of the weight demanded of it. The relation is purely a contingent matter, depending on innate structure. Suppose that evidence that "each other" is a reciprocal expression suffices (by virtue of the opacity principle) for the child to know that "the candidates wanted me to vote for each other" is not a well-formed sentence meaning that each wanted me to vote for the other. To say that this case of *knowledge that* is literally "justified" by the observation that "each other" is a reciprocal would undermine the concept of justification entirely; for a Martian lacking the principle of opacity, we would have to say that the same evidence justifies his contrary knowledge that the sentence in question *is* well-formed with the meaning that each wanted me to vote for the other. But then the concept of "justification" has disappeared. Similar observations apply in the case of knowing that an object will emerge from behind a screen at a particular point, that we will fall if we step over a cliff, and so on.

What of Edgley's paradigm case: knowing that it will snow. Suppose that the operative principle is the true principle *P*: under certain atmospheric conditions (leaden skies, plunging temperatures, etc.) it will snow. Consider a series of individuals $x_0, x_1, x_2, \ldots$ where x_i, by virtue of his innate constitution, attains a cognitive state that includes P after i instances are observed. For x_0, the principle is innate; for the others, made operative by some experience. Suppose there is also an individual y who attains P by triggering experience, say, observation of fallen snow, or a "snow pill." For each of these individuals, observation of atmospheric conditions provides good reasons for certainty that it will snow; each uses P to infer that it will snow and therefore knows that it will snow, according to Edgley's paradigm. But only some of these individuals know the principle P that each is using to derive his knowledge that it will snow; namely, x_i for sufficiently large i. In contrast, all of them "cognize" P, as I have defined the term. An individual who is claimed not to know P might be able to tell us that it is by virtue of P that he has inferred that it will snow, i.e., that P provides the basis for his knowledge that it will snow. He might even be able to tell us that P is grounded in past successes beyond his own experience, but since these are not the reasons he *has* for his certainty that P, he still does not know that P. Frankly, my intuitions are too uncertain to enable me to decide whether or not x_0, y, or x_i for i small should properly be said to know the principle P. Given other paradigm cases of knowledge, such as those already discussed, I would be inclined to say that a coherent and useful concept for the study of the origins and nature of what we call "knowledge" should have the properties of "cognize" throughout: that is, the person has (perhaps tacit) knowledge of P. Furthermore, it is unclear that to identify "cognize" with "know" is much of a departure from ordinary usage (not that that is terribly important in this connection). However large or small, the step from "know" to "cognize" is one that should be taken, I think, if we hope to resurrect a coherent and significant concept of knowledge from ordinary usage.

While I think that Edgley is right to think of his as a "paradigm case," it is a misleading one for his purpose, since the principle P seems so obviously acquired rather than innate in fact (though not in principle; there could be an organism for which P is innate). Consideration of no less typical cases, such as a child's knowledge that an object will emerge from behind a screen at a particular point or that a linguistic expression has some property, seems to me to cast serious doubt on the conditions he requires for knowledge, and correspondingly, to diminish the force of the argument against innate knowledge.

For examples such as Edgley's paradigm case—knowing that it will snow—standard formulations seem more or less adequate in fact (though not in principle); e.g., Dewey's characterization of knowledge as belief "held with assurance especially with the implication that the assurance is justified, reasonable, grounded."[11] And surely having good reasons, etc., is in fact required for explicit support of knowledge claims in such cases as this. Perhaps these are the most important cases to consider for normal life, just as the idiosyncratic aspects of language merit more attention in normal life than the genetically-determined universal aspects; it is the idiosyncracies that are the subject matter for dictionaries and traditional or pedagogic grammars, for good reasons. In normal life we can generally take for granted the common understanding that results from shared biological endowment. The important knowledge claims are those that require justification. The concerns of the scientist seeking to determine human nature and those of the person living his or her life are virtually complementary. Specifically, the concerns of a linguist seeking to determine the nature of language are virtually complementary to those of a person trying to learn a language; and in a partially similar way, those elements of our knowledge that do in fact require explicit grounding are the ones to which our efforts are dedicated and which we must be most scrupulous to try to establish. But to understand how states of knowledge are attained and what kinds of structures enter into them, it seems necessary to investigate in a fundamental way the scaffolding, schematisms, and principles that are part of our biological nature, and to depart from the assumption that knowledge of empirical fact is necessarily grounded in experience.

To summarize, I will continue to use the term "know" in the sense of "cognize," in the belief that we thus move towards an appropriate concept for the study of the nature and origins of what all agree to be *knowledge that* or *knowledge of*. It seems doubtful that there is a useful sense of such notions as "justification," "grounding," "reasons," etc., in which justification, having good reasons, etc., is in general a necessary condition for knowledge (including *knowing that*)—nor a sufficient condition for true belief to be knowledge, as the Gettier examples show. Rather, having knowledge should be analyzed at least in part in quite different terms, in terms of possession of certain mental structures, I believe.

It is sometimes argued that though knowledge might in principle be innate, it must nevertheless be grounded in experience through evolutionary history; for example, by Alvin Goldman, who argues that it is at least dubious and perhaps false that "justification is at least a necessary condition of knowing."[12] But while a causal theory of knowledge of the sort that Goldman suggests might well be correct in essence, there is no reason to require, as he does, that evolutionary adaptation play some special role. There is no reason to demand and little reason to suppose that genetically-determined properties invariably result from specific selection—consider the case of the capacity to deal with properties of the number system. They might, for example, arise from the functioning of certain physical laws relating to neuron packing or regulatory mechanisms, or they might be concomitants of other properties that are selected, or they might result from mutation or genetic engineering. I see little reason to withhold the term "knowledge," restricting it to cases in which there has been specific evolutionary adaptation in the remote past. Neither ordinary usage nor epistemological concerns nor a principled theory of knowledge and belief seem to me to lend any support to such a move. If there is, as I believe, good reason to construct such a theory in terms of mentally represented cognitive structures (for example, knowledge of a grammar or of properties of the world of experience), then it becomes a question of fact, not doctrine, to determine the character and origin of these structures. It is an open empirical question what if any role experience or phylogenetic development may play.

It is commonly argued that language is not only learned but taught by conditioning and training. Strawson and Quine, for example, have been insistent on this point.[13] Presumably this, at least, is a question of fact, and the facts seem to show pretty clearly that the assumption is incorrect. Some agree that language is neither taught nor "consciously learned," thus rejecting part of this picture, but in my opinion, without going far enough. For example, Michael Williams suggests that we should reject the position that acquisition of "conceptual abilities, especially those which come with the learning of language" must result from a process of "conscious learning" or training.

"The alternative to this kind of empiricism," he writes, "is not a doctrine of innate ideas, though it might be a doctrine of innate predispositions to respond more readily to some stimuli than to others," a view that he says is much influenced by Wittgenstein.[14] He does not indicate what he means by "a doctrine of innate ideas"; I have suggested elsewhere that significant elements of traditional doctrines of "innate ideas" can be resurrected in an intelligible and suggestive form. But consider the alternative that he considers reasonable. First, would any empiricist of however narrow a variety deny that there are innate predispositions to respond more readily to some stimuli than to others? Is any empiricist, for example, committed to the belief that we have no innate predisposition to respond to light in the visible range more readily than to radio waves? Williams's alternative to empiricism is no alternative at all. Nor is there any reason to insist, as he and many others do, that rejection of some version of empiricist psychology may go no further than postulation of innate predispositions, unless, of course, we understand the latter concept so broadly as to include, for example, a "dispositional" theory of "innate ideas" of the sort that Descartes advanced, in which case the proposal loses any significance.

Against an approach to the study of knowledge of the sort that I have been describing, it is commonly argued that it would not permit us to distinguish properly between, say, knowing a language and knowing how to ride a bicycle. Thus in the latter case too one might say that the bicycle rider "cognizes" both "the rules of riding he can articulate—push with the feet on the pedals—and those that he cannot, even though his practice is in accord with them—e.g., lean into a curve. But nothing much of interest may turn out to have been attributed when we attribute to him the [cognizing] of a rule of riding."[15] I have discussed similar objections elsewhere, explaining why I think they are misguided.[16] Let's consider Donnellan's specific case. True, there would be little point to a concept of "cognizing" that did not distinguish "cognizing the rules of grammar" from the bicycle rider's knowing that he should push the pedals or lean into a curve, given what we assume to be the facts of the matter. But it seems easy enough to make the relevant distinction. In the case of riding a bicycle, there is no reason to suppose that the rules in question are represented in a cognitive structure of anything like the sort I have described. Rather, we take bicycle riding to be a skill, whereas knowledge of language and its concomitants, for example, knowledge that reciprocal expressions have the properties I mentioned, is not a skill at all. The skill in question might, perhaps, be based on certain reflex systems, in which case it would be incorrect to attribute a cognitive structure in the sense of this discussion to the person who exercises the skill. In contrast to the case of language, nothing seems to be explained by attributing to the bicycle rider a cognitive structure incorporating the rules with which his practice accords. But suppose we are wrong, and in fact the bicycle rider does have a representation of certain physical principles in his mind and uses them to plan or compute his next act. In this case, we *should* attribute to him a cognitive structure, and in fact, it would be quite appropriate to say that he cognizes these principles as he does the rules of his language. The question, I take it, is basically one of fact.

To help clarify the issue, consider two missile systems, each of which is designed to send a rocket to the moon. One of them operates along lines once proposed by B. F. Skinner; it has several pigeons looking at a screen that depicts what lies directly ahead, trained to peck when the rocket veers off course, their pecking restoring the image of the moon to a focused position on the screen. Consider in contrast a system that incorporates an explicit theory of the motions of the heavenly bodies and information about its position and velocity and that carries out measurements and computations using its internalized theory to adjust its course as it proceeds. This rocket might hit the very same spot as the servomechanism with the pigeons, but it would do so in a very different way. Mere investigation of behavior might tell us little, perhaps nothing. A deeper look might be required to distinguish the two systems. In the second case, but not the first, inquiry might lead us to attribute to the missile something like a "mental state." That is, it might lead us to formulate an abstract characterization of perhaps unknown mechanisms, postulating a system which involves the cognizing of certain principles and computation involving these principles and certain representations. In the first case, such an account would be factually wrong. I think that the two cases fall on opposite sides of an important divide, and that the second—the cognizing missile—shares properties with human knowledge. It also lacks crucial properties; for example, it is a task-oriented device, whereas knowledge of language, for example, is not.

No doubt one can construct other cases that are not so readily distinguished. This could be a valuable exercise, which might contribute to an understanding of just what distinguishes knowledge (cognizing) in the sense of this discussion from skill and ability. But the many examples of the sort just mentioned that appear in the literature do not seem to me very helpful in this regard because they are too easily handled. Nor do they suggest any problem in the course I have been pursuing, so far as I can see.

A recurrent theme throughout this discussion has been the question whether it is legitimate to adopt the standard "realist" assumptions of the natural sciences in studying language, and cognition more generally. I have been assuming that the questions I have been raising are (rather obscure) questions of fact. Thus, it is a question of fact whether knowledge of grammar is represented in the mind along the lines I have been suggesting, or in other ways, or not at all; or whether such knowledge arises from some sort of learning or differential response to stimuli or in some other way, perhaps through the unfolding of a fairly detailed genetic program under the triggering and partially shaping effect of experience; or whether my knowledge that the typewriter before me will not suddenly fly away is grounded in experience with similar objects or derives in significant part from a conceptual system that has its roots in human biological endowment and is only modified and sharpened in certain ways by experience, clearly a very different picture, which is susceptible to considerable further refinement. I am taking these to be empirical questions, so that we cannot specify in advance what categories of evidence may be relevant to advancing our understanding of them or settling them. Is it correct to regard these questions as empirical?

In the natural sciences, when a theory is devised in some idealized domain, we ask whether the theory is true and try to answer the question in various ways. Of course, we expect that the theory is probably false, and even if on the road to truth, that it does no more than describe at some appropriate level of abstraction properties alleged to be true of whatever the real elements of the world may be when considered at this level of description; it has, in short, some of the properties of so-called "functionalist" theories in psychology. There is a familiar morass of problems about just what is meant when we take a theory to be true: what is the status of its theoretical entities, its principles, its idealizations?; how have the facts been recast through the medium of the experimental situation or our perceptual and cognitive faculties? I am not now concerned with these questions, but rather with some special and additional ones that are held to arise, beyond these, when we turn to psychology.

Presumably these problems arise somewhere on the boundary between physiology and psychology. Consider again the study of vision. Suppose that some series of experiments leads to the conclusion that particular cells are sensitive to lines with certain orientations. In this case, no special problems are held to arise, though of course the conclusion is underdetermined by evidence, the cell is abstracted from its environment, nothing is said (at this level) about the mechanisms that might be responsible for what the cell is alleged to be doing, the results are obtained under highly idealized conditions built into the experimental situation and apparatus, and so on. Suppose next that it is proposed that identification of objects involves analysis into stick-figures or geometrical structures, though nothing is said or known about neural mechanisms that might carry out such analysis. Is the situation fundamentally different in some way, apart from the fact that the theory abstracts still further from the physical and chemical properties of the brain? It is not clear why one should assume so. That is, in this case there seems no reason to refrain from taking the theory to be true, then seeking evidence to verify, disconfirm or sharpen it, proceeding to search for mechanisms with the properties postulated, and so on.

Let us turn now to the problem that seems to many people to

be more disturbing. Consider the elements postulated to account for the facts used for illustration earlier: the rule of movement, the principles of opacity and locality, the representations postulated, etc. Suppose that all of this can be made as precise as one pleases and that the system meets some very high level of success in explaining such facts as those mentioned over a substantial range. Suppose further that by assuming elements of this structure or conditions holding of it to be innate we can go on to explain how it is that children presented with some information—say, that "each other" is a reciprocal expression rather than the name of a tree—reach the conclusions they do about such facts as those mentioned. Are we permitted to regard the theories of particular and universal grammar so constructed as true, respectively, of the steady state attained in language acquisition and of the initial state common to the species, so that we then proceed to test, refine and extend them, search for mechanisms with the properties they codify, and so on? It is this step, as we have seen, that gives rise to various qualms and objections. It is commonly felt to be unwarranted, requiring different sorts of evidence; or it is held that there is no fact of the matter (as advocates of "indeterminacy" would maintain). The question is, what boundary have we crossed that requires us to abandon normal scientific practice, with all of its familiar pitfalls and obscurities?

What is commonly said is that theories of grammar or universal grammar, whatever their merits, have not been shown to have a mysterious property called "psychological reality." What is this property? Presumably, it is to be understood on the model of "physical reality." But in the natural sciences, one is not accustomed to ask whether the best theory we can devise in some idealized domain has the property of "physical reality," apart from the context of metaphysics and epistemology, which I have here put aside, since I am interested in some new and special problem that is held to arise in the domain of psychology. The question is: what is "psychological reality," as distinct from "truth, in a certain domain"?

As has been evident throughout, I am not convinced that there is any such distinction, and see no reason not to take our theories tentatively to be true at the level of description at which we are working, then proceeding to refine and evaluate them and to relate them to other levels of description, hoping ultimately to find neural and biochemical systems with the properties expressed in these theories. Perhaps we can gain some insight into the question, if there is one, by asking how it arose.

The first discussion of "psychological reality" that I know of in this connection was in the classic paper of Edward Sapir's on "the psychological reality of the phoneme."[17] We can reconstruct Sapir's argument—unfairly to him, though in accord with subsequent interpretation—as proceeding in essentials as follows. Considering first what is often called "linguistic evidence," Sapir arrived at a phonological analysis for a certain language: an abstract system of rules and underlying representations that offered a plausible account of the linguistic data. The phonological analysis was not empirically vacuous over the domain of "linguistic evidence." It had some predictive power in the language for which it was offered (e.g., with regard to previously unanalyzed forms) and also had indirect empirical content in that the principles on which it was based could be tested for validity in other languages, or in study of language change, and so on. In our terms, his principles of phonological analysis can be regarded as elements of universal grammar and one should then ask whether they yield, in each language, the best account of phonetic organization for this language, with the proper predictive consequences, the most far-reaching explanatory principles, etc. So far, what Sapir was doing was standard linguistics, though unusually well-conceived.

But he then proceeded to raise a new question: do the phonemes he postulated have "psychological reality"? To answer this question he turned to other kinds of data, what is sometimes called "psychological evidence," that is perceptual tests of various kinds that we need not go into here. The outcome of these tests convinced him that his theoretical constructions had "psychological reality."

Sapir was sharply criticized in subsequent years for venturing to claim that his constructions had "psychological reality" instead of putting them forth merely as fictions convenient for some purpose.[18] But another question arises. Why didn't the "linguistic evidence" suffice to establish "psychological reality"? Perhaps the answer is that it was too weak; after all, phonology is a finite system with limited predictive content. But that does not seem to be the right answer. In fact, in this case the "linguistic evidence" may well be more persuasive than Sapir's "psychological evidence." Furthermore it is clear from the ensuing debate[19] up until the present that no matter how powerful the "linguistic evidence" might have been, it would not have sufficed to establish "psychological reality." It is claimed that some new *category* of evidence is required, and this, however weak and inconclusive, could support a claim to "psychological reality."

In short, the evidence available in principle falls into two epistemological categories: some is labelled "evidence for psychological reality," and some merely counts as evidence for a good theory. Surely this position makes absolutely no sense, but it remains implicit in discussion of the matter by psychologists and linguists to the present.[20] I suspect that something of the sort also may lie behind the wariness about inner mechanisms or "the psychological form in which competence exists" (see p. 72) expressed by many philosophers concerned with language and mind, for example, those I discussed in the last lecture.

What we should say, in all these cases, is that any theory of language, grammar, or whatever carries a truth claim if it is serious, though the supporting argument is, and must be, inconclusive. We will always search for more evidence and for deeper understanding of given evidence which also may lead to change of theory. What the best evidence is depends on the state of the field. The best evidence may be provided by as yet unexplained facts drawn from the language being studied, or from similar facts about other languages, or from psycholinguistic experiment, or from clinical studies of language disability, or from neurology, or from innumerable other sources. We should always be on the lookout for new kinds of evidence, and cannot know in advance what they will be. But there is no distinction of epistemological category. In each case, we have evidence—good or bad, convincing or not—as to the truth of the theories we are constructing; or if one prefers, as to their "psychological reality," though this term is best abandoned, as seriously misleading.

Of course, we may choose for one or another reason to limit the evidence under consideration, but there are hazards in this course. For example, consider Michael Dummett's account, in a series of important papers, of what he is doing in constructing a theory of meaning:

A theory of meaning of this kind is not intended as a psychological hypothesis. Its function is solely to present an analysis of the complex skill which constitutes mastery of a language, to display, in terms of what he may be said to know, just what it is that someone who possesses that mastery is able to do; it is not concerned to describe any inner psychological mechanisms which may account for his having those abilities . . . since what is being ascribed to a speaker is *implicit* knowledge, the theory of meaning must specify not merely what it is that the speaker must know, but in what his having that knowledge consists, i.e., what counts as a manifestation of that knowledge . . . [namely] . . . specific practical abilities, the possession of which constitutes a knowledge of . . . propositions [of the theory of meaning].[21]

Dummett's theory of meaning is concerned with empirical fact and attributes implicit knowledge to the speaker, an "implicit grasp of certain general principles, naturally represented as axioms of the theory [of meaning], [which] has issued in a capacity to recognize, for each sentence in a large, perhaps infinite, range, whether or not it is well-formed, a capacity naturally represented as the tacit derivation of certain theorems of the theory . . . [to each of which] . . . corresponds a specific practical ability," such as the ability to recognize well-formedness, "to use the language to say things," and so on.[22]

In short, Dummett's theory of meaning will incorporate statements about the speaker's capacities, practical abilities, implicit knowledge, and the like, which are taken to be true statements. But he is not proposing a psychological hypothesis concerning "inner psychological mechanisms."

One might ask at this point, once again, what is the distinction between a theory held to be true of the speaker's capacities and implicit knowledge, on the one hand, and a "psychological hypothesis," on the other. I see no distinction. One might argue that for some particular purpose, say Dummett's, it is unnecessary to go beyond a certain level of theoretical description, just as in studying some question of astronomy it may be appropriate to regard heavenly bodies as mass points. But just as a theory of the latter sort would incorporate "physical hypotheses" spelled out at a certain level of abstraction from inner structure, so Dummett's theory of meaning is a "psychological hypothesis," though one that abstracts away from many questions that can be raised about inner mechanisms.

What would count as a theory that goes beyond Dummett's aims and actually proposes what he would regard as "psychological hypotheses" concerning "inner psychological mechanisms?" That question, once again, does not seem easy to answer. Apparently, Dummett believes that a certain limited domain of factual evidence suffices for his purposes in constructing a theory of implicit knowledge and human capacities, though he does not indicate what these limits are or why evidence that falls beyond them is necessarily irrelevant to his purposes. One must be wary of the fallacies noted in the case of arguments against the "museum myth."[23] To elucidate his point, Dummett says that "If a Martian could learn to speak a human language, or a robot be devised to behave in just the ways that are essential to a language-speaker, an implicit knowledge of the correct theory of meaning for the language could be attributed to the Martian or the robot with as much right as to a human speaker, even though their internal mechanisms were entirely different." Implicit in this formulation is some notion of "essential behavior" that suffices to elucidate "speaking a human language," as distinct from "inessential behavior" or other nonbehavioral evidence that may bear on what the "inner psychological mechanisms" really are but does not bear on "an analysis of the complex skill which constitutes mastery of a language." What the basis for the distinction may be, Dummett does not explain; I am skeptical about the possibility of drawing a principled and coherent distinction.

No matter how broadly we cast our net in seeking evidence, it will always be true that our theories leave open innumerable questions about mechanisms. This will remain true no matter how far an inquiry into language and its use proceeds. When should we be willing to say that we *are* presenting psychological hypotheses and describing "inner psychological mechanisms?" As far as I can see, we should be willing to say at every stage that we are presenting psychological hypotheses and presenting conditions that the "inner mechanisms" are alleged to meet, just as we say that we are offering physical hypotheses when we study heavenly bodies as mass points or as consisting of certain chemical elements, or when we describe them in terms of elementary particles, or whatever the science of tomorrow may unearth, up to the point of Descartes's clocks (if there is an absolute point where inquiry necessarily terminates).

In fact, we might take the analogy more seriously. A study of the heavenly bodies as mass points would be rash indeed were it to conclude that no further evidence about inner structure could possibly bear on its concerns. Correspondingly, it seems to me less than clear that there is a certain limited domain of evidence concerning behavior "essential" to Dummett's theory, while other evidence is in principle irrelevant. However fully his enterprise succeeds in his own terms, it is making claims— which appear to be factual claims—about capacities, implicit knowledge and the like, and it is difficult to imagine why these claims should be immune in principle from certain domains of evidence dismissed in advance as inessential. This is true, at least, if he is attempting to construct a theory of *human* language and *human* capacities, as his references to the capacities and implicit knowledge of speakers seem to imply. In contrast, if he were attempting an analysis of the concept "language," say, along the lines proposed by Thomason in remarks I discussed in the first lecture, perhaps some such distinction would be possible, though it is not at all clear in what terms it might be cast or what the criteria for success would be.

I think that these remarks bear directly on Dummett's central concerns. I cannot really try to do justice to the subtlety and complexity of his argument, but a few quotes may bring out its flavor. He wants to construct "an account of the sort of understanding which a speaker of the language has," and assumes that "Of course, what he has when he knows the language is practical knowledge, knowledge how to speak the language," a "practical ability" to do certain things. This is what constitutes knowledge of a language. Furthermore, language is learned: "when someone learns a language, what he learns is a practice; he learns to respond, verbally and nonverbally, to utterances and to make utterances of his own." In the course of this learning, certain predicates are learned or "introduced" into the language through the medium of certain types of propositions; thus the language learner comes to understand the predicate *good at doing so-and-so* "by means of" the subjunctive conditional "If X were to attempt to [do so-and-so], he would quickly succeed." [24]

Given these alleged facts, we reach an "impasse" if we try to found the theory of meaning on the notion of truth, Dummett argues. The reason lies in two regulative principles concerning this notion: the first holds that "If a statement is true, there must be something in virtue of which it is true"; the second, that "If a statement is true, it must be in principle possible to know that it is true," [25] and "possibility in principle" must be construed not in terms of superhuman powers, but of our own. Certain sentences of language are unproblematic: namely, those that are "decidable," that is, for which there is an effective procedure for determining when their truth conditions hold, for "conclusively establishing" that they hold. These unproblematic cases are observation sentences and statements reduced to these by verbal explanation. But difficulties arise "because natural language is full of sentences which are not effectively decidable" in this sense; that is, sentences for which there is "no effective procedure for determining whether or not their truth conditions are fulfilled."[26] In the case of such a sentence, "we are at a loss to explain in what a speaker's implicit knowledge of the truth conditions of the statement can consist, since it apparently cannot be exhaustively explained in terms of the actual use which he has learned to make of the sentence."[27] In other words, for these "undecidable" sentences, "we cannot equate a capacity to recognize the satisfaction or non-satisfaction of the condition for the sentence to be true with a knowledge of what that condition is," the reason being that we may not be able to recognize when the condition holds: "hence a knowledge of what it is for that condition to hold or not to hold, while it may demand an ability to recognize one or other state of affairs whenever we are in a position to do so, cannot be exhaustively explained in terms of that ability," so that "there is no content to an ascription of an *implicit* knowledge of what that condition is, since there is no practical ability by means of which such knowledge may be manifested";[28] "the difficulty about a theory of meaning based on the notion of truth . . . arises from the fact that the truth of many sentences of our language appears to transcend our powers of recognition."[29]

Given these alleged difficulties in a truth-based theory, Dummett proposes a "verificationist theory" of meaning in which the verification of a sentence consists "in the actual process whereby in practice we might come to accept it as having been conclusively established as true."[30] He suggests as the proper goal a theory in which "the meaning of each sentence is given by specifying what is to be taken as conclusively establishing a statement made by means of it, and what as conclusively falsifying such a statement." This must be "done systematically in terms only of conditions which a speaker is capable of recognizing." In general, understanding of a sentence consists "in a knowledge of what counts as conclusive evidence for its truth."[31] The theory of meaning should make explicit the actual basis on which we judge the truth values of our sentences, thus explaining meanings in terms of actual human capacities for the recognition of truth. We have the capacity to recognize that the sentence "the book is on the table" is conclusively established as true, Dummett maintains, but lack this capacity for subjunctive conditionals, statements in past and future tense, or quantification over unsurveyable or infinite totalities.

Dummett's argument includes what appear to be factual assertions about our knowledge and capacities. It may seem innocuous enough to begin by saying that of course, knowledge of a language is knowledge how to speak the language. But as this idea is spelled out in an analysis of knowledge of language as a system of practical abilities to do such-and-such, questions of fact begin to intrude, for example, those I have already discussed. The range of facts potentially relevant is vast and unknown. These facts might convince us that it is a serious mistake to think of knowledge of language as a collection of learned practices to respond and "make utterances" used for particular ends. If what I have suggested is true—and it does not seem false a priori at least; we can imagine an organism so constructed—then there will be little hope of developing a theory of understanding unless we study not only capacities to do such-and-such but also the mental structures that enter into the exercise of such capacities, exploring the properties of these mental structures and separating out their various strands, distinguishing grammatical from pragmatic competence, perhaps distinguishing the computational structure of language from conceptual systems of a different sort, perhaps finding that the interaction of these systems specifies truth conditions (or more indeterminate conditions) over a range that does not relate at all to Dummett's distinction in terms of "effective decidability." Furthermore, his assumptions about learning are also not true a priori, and indeed appear to be dubious or false.

What is more, if some range of evidence convinces us that Dummett is proceeding in entirely the wrong way from the start, ignoring crucial features of human capacities and human knowledge, then little force remains behind the program of developing a verificationist theory of meaning.[32] I think that this is just as well, because its conclusions seem to me rather paradoxical. I do not see what sense can be made of the claim that the truth of the statement "the book is on the table" can be conclusively established or that we know what would count as conclusive evidence for its truth or that we have actual capacities for recognizing this conclusive evidence, as contrasted with such statements as "it rained yesterday," or "if it were to rain the grass would get wet," or "he is good at high-jumping," or "people who watch television suffer brain damage," or "the sun is always shining somewhere."

To see how paradoxical his conclusions are, consider the following crucial principle. According to Dummett, "If we are able to understand a description of a state of affairs which we are incapable of recognizing as obtaining, and to entertain the supposition that it *does* obtain, then there is no reason not to conceive of meaning as given in terms of truth conditions which we cannot in general recognize."[33] But he feels he has shown that we cannot so conceive of meaning, so it follows that we cannot understand a description of a state of affairs which we are incapable of recognizing as obtaining and entertain the supposition that it does obtain. Consider now some universal statement about an unsurveyable domain, say, "the universe is constantly expanding," i.e., at every moment in time, its size is increasing—the discovery that turned Woody Allen into a neurotic. Can we recognize this state of affairs as obtaining? No, Dummett insists. It therefore follows that we cannot understand the description of this state of affairs and entertain the supposition that this state of affairs does obtain. This seems an odd conclusion, to say the least; it offers too easy a cure for Woody Allen's neurosis. It seems to me that such conclusions can be traced to a complex of leading ideas about language, practical abilities, learning, capacities and skills, and implicit knowledge that are highly misleading at best, and when presented clearly as empirical hypotheses, apparently false. At the very least, factual evidence seems relevant to assessing them, and we cannot set limits in advance on the nature of this evidence.

Dummett's argument is based on other factual assumptions of a rather dubious nature. Thus he argues that "A language, in the everyday sense, is something essentially social, a practice in which many people engage"; correspondingly, "an individual's always partial, and often in part incorrect, understanding of his language . . . needs to be explained in terms of the notion of a shared language, and not conversely."[34] This amounts to a denial of the legitimacy of the idealization to a homogeneous speech community that I discussed in lecture 1, noting that the denial entails consequences that seem quite absurd. Dummett offers only one reason for holding this view (though he says there are others), namely, Putnam's observation that each of us will defer to "experts" to explain the meaning of terms that we do not fully understand. But while this is no doubt a fact in a sufficiently complex society—perhaps any actual society—it by no means compels us to accept Dummett's conclusion. From this observation we may conclude merely that each person has an internalized grammar that leaves certain questions open, and is willing to turn to others to answer the open questions. But it does not follow that there exists a "shared language," a kind of "superlanguage," in terms of which each individual's understanding of his own language must be explained.

It is unclear that this notion of a "superlanguage" is even coherent. Speakers of what is loosely called English do not have partial knowledge of some English superlanguage, but rather have knowledge of systems that are similar but in part conflict.[35] Their pronunciation differs, their sentence structure differs in part, and so do their interpretations of words, no doubt. How broadly should the "superlanguage" German extend? To Dutch? If not, why not, since it will presumably cover dialects that differ from one another more or less in the way some of them differ from Dutch. It is very doubtful that one can give any clear or useful meaning to the "everyday sense" of the term "language" that Dummett seems to have in mind. The fact that this may be an "everyday sense" is beside the point. Dummett is aiming at a theory that will be true of people's capacities and implicit knowledge, and as has commonly been the case elsewhere, such an enterprise may have to depart from concepts that serve well enough in ordinary life, such as the concepts "knowledge" and "language." To establish his point, Dummett would have to give a clear account of a notion of "language" as "a practice in which many people engage" and explain the status of this object, given that each individual has only a partial and often incorrect understanding of this "language," and given the internal inconsistencies of any such "superlanguage." And having done this, he would have to show that it is necessary (or even possible) to account for the various "idiolects" of an individual, hence what that individual implicitly knows, in terms of this phenomenon of shared social practice. I doubt that either of these tasks can be accomplished; certainly, neither has been attempted in any serious way.

The potential relevance of further facts can be seen if we recall that one of the practical abilities that every speaker is alleged to have is the capacity "to recognize, for each sentence in a large, perhaps infinite, range, whether or not it is well-formed."[36] While the statement is a bit vague, we might interpret it as implying that a language must be a recursive set. The notion of language as "shared practice" seems irrelevant here, even if some sense can be made of it, since Dummett is speaking of a person's actual capacities; I have already discussed the problems inherent in the view that such practices can exist over an infinite or indeterminate range in the absence of any mental representation of implicit knowledge that determines them. Presumably, then, Dummett's factual assumption is that the grammar represented in a speaker's mind generates a recursive language. But is this claim true? Perhaps it is in fact, but it hardly seems true a priori. If it is even possible that mentally represented grammars do not generate recursive sets—and it is possible—then we have an additional reason to reject an analysis of language or knowledge in terms of capacities and practical abilities. And if the facts show, as they might, that the possibility is furthermore realized, we would have an additional (though unnecessary) reason to reject this entire approach to

"understanding of language," and "understanding" more generally.

I have argued that the grammar represented in the mind is a
"real object," indeed that a person's language should be defined
in terms of this grammar, and that the vague everyday notion of
language, if one wants to try to reconstruct it for some purpose,
should be explained in terms of the real systems represented in
the minds of individuals and similarities among these.[37] We are
now asking whether there is some reason of principle why these
grammars must generate recursive sets. No serious argument
has ever been advanced in support of such a claim. There are
arguments in the literature that languages *are* recursive sets;
these arguments do not claim to show necessity,[38] so they are
not really relevant here, but it is perhaps worthwhile to survey
them nonetheless. The *possibility* that languages are nonrecursive, however, is granted by everyone who has seriously discussed the subject, and the question whether this possibility is
realized remains an open one.[39]

The earliest discussion of the issue was by Hilary Putnam in
an important paper in 1961.[40] He offers several arguments in
support of the conclusion that languages are recursive. The
issue was taken up again by William Levelt, who gives similar
arguments.[41] Both Putnam and Levelt are properly cautious;
Putnam observes that the arguments are not decisive, and Levelt
says only that it would be "a rather unattractive situation" if
grammars generated nonrecursive sets. The arguments reduce to
these. First, it is alleged that speakers can in fact classify sentences into grammatical and ungrammatical. That is true,
though it is also true that they often cannot. Levelt argues that it
is "more elegant" to ascribe the failure of intuition to "psychological circumstances." I do not see why this is the case; rather,

the question of fact remains open. The argument as a whole seems quite weak. People can also often decide whether sentences of arithmetic are true or false. In fact, as soon as sentences become moderately complex, judgments begin to waver and often fail, which is neither surprising nor particularly important, but leaves the question of existence of a decision procedure wide open. Putnam offers a related argument: that people can often classify nonsense sentences as grammatical or not. Again, this is true, but not really pertinent. A third argument, offered by both Putnam and Levelt, has to do with learnability. Levelt goes so far as to say that "a non-decidable language is unlearnable," which is surely false (though true under his technical definition of "unlearnable," from which it follows that this is the wrong one).[42] It might be that universal grammar provides exactly 83 possible grammars, all of which generate nonrecursive sets, and that the task of the learner is to select among them, which might easily be possible from finite data, depending on the character of these sets. Or, to be more realistic, universal grammar might provide a very large set[43] of possible grammars arrayed in some manner in a hierarchy of accessibility. Many of these grammars might generate nonrecursive sets but be early in the hierarchy, easily learned. In contrast, some "grammars" which generate recursive sets—specifically, finite sets—might be quite inaccessible or perhaps not in the set of possible grammars at all, hence never learned or perhaps even unlearnable through the exercise of the language faculty.[44] Recursiveness and "learnability" (in any empirically significant sense of this notion) are unrelated conceptually. Hence this argument collapses entirely. Levelt offers one additional argument, a methodological one, namely, that we want to find the most restrictive possible theory of universal grammar. That is true, but again irrelevant. As has often been pointed out,[45] it might even turn out that universal grammar provides a potential grammar for every recursively enumerable set, but that these grammars are so arranged in accessibility that finite data of the sort available to language learners will unerringly choose a single grammar.[46] The theory would meet the methodological condition that Levelt poses, which is better construed, I believe, as an empirical condition on "learnability," but without limiting the class of languages to recursive sets. As noted, some nonrecursive sets may be more accessible than some recursive (specifically, finite) sets. In short, these arguments lead nowhere.

An empirical argument in support of the thesis that human languages are, in fact, recursive has been advanced by Stanley Peters on the basis of joint work with Robert Ritchie, which has been seriously misinterpreted.[47] Peters and Ritchie showed that if the rules of a transformational grammar meet a certain condition (their "survivor property"), the languages generated will be recursive, and Peters offered evidence that in fact known rules do meet this condition. Without pursuing the issue any further, it seems that this is one kind of argument that might support the thesis of recursiveness, though obviously it would not, and is not intended to show that recursiveness is a logically necessary property of language.[48] In short, while languages may be recursive, there is no reason to suppose that this must be so. Knowledge of language, then, cannot be analyzed in terms of practical abilities in Dummett's sense, and evidence of any sort may ultimately prove relevant to his enterprise, so it appears.

In discussing languages and grammars in the preceding lecture I mentioned that it might turn out that grammars do not generate languages at all. Given the epiphenomenal nature of the notion "language," this would not be a particularly disturbing discovery. It would mean that the real systems that are mentally represented do not happen to specify recursively enumerable languages. This might happen for many possible reasons. It might turn out that the grammar has parameters that must be fixed in terms of other systems (say, the conceptual system) for actual representations of sentences to be generated,[49] and these other systems might have all sorts of exotic properties. Or the rules of grammar might be inherently indeterminate in some respect, even though formulated with perfect precision. In this case, "language" would simply not be a well-defined notion (in the sense of "recursively defined"), a conclusion that would not affect the preceding discussion, or the practice of linguistics and psychology, in any significant way. It would simply be an empirical discovery, more or less interesting, about the systems that are mentally represented and the universal grammar from which they arise, on a par with other empirical discoveries that lead us to modify theories dealing with these matters.

A different sort of argument to the effect that languages are not recursively enumerable has been advanced by Jaakko Hintikka in a series of papers. His argument does not go through, but it illustrates a possible form of argument that might establish that human languages are not recursively enumerable (and does show that "possible languages" not too unlike human languages are indeed not recursively enumerable), and is worth investigating for that reason. Hintikka believes that the argument has "striking consequences . . . for the methodology of theoretical linguistics" and that "there is no doubt about [its] tremendous potential interest and importance."[50] I do not see what consequences it would have (apart from leading to a modification of theories of language and grammar) if it were correct, but nevertheless the point is of some potential interest. The argument runs as follows.

Consider sentences using the word "any." As has often been remarked, "any" differs from "every" in that in an interesting range of cases, a sentence containing "any" is grammatical only if the word is within the syntactic domain of a logical operator that falls within its (semantic) scope; "any" is therefore sometimes called a "wide-scope" quantifier. Let us assume it to have the meaning of the universal quantifier. To take a simple case, we can say "John doesn't know anything," meaning "for all x, John doesn't know x." But we cannot say "John knows anything," meaning "for all x, John knows x." To account for such facts as these, Hintikka proposes his "Any-thesis," which reads as follows:

The word "any" is acceptable (grammatical) in a given context X—any Y—Z if and only if an exchange of "any" for "every" results in a grammatical expression which is not identical in meaning with X—any Y—Z.

Replacement of "any" by "every" in "John doesn't know anything" changes the meaning from "for all x, John doesn't know x" to "not for all x, John knows x." But in the ungrammatical example, "John knows anything," replacement of "any" by "every" preserves the meaning "for all x, John knows x."

Assuming the Any-thesis to be correct, Hintikka then shows that if we take identity in meaning to be logical equivalence, it is possible to construct predicates such that there is no decision procedure to show whether interchange of "any" and "every" will change meaning, and further that the class of grammatical sentences is not recursively enumerable, that is, not generated by any generative grammar.

Before turning to the consequences Hintikka draws, let us ask whether the argument is successful. Assuming the Any-thesis to be the right idea in essence (which is not obvious), his argument still fails because we get exactly the same results, in the moderately clear cases at least, if we replace the phrase "identical in meaning" in the Any-thesis with "identical in form" under a quantifier rule, which we may think of as mapping a syntactic representation into a representation in standard logical notation.[51] This rule we can think of as being one of the rules that assign the representation of meaning given by the grammar. Thus, "John knows anything" and "John knows everything" both map into "for all x, John knows x" under the quantifier rule, but "John doesn't know everything" maps into "not for all x, John knows x" whereas "John doesn't know anything" maps into "for all x, John doesn't know x" since the rule treats "any" as a wide-scope quantifier. But differences in form are checkable, so the argument collapses.[52] The Any-thesis can be restated within a kind of "pure syntax"; in this case, what we might call "the syntax of logical form."

Suppose that the argument, or another like it, were correct. What would follow? Hintikka points out that it would show that the syntactical component is not independent of the semantical one, since syntactic acceptability of any-sentences depends on their meaning. The conclusion does not follow under the reconstruction just suggested. But suppose that it did follow. How significant would that be? It would be as significant as a demonstration, should one be given, that a theory of rules dealing with morphological or phonological variants makes reference at some point to a notion of "related word" that has a semantic element. It would, in other words, support what I have called elsewhere, a "parametrized version" of the thesis of autonomy of syntax.[53] It is worth knowing the answer to the question, but it does not seem particularly rich in consequences.

Hintikka maintains that the argument is "a clear-cut counter-example to generative grammar." If the argument were valid, it might be a counter-example to the belief that a generative grammar, represented in the mind, determines the set of well-formed sentences.[54] It in no way impugns the belief that a generative grammar is represented in the mind, but rather implies that this grammar does not in itself determine the class of what we might choose to call "grammatical sentences"; rather, these sentences are the ones that meet both some condition that involves the grammar and a condition lacking a decision procedure. Again, that would be interesting to know if true, but the consequences seem slight. It would be on a par with other versions of a para-metrized autonomy thesis, which might well lead to various forms of ill-definedness of language, as already noted. I see no consequences, striking or otherwise, for the methodology of linguistics or psychology, once we recognize that the fundamental concepts are *grammar* and *knowing a grammar*, and that *language* and *knowing a language* are derivative.

There is nothing in "the concept of language" (whatever that may be) that rules out Hintikka's conclusions, so far as I can see. Human languages might accord with these conclusions, and perhaps even do. It will still be proper to say that the fundamental cognitive relation is "knowing a grammar," but we will now conclude that a grammar does not in itself define a language (not an unreasonable conclusion in any event, for reasons already mentioned), and that in fact languages may not be recursively definable, even though the conditions that they meet are represented in the mind, hence brain. In this case, various questions would remain to be settled as to what we would choose to call "a language," but they do not seem to be particularly interesting, because the notion "language" itself is derivative and relatively unimportant. We might even dispense with it, with little loss. I see nothing objectionable or paradoxical about such conclusions, nor do they seem to raise any particular problems, though they would, once again, reinforce the distinction between knowledge and capacity, between possession of a mental structure and practical skills.

Note that these conclusions would not bear on the question of learnability, any more than the question of recursiveness does. There is no reason why one cannot learn Hintikka's Anythesis or even why it cannot be rooted in some innate principle, perhaps one that comes into play under the effect of experience.

In fact, we can make up simple examples of "languages" very much like the ones we speak that are not recursively enumerable. In particular, we can do this when certain words have "numerical properties," roughly speaking. Take the words "between" and "among" in a variety of English that allows "I find it hard to choose between A and B" and "I find it hard to choose among A, B and C," but does not allow interchange of "between" and "among" in these cases. Imagine a very similar language (maybe an actual variety of English) that extends the operative principle from conjunctions to sets. Thus the sentence "I find it hard to choose between the prime numbers that are less than four" is grammatical, but not "I find it hard to choose between the prime numbers that are less than six." Here we must say "among" in place of "between," because the set has more than two members. Since we can formulate conditions on numbers of arbitrary complexity, consideration of sentences of the form "I find it hard to choose between the numbers meeting the condition C" would show that the set of grammatical sentences is neither recursive nor recursively enumerable, and in fact can be extremely "wild." The grammar for this language would be the generative grammar for English plus a stipulation such as the one I just gave for the words "between" and "among." No consequences of any great moment ensue, so far as I can see, though the language would not be defined by any recursive procedure.

There are two final points on which I would like to comment briefly in connection with the notion "knowledge of grammar." The first has to do with consciousness, the second with learning.

As I am using the term, knowledge may be unconscious and not accessible to consciousness. It may be "implicit" or "tacit." No amount of introspection could tell us that we know, or cognize, or use certain rules or principles of grammar, or that use of language involves mental representations formed by these rules and principles. We have no privileged access to such rules and representations. This conclusion appears to be inconsistent with requirements that have been widely enunciated. Kant, for example, insisted that "All representations have a necessary relation to a *possible* empirical consciousness. For if they did not have this, and if it were altogether impossible to become conscious of them, this would practically amount to the admission of their non-existence."[55] Similar doctrines are familiar in contemporary philosophy. John Searle writes that "It is in general characteristic of attributions of unconscious mental states that the attribution presupposes that the state can become conscious, and without this presupposition the attributions lose much of their explanatory power." Specifically, when I claim that there are unconscious rules for performing speech-acts I believe that if I have stated the rules correctly then the intelligent native speaker should be able to recognize the rules as rules he has been following all along . . . if the rules are indeed the rules of English then English-speakers ought to be capable of a sense of how they guide their speech behavior in so far as their speech behaviour is a matter of following the rules of English . . . it would seem at least *prima facie* to be a condition of adequacy of any theory purporting to state the rules that the speaker should be in principle capable of an awareness of how the rules enter into his behaviour.[56]

And Steven Davis asserts that

a necessary condition for someone to know the rules which govern some activity is that he must be able to say or show us what the rules are . . . we can say that someone follows a rule only if he knows what the rule is and can tell us what it is . . . Consequently, Chomsky cannot claim that speakers use rules in determining facts about sentences of their language or in speaking and understanding sentences of their language.[57]

Both Searle and Davis, and many others who have written in a similar vein, insist that the most that can be said is that what speakers do is in accordance with rules, or is described by rules, unless these rules are accessible to consciousness.

I have already indicated why I think that the last conclusion is wrong,[58] why it is reasonable to suppose that the rules of grammar are mentally represented and used in thought and behavior, much as in the case of the "cognizing missile" discussed earlier (but also with crucial differences, as noted). Furthermore, this approach to knowledge and understanding has not simply been proposed as a possibility, but explored in some detail, I think with a considerable measure of success. To the best of my knowledge, it is unique in this respect. For example, facts such as those offered earlier as illustration relating to the possibilities for question-formation and the choice of antecedents can be explained on the assumption that the speaker-hearer has internalized a rule system involving the principles of locality and opacity and that judgment and performance are guided by mental computation involving these internally-represented rules and principles, which are surely not accessible to consciousness. There are a great many other examples. I know of no other account that even attempts to deal with innumerable facts of this nature, and I know of no proposed explanation for the fact that our judgments and behavior accord with certain rule systems other than the assumption that computation involving such rules and the representations they provide takes place in the mind—exactly the further assumption one would make without hesitation in the study of perception and other topics. Unless some principled objection to this approach can be discovered, to reject it out of hand in the absence of any coherent alternative is simply a variety of dogmatism, deserving of no comment. The critic's task is to show some fundamental flaw in principle or defect in execution or to provide a different and preferable account of how it is that what speakers do is in accordance with certain rules or is described by these rules, an account that does not attribute to them mental representation of a system of rules (rules which in fact appear to be beyond the level of consciousness). If someone can offer such an account of how it is that we know what we do know, e.g., about reciprocals, or judge as we do judge, etc., there will be something to discuss. Since no such account has been forthcoming, even in the most primitive or rudimentary form, there really is nothing to discuss.

As the quotes above indicate, the issue is not simply whether we should use the word "knowledge" in connection with knowing rules. The issue is whether this is a permissible approach to developing a theory that will account for parts of what everyone agrees to be knowledge, or if one wants to drop the term, that will account for what is taken to be in the domain of knowledge, thought, language, action and behavior.

Davis reaches his conclusions by "generalizing" from the rules of chess, but this argument is without merit. Chess is, in fact, a trivial game from the point of view of its rule structure, and one that is (generally) explicitly taught; hence the rules are known consciously. No generalization is possible from this special case. The problem remains exactly where it was.

Searle, in contrast, offers no argument at all. He merely stipulates that mental states must be accessible to consciousness, claiming without argument that otherwise attribution of mental states loses "much of its explanatory power." This latter statement is simply false; in principle explanations constructed in these terms could be of arbitrary depth and success, and in fact some seem to have a fair degree of explanatory force, a fact that Searle does not explore. In these cases, nothing turns on consciousness. Searle's statement that his own rules for speech-acts are accessible to consciousness has as much merit as Davis's reference to rules of chess. Evidently, it provides no basis for generalization, or for his *prima facie* condition that a person must be aware of the rules that enter into his behavior. This remains sheer dogmatism, supported by no hint of argument. Notice that we are speaking of factual claims throughout.

The fact of the matter is that many explicit empirical problems have been formulated and investigated, of which the examples cited earlier serve as illustrations, and some success has been reached in constructing explanations for the facts along

lines that Searle rejects, but in no other way. No valid objection
has been offered to this approach (putting aside observations
concerning indeterminacy and inconclusiveness, which are correct, but merely underscore the fact that the investigation is an
empirical one). As far as I can see, then, the only proper course
is to take note of these attitudes, and then to disregard them, at
least until some coherent argument or alternative is offered.

Searle remarks correctly that speakers of English do not recognize the rules of grammar as being those they follow, and also
that the rules proposed are "abstract and complicated" and "are
a long way from having the intuitive plausibility that ordinary
grammar-book rules have." Let us consider the merit of these
objections—they are offered as objections—to an approach of
the sort I have been outlining.

Since the rules are not recognized by speakers as being those
they follow, and in fact appear to be inaccessible to consciousness or introspection, Searle concludes that "For the most part
the rules remain mere hypotheses." With the conclusion I of
course agree, apart from the words "mere" and "for the most
part." What he should have said, simply, is that "the rules are
hypotheses," or that theories attributing mental representations
of these rules offer hypotheses. That is to say, the theories in
question have empirical content, not a criticism in my book at
least. The words "mere" and "for the most part" suggest that
Searle has seriously misunderstood the work on which he is
commenting, apparently taking it to be an attempt at some sort
of conceptual analysis.

There is a further problem. Note that Searle argues that "for
the most part the rules remain mere hypotheses" on the grounds
that speakers do not recognize them as being rules they follow.
As already noted, this is no argument at all. But suppose that

someone were able to construct an alternative theory involving rules accessible to consciousness that had something like the coverage or explanatory force of theories involving inaccessible rules. That would certainly be an interesting result, though it obviously would not move us beyond the domain of "mere hypotheses," that is, beyond the domain of statements with empirical content. A person's judgments about what he does have no uniquely privileged status, but simply constitute evidence to be set alongside of other evidence. But again, the question is academic. So far as I know, explanatory principles with any merit bearing on the domain of facts of the sort that I have been considering are in general inaccessible to consciousness, and there is no reason to expect otherwise. The doctrine of accessibility in any of its traditional or contemporary forms seems to me entirely without antecedent plausibility, and without empirical support.

As for the fact that the rules do not have the intuitive plausibility of those of ordinary grammar books, that is true and surely to be expected, for reasons that have been discussed many times. As briefly noted earlier, ordinary grammar books are concerned with a domain of facts that is virtually complementary to what is most significant for the project I have been discussing. That is, ordinary grammar books, quite properly for their purposes, tacitly assume a principled grammar (generally without awareness) and deal with idiosyncracies, with the kinds of things that could not be known without experience or instruction. For example no grammar book devised, say, for teaching English, would, or should, deal with the simple properties of questions or of reciprocals that I mentioned. Rather, it should deal with basic facts of word order and inflection, or with the fact that "each other" is a reciprocal in contemporary English as distinct

from languages that do not formally distinguish reflexive and reciprocal, and so on. Such comments on the language no doubt
have great intuitive plausibility, but there is surely no reason to
expect that this will remain true when we consider such principles as locality or opacity in an attempt to explain facts many of
which any ordinary grammar book simply disregards, as it
should, insofar as these facts and the principles that underlie
them can be assumed to be available to the person using the
grammar, once the idiosyncracies are presented.

To conclude these remarks, I would like to turn briefly to the
notion "learning." I have been suggesting that knowledge of
grammar, hence of language, develops in the child through the
interplay of genetically determined principles and a course of
experience. Informally, we speak of this process as "language
learning." It makes sense to ask whether we misdescribe the process when we call it "learning." The question merits some
thought, I believe. Without attempting to inquire into too many
subtleties or to settle the question, I would like to suggest that in
certain fundamantal respects we do not really learn language;
rather, grammar grows in the mind.

When the heart, or the visual system, or other organs of the
body develop to their mature form, we speak of growth rather
than of learning. Are there fundamental properties distinguishing the development of physical organs and of language
that should lead us to distinguish growth, in the one case, from
learning, in the other? Perhaps, but it is not obvious. In both
cases, it seems, the final structure attained and its integration
into a complex system of organs is largely predetermined by our
genetic program, which provides a highly restrictive schematism
that is fleshed out and articulated through interaction with the
environment (embryological or post-natal). There are certain

processes that one thinks of in connection with learning: association, induction, conditioning, hypothesis-formation and confirmation, abstraction and generalization, and so on. It is not clear that these processes play a significant role in the acquisition of language. Therefore, if learning is characterized in terms of its distinctive processes, it may well be that language is not learned.

Can we distinguish learning from growth in terms of the nature of the state attained—say, a system of belief or knowledge, with facts or principles stored in the memory accessible to mental computation in the case of learning, or something of this sort? If we do, then it is not clear that any coherent notion of "learning" will remain. It is entirely possible that significant components of such cognitive states are "wired in," taking their explicit shape in the mind in perhaps something like the way that the distribution of horizontal and vertical receptors in the visual cortex is fixed within certain innately-determined bounds by the character of presented visual experience. Knowledge of behavior of objects in visual space or of principles and rules of language, and much else, arises in ways that do not seem crucially different from other forms of growth or selection from a set of highly restricted alternatives, so far as we know.

Dennett has suggested that we think of "learning" as what he calls "self-design." In some cases of transition from state to state, the new design *"exists ready made* in the old design in the sense that its implementation at this time is already guaranteed by its old design" (presumably, given some triggering event). In other cases, "the old design does not determine in this way what the new design will be"; rather the design process generates alternatives which are tested "against a whole array of requirements and constraints."[59] If the "whole array of requirements and constraints" is taken to be confirmation by evidence, "simplicity" in some sense relevant to choice among theories, and the like, then self-design, i.e., learning, seems pretty much like what Peirce called "abduction," a process in which the mind forms hypotheses according to some rule and selects among them with reference to evidence and, presumably, other factors. It is convenient sometimes to think of language acquisition in these terms, as if a mind equipped with universal grammar generates alternative grammars that are tested against the data of experience with the most highly-valued one selected; I have occasionally used this metaphor, but I don't think that it should be taken too seriously. If we take it partially seriously, then under this concept of learning as "abduction" or "self-design," the question whether language is learned or grows will depend on whether the mind equipped with universal grammar presents a set of grammars as hypotheses to be selected on the basis of data and an evaluation metric, or whether the steady state grammar arises in another way—for example, by virtue of a hierarchy of accessibility (stated, perhaps, in terms of the very same evaluation metric) and a process of selection of the most accessible grammar compatible with given data. The distinction between such alternatives lies so far beyond conceivable research that the question whether knowledge is the result of learning or growth is hardly worth considering, if learning is characterized in these terms. It is open to question whether there is much in the natural world that falls under "learning," so conceived, if the metaphors are taken seriously.

There is an interesting discussion of related questions by the immunologist Niels Kaj Jerne.[60] He distinguishes between instructive and selective theories in biology, where an instructive theory holds that a signal from the outside imparts its character to the system that receives it, and a selective theory holds that change of the system takes place when some already present character is identified and amplified by the intruding stimulus. He argues that "Looking back into the history of biology, it appears that wherever a phenomenon resembles learning, an instructive theory was first proposed to account for the underlying mechanisms. In every case, this was later replaced by a selective theory." The primary example that he deals with is the development of antibodies by the immune system. This was first assumed to be a kind of learning process in which the antigen played an instructive role, the reason being that the number of antigens was so immense, including even artificially synthesized substances that had never existed in the world, that no other account seemed conceivable. But this theory has been abandoned. An animal "cannot be stimulated to make specific antibodies, unless it has already made antibodies of this specificity before the antigen arrives," so that antibody formation is a selective process in which the antigen plays a selective and amplifying role.

As another example, Jerne cites the familiar Darwinian account of a factory wall covered with brown moths, later found to be covered with white moths after it is painted white. Darwinian theory offers a selective account based on the fact that moths of lighter color were already present before the new signal arrived. "In this case, the signal that entered into the system, i.e., the color change, was not even received by the moths, but by the birds" that fed on them.

After reviewing a number of such examples, Jerne turns to some speculations on the central nervous system. He notes certain analogies to the immune system. Both systems develop through experience, with change of state induced by outside elements. Both appear to be learning in response to these external events, and the changes are not transmitted to the offspring. He suggests that learning from experience may be "based on a diversity in certain parts of the DNA, or to plasticity of its translation into protein, which then controls the effective synaptic network underlying the learning process." If such speculations are valid, "It thus remains to be asked if learning by the central nervous system might not also be a selective process; i.e., perhaps learning is not learning either." The air of paradox in this last remark can be dissipated if we think of the term "learning" as a rigid designator, perhaps commonly misapplied; or to take a standard example, as analogous to such terms as "witch," commonly applied at one time but always misapplied.

Jerne suggests, finally, a distinction between learning and selection in terms of level of analysis, a distinction that would explain why accounts in terms of learning come to be replaced by accounts in terms of selection as inquiry proceeds. Keeping to the interaction of the whole system and an external signal, we see what appears to be an "instructive process"; the system changes and the change is caused by the stimulus. Thus in the case of the moths, one might say that the signal of painting the wall white " 'instructed' the population of moths to mimic the color change," even though the moths never received the signal.[61] But processes which are "instructive" at the system level, in this sense, "imply selective mechanisms, through which products that are already present in the system prior to the arrival of the signal are selected and amplified." So when we analyze an "instructive" process we find that learning is not learning either.

I don't think that the notion of selection from preexisting materials is rich enough to provide an analysis for the large-scale interactions that are loosely called "learning," but it may be a step along the way. It is possible that the notion "learning" may go the way of the rising and setting of the sun.

Outside of cognitive capacities that are part of our intrinsic nature, modification and fixing of belief may proceed by trial-and-error, conditioning, abstraction, induction and the like; that is, in domains in which the mind is equipped with no special structure to deal with properties of the task situation.[62] Learning theory will then reduce to the study of tasks and problems for which we have no special design, which are at the borders of cognitive capacities or beyond, and are thus guaranteed to tell us very little about the nature of the organism. This is not, of course, to demean the content of what is learned. As noted earlier, what is significant for human life is not necessarily significant for the person inquiring into human nature. In the case of "language learning," mechanisms of association (etc.) may be involved in the acquisition of idiosyncracies (e.g., specific inflectional patterns and choice of vocabulary items), though even here, it is highly likely that powerful intrinsic constraints guide the course of development. For example, the rate of vocabulary acquisition is so high at certain stages of life, and the precision and delicacy of the concepts acquired so remarkable, that it seems necessary to conclude that in some manner the conceptual system with which lexical items are connected is already substantially in place.

From the point of view of the study of human nature, the most interesting aspects of learning (as distinct from growth of knowledge and belief), may well turn out to be those to which Dennett's remarks direct our attention: essentially, Peircean abduction. In some domains—acquisition of language, object perception, etc.—the growth of our knowledge just happens to us, in effect. The mental faculty grows from its initial to its steady state without choice, though not necessarily without effort or willed action.[63] In other domains—the natural sciences, for example—the growth of knowledge involves deliberate inquiry involving hypothesis formation and confirmation, guided no doubt by "abductive" constraints on potential hypotheses as well as other equally obscure factors that enter into choice of idealization and the like. The basic elements of rational inquiry may have some of the properties of such cognitive systems as the language faculty, though the ways in which they are employed are surely quite different: scientific knowledge does not grow in the mind of someone placed in an appropriate environment. The study of human knowledge should, it seems, consider a number of rather different types of system: the growth of "natural" faculties such as those that provide common sense understanding of the physical and social world or language;[64] learning by association, conditioning, induction and the like on the periphery of fixed cognitive capacities; deliberate inquiry employing "abductive" constraints on intelligible hypotheses and other elements of so-called "scientific method." In each of these domains, elements of our knowledge appear to be innate and still other elements ungrounded, in any reasonable sense of the term.

If we hope to assimilate the study of human intelligence and its products to the natural sciences insofar as possible and to learn something about human nature in this way, we would do well, I think, to devote particular attention to those domains in which rich and complex mental structures arise under minimal exposure to the environment, language being a striking example, though for reasons already discussed, no more "typical" than others.

4

Some Elements of Grammar

So FAR IN these lectures, I have been suggesting that it is reasonable to study the human mind and its products in the manner of the natural sciences, rejecting a curious dualism that appears in much contemporary thought and that seems to me to have considerably less warrant than the metaphysical dualism it succeeded. I have in mind the several variants of the bifurcation thesis and the general wariness over attribution of inner mechanisms of mind or attempts to determine "the psychological form in which competence exists," and in general, the unwillingness to regard our theories as offering "psychological hypotheses" or to understand and interpret them in the ways that we take for granted in the natural sciences.

To conclude these remarks, I would like to consider a bit more closely the cognitive system that has, so far, proven most amenable to detailed study, namely, the language faculty in the sense of the preceding discussion. In the second lecture I discussed in a very general way some of the properties we should expect to find in the theory of universal grammar, regarded as an element of the human genotype: namely, we should expect to find a unified system of principles with a fairly rich deductive structure and some open parameters to be set by experience. Then complex systems of knowledge can develop, superficially quite distinct from one another but fundamentally organized along similar lines, triggered and partially shaped by limited experience, though the resulting knowledge is not grounded in experience in any sense of this term adequate to provide warrant, reasons, or justification. Much the same is possible in principle, and may well be true in fact, in other cognitive domains as well.

I mentioned that in the past few years there has been some work leading towards the construction of systems of this sort. A number of approaches are currently being developed, similar in some respects but divergent in others. No one, surely, expects that any of them are correct as they stand. Each such approach is far too restricted in its basic principles and deductive structure and inadequate in its choice of parameters, and thus remains incapable of accounting for either the richness and specificity of actual grammars, on the one hand, or their apparent diversity, on the other. Furthermore, each is faced with a vast range of unexplained phenomena and what appears to be—and may actually be—counter-evidence, exactly as we should anticipate for a long time to come, in fact indefinitely, if the field remains a living one. This work seems to me quite promising. Perhaps for the first time in the long and fruitful history of inquiry into language, it begins to provide a glimpse of the kind of theory that might account for crucial aspects of human knowledge in this, and I would guess other domains.

Keeping to an informal presentation and thus cutting many corners, I would like to sketch what I think may be some properties of the universal grammar that provides the basis for knowledge of language and thus our knowledge of particular facts about language. My purpose is rather limited in these informal remarks; it is primarily to illustrate the kinds of evidence and argument that can support specific assumptions about such rules and representations. I will keep for the most part to examples that appear in the technical literature, and will discuss their possible import and also some questions that arise at or near the borders of much current research.

Let's begin with some simple assumptions. The basic elements we consider are sentences; the grammar generates mental representations of their form and meaning. I will call these representations, respectively, "phonetic form" and "LF" (which I will read, "logical form," though with a cautionary note). For reasons already discussed, determination of the elements of LF is an empirical matter not to be settled by a priori reasoning or some extraneous concern; for example, codification of inference. I use the term, I hope not too misleadingly, because this representation does in fact seem to express some basic properties of what is taken to be "logical form" from other points of view.

When I speak of sentences, I really have in mind their representation in phonetic form. Sentences are composed of words organized into phrases. Or to put the matter as I would prefer, there are mental representations of sentences as strings of words and structures of phrases, mapped into phonetic form by rules with some extremely simple properties, including these: each word is mapped into a phonetic form, and the phonetic form of the sentence is the string consisting of the successive images under this mapping of the words (ignoring nonsegmental phonology and interword phonetic effects); the phrase representation of a sentence (its "phrase-marker," in technical terminology) is a set of strings, one of which is the string of words, and is thus mapped into the word representation by simply eliminating the other elements of the phrase representation, which one may think of as a labeled bracketing or a tree-diagram of the familiar sort.[1] This amounts to saying that sentences are composed of words with a proper bracketing into phrases of various types:

Noun Phrase, Sentence, etc. For example, the sentence "what is it easy to do today" consists of seven words.[2] It belongs to the phrase category "Sentence" and is barely organized into phrases at all (apart from lexical categories) apart from this. Whatever further phrase structure there may be is not very revealing as to the character of the sentence, the relations among its parts, or its representation in LF. For example, nothing in the phrase structure expresses the fact that the interrogative *what* is in some important sense the direct object of *do*. This representation in phrases I will call the "surface structure" of the sentence.

Much of the early work in generative grammar was concerned with overcoming the inadequacies of certain theories of phrase structure modelled in part on procedures of constituent analysis in structural linguistics and in part on formal systems devised for the study of formal languages. The most extensively studied approach, and one that I think is basically correct, is what has been called "transformational generative grammar," which has been developed in a number of different forms in the past twenty-five years. The fundamental idea is that surface structures are formed through the interaction of at least two distinct types of rules: base rules, which generate abstract phrase structure representations; and transformational rules, which move elements and otherwise rearrange structures to give the surface structures. In the case of the sentence "what is it easy to do today," the abstract base-generated structure might be something like (1):

(1) [s [NP it] [VP is [AP easy [s NP [VP to do [NP what]]]] today]][3]

A transformational rule then forms the surface structure by moving the embedded Noun Phrase *what* and the copula *is* to the front of the sentence, modifying the structure accordingly.

Theories have, of course, been successively modified over the years. This inevitable development in a living subject has given rise to various qualms on the part of people who are seriously misguided about the nature of substantive empirical research and who feel that a theoretical framework is discredited if it is constantly being revised (and, we hope, improved), an astonishing view that is, unfortunately, not uncommon outside of the natural sciences. It has also led to some terminological confusion as notions that were, at one time, characterized in terms of certain properties have come to be characterized in terms of others. In the hope of avoiding further confusion, I will introduce some new terms suggestive of earlier ones. Let's say that the base generates "D-structures" ("deep structures") and that the transformations convert these to "S-structures," which are converted to surface structures by rules of various sorts.

Recent work has suggested that the base rules fall within the restricted framework of what has been called "X-bar theory,"[4] and that the transformational mapping to S-structure can be reduced to (possibly multiple application of) a single general rule: "Move α," where α is an arbitrary phrase category. While such a rule will overgenerate wildly, there are a number of far-reaching principles, some of which I will discuss, that interact with it to overcome this problem in a natural way, so it appears. As the single example just cited suggests, D-structures provide an analysis into phrase structure that is much more revealing than surface structure, as to the logical form of the sentence. In particular, it seems to be the case that thematic relations in the sense mentioned in Lecture 2 are determined directly and in a simple way by the D-structures.[5]

Consider the S-structure that results from moving the phrase *what* in the base form (1) to give ultimately "what is it easy to do today." In the earliest work it was assumed that when *what* is moved, nothing is left behind in the place that it formerly occupied. Another possibility suggested in work of the past ten years is that movement leaves behind a "trace," which we can understand to be a phonetically null category; thus when *what* is moved by a mental computation in the example cited, the position from which it is moved retains the category Noun Phrase, but now lacking a phonetically realized element; movement vacates the category but does not eliminate it. The structure resulting from the transformation would be something like (2):

(2) [NP what] [S [NP it] [VP is [AP easy [S NP [VP to do [NP *e*]]]] today]] [6]

The empty category that I am calling "trace" (namely, [NP *e*]) is a real element of mental representation, in this view, though it happens to have no phonetic content; it may, however, and apparently does have phonetic reflexes.

I am assuming it to be a question of empirical fact whether mental representations at the level of S-structure include trace in this sense. I think there is substantial evidence that they do. I will briefly return to this question; let's assume for the moment that S-structures do contain trace, which we can think of loosely as a bound variable, introduced by a movement rule. Notice that on this assumption, S-structures are considerably more abstract than surface structures, since they contain unrealized categories in D-structure positions. Whereas surface structures offer no proper basis for assigning logical form, as has been argued extensively and I think persuasively, the more abstract S-structures including trace are much more reasonable candidates for semantic interpretation. Consider again the single example just discussed. In the surface form "what is it easy to do today" the surface structure gives no indication that the word *what* is to be understood as the direct object of the verb *do*, a fact crucial for assignment of thematic relations and thus for determining the meaning of the sentence. This relation between *do* and *what* is expressed directly in the D-structure (1) generated by the base, since in this abstract structure we have the actual phrase *do what*, identified as a Verb Phrase, exactly analogous to *do the job*. But while the relation is not expressed in the surface structure, it is expressed in the S-structure (2); in fact, it is expressed in a more perspicuous form than in the D-structure. If we think of the word "what" as being rather like a quantifier binding its trace as variable, then the S-structure is, in effect, of the form (3):

(3) for which x, it is easy [$_s$ NP [$_{vp}$ to do x]] today

Or to put it a bit differently, the S-structure maps directly onto a logical form similar to (3) simply by a rule giving the meaning of the quasi-quantifier *what*. In (3) the variable x bound by the quasi-quantifier *for which* x is in the proper structural position for assignment of thematic relations by the same rules that apply in the sentence "it is easy to do the job today," and can be regarded as functioning as a name-like bound variable in this position. Note that the S-structure has advantages over the D-structure in this regard, since the phrase *what* is better construed as a quasi-quantifier binding a variable than as some kind of referential expression, as the D-structure suggests if directly interpreted.

Considerations of this sort suggest that it is, in fact, S-structures rather than D-structures that are directly associated with logical form. The D-structures generated by the base rules give the fundamental syntactic configurations that determine the-

matic relations and in this respect enter into semantic interpretation; application of the transformational rule converts the D-
structure to an S-structure which is readily associated with an
appropriate representation in LF in ways that I want to discuss.
Through the mechanisms of trace theory, the base-generated
syntactic configurations that determine thematic relations are
"carried over" to S-structure, which can therefore serve as the
single "input" for conversion to LF. The S-structure is also associated by other rules with a phonetic form. The mapping of
S-structure to phonetic form with its surface structure involves
rules of deletion, other sorts of movement rules, and rules of
other types as well; thus in various respects, S-structure is more
abstract than surface structure, though I will consider here only
one of these respects: namely, the presence in S-structure of
phonetically unrealized empty categories, including trace.

We therefore have a picture of grammar of approximately the
following form: base rules constrained by X-bar theory give
D-structures which are mapped into S-structures by (possibly
repeated) application of the rule "Move α," α an arbitrary category, and then assigned a representation in phonetic form with
surface structure on the one hand, and a representation in LF
on the other. The rules associating S-structure with phonetic
and logical form are sometimes called "rules of interpretation."[7]

Recall that much of the work of the 1950s and 1960s was
devoted to showing how grammatical transformations could
overcome in a unified way a large variety of apparently disparate
problems that would arise in theories that generate surface structure directly by phrase structure grammars.[8] I think that the
argument developed in this work was basically sound, but now,
with trace theory and the more abstract notion of S-structure
including trace, we can raise a new and more subtle question:

should the base generate S-structures directly or should it gener-ate D-structures which are mapped by the rule "Move α" into S-structures? It is not entirely obvious that this is a real empiri-cal question, as was the former one. That is, it might be that these two theories are simply two ways of understanding a single and somewhat more abstract theory, yet to be properly formu-lated, which expresses the fundamental properties shared by these two variants. It might be, to use a loose analogy, that both transformational grammar and the variant just suggested relate to this deeper theory more or less in the way that the set of rota-tions of figures in a plane and the set of natural numbers under addition relate to group theory, that is, as specific realizations of the more abstract theory that expresses the fundamental proper-ties with which we should properly be concerned in a theory of the mind that seeks to formulate the rules and representations of a system of knowledge. Or it may be that there really is an em-pirical issue here, but one that is going to be considerably harder to resolve than the question of phrase-structure-versus-transformational-grammar that motivated earlier work. The question was noted in the earliest work on trace theory, and has not been resolved, or indeed formulated with sufficient clarity.[9]

To illustrate some considerations that might bear on the issue, consider idiomatic expressions such as "take care of," "take advantage of," "take exception to," "make much of," "make mention of," "kick the bucket," etc. These are idiomatic in the sense that their meaning is noncompositional, requiring a separate lexical rule analogous to the rule that gives the sense of a word; in other respects, these idioms differ in various ways, most of which need not concern us here. These idiomatic ex-pressions have several relevant properties. In the first place, they typically have the syntactic form of nonidiomatic expressions and, in fact, sometimes have a perfectly reasonable literal meaning if understood as nonidiomatic. For example, "John kicked the bucket" can mean either that John hit the bucket with his foot or that he died. And "John took advantage of Bill," while it has no literal reading, has essentially the same syntactic structure as "John took food from Bill," namely: NP-V-NP-PP, with further labelled bracketing. From the point of view of their semantics, the idiomatic expressions are like lexical items: thus, "John took advantage of Bill" is analogous to "John exploited Bill," etc. In some cases the idiomatic expressions behave syntactically as if they were single words. Thus corresponding to the sentence "John took care of Bill" we have either of two passives: "care was taken of Bill," analogous to "food was taken from Bill," or "Bill was taken care of," analogous to "Bill was nurtured" (whereas, in contrast, the nonidiomatic "John took food from Bill" cannot be passivized as "Bill was taken food from"). These properties of idiomatic expressions can easily be accounted for by "idiom rules" that apply at the level of D-structure and are analogous to rules of the lexicon.[10] Thus, the base rules will freely generate "John kicked the bucket" and "John took advantage of Bill" with syntactic structures that are realized for nonidioms, and an idiom rule will tell us that "kicked the bucket" can be assigned to the category Verb with the meaning *die*, while "take advantage of" can be assigned to the category Verb with the meaning *exploit*.[11]

Note that idioms provide evidence for the reality of the abstract levels of S-structure and D-structure. Suppose that we were to think of a grammar as a system of rules assigning surface structure representation to meanings, somehow represented in the mind—a rather traditional view. On this view, the meaning *John exploited Bill* is represented in the mind, and a rule assigns it the structure *John took advantage of Bill*. Idiom rules are highly idiosyncratic. The question then arises: why do the idiom rules characteristically form independently generated structures, sometimes with literal meanings?; why do these rules constitute a mapping into the set of structures generated quite apart from idioms? Given the idiosyncratic nature of the idiom rules, the grammar would be no more complex if, say, the meaning *John exploited Bill* were mapped by an idiom rule into *John Bill advantage of took*, the meaning of "they made much of Bill's achievements" were mapped into some permutation of the words, etc. The fact that idiom rules characteristically map into the class of independently generated nonidiomatic structures, sometimes with literal readings, would be an accident if meanings were simply mapped into formal structures. But if the relation between form and meaning is more indirect, mediated through D-structures and S-structures, it follows that idioms must have the form of independent generated structures, as is in fact overwhelmingly the case. Thus the properties of idioms provide an argument—a compelling one, I believe [12]—in support of a conception of grammar with an independent syntactic component generating structures that are associated with representations of form and meaning, as contrasted with a perhaps more traditional view that the grammar simply assigns form to meanings in some manner.

Furthermore, other properties of idioms provide a more complex argument both for the preceding conclusion and for the existence of base-generated D-structure distinct from S-structure. The reason lies in a certain asymmetry between S- and D-structure revealed by investigation of idioms. We have noted two categories of idioms: such idiomatic expressions as "John took care of Bill" can undergo movement rules, giving "care was taken of

Bill" or "care seems to have been taken of Bill." Others, such as "kick the bucket," cannot; there is no idiomatic reading for "the bucket was kicked by John" or "the bucket seems to have been kicked by John." To put it loosely, there are idioms that appear at both the D- and S-structure levels, and idioms that appear only at the D-structure level. But idioms that appear only at the S-structure level are very rare; we can regard this possibility as excluded in principle, with such marginal exceptions as should be expected in the case of idiomatic constructions. This is a general fact that requires explanation. It can be easily explained on the assumption that idiom rules apply at the level of D-structure, marking some idioms as immune to movement rules.[13] A related fact is that while some idioms undergo movement, as in "excellent care was taken of the orphans," "excellent care seems to have been taken of the orphans," "much seems to have been made of Bill," etc., we do not find the same idiomatic interpretation in such structures as "excellent care is hard to take of the orphans" (analogous to "food is hard to take from the orphans"), "much is easy to make of Bill," etc. There is good reason to believe that the latter construction does not involve movement of a Noun Phrase to the subject position; rather, the subject of the main clause is base-generated in place. Correspondingly, interpretation as an idiom is ruled out in principle if idiom rules apply at the D-structure level.[14] Note finally that at the D-structure level idioms are generally contiguous or at least local, whereas in S-structures they may be "scattered," as in "excellent care seems to have been taken of the orphans," so that a D-structure idiom rule is much simpler than a corresponding set of rules applying to the various reflexes that appear at the level of S-structure. Note that idioms are also "scattered" at the level of LF, if, for example, we assume the existence of a quantifier rule such as the one discussed on p. 125, above (e.g., "what kind of care was taken of the orphans," "they took no care of the orphans," etc.), though questions arise about the proper interpretation in such cases as these, questions that have considerable further import that has yet to be properly investigated.

These properties of idioms provide evidence in support of an independent syntactic component mediating the relation between sound and meaning in terms of D- and S-structures, and also in support of the existence of D-structures as distinct from S-structures, related to the latter by grammatical transformation.

These remarks illustrate the kind of consideration that bears on the question whether S-structures are generated directly by base rules or transformed from base-generated D-structures—if indeed it is a real question, which is not entirely clear, as noted.[15] But it is important to observe that whatever the answer to the question (if it is a question) may be, it is not to be confused with a quite different question, the one that motivated much earlier work: namely, whether grammars should be transformational in character. Both answers to the question in this case presuppose that they should, though one answer adopts the rule "Move α," whereas the other adopts new interpretive rules that may or may not ultimately be empirically distinguishable from the transformational rule "Move α." Furthermore, both answers presuppose the distinction between surface structure and a more abstract representation of syntactic form (namely, S-structure), which is generated by base rules (or base rules plus the movement rule) and is interpreted to yield surface structure on the one hand and LF on the other. Thus both answers accept the basic premise that has guided transformational grammar: namely, that the rules relating surface structure and logical form should be "factored" into several components, including base rules of a very simple nature that satisfy some general conditions (perhaps those of X-bar theory), and at least two kinds of rules of interpretation, those that map abstract structures (S-structures) to surface structure and those that map abstract structures (again, S-structures) to LF; and that only under such factoring of the relationship between representations of sound and meaning can the fundamental properties of the system of grammar be revealed. The answers differ with regard to a different question: is there a further factoring of rules into base rules that generate D-structures and a rule of movement, or is there a further factoring into base rules that generate S-structure and new kinds of interpretive rules that play the role of the movement rule.[16]

A fallacy that should be avoided, in this connection, is the assumption that the general theory is "simpler" or more restrictive if the transformational component (now reduced to the rule "Move α") is eliminated completely—or, comparably, if the phrase structure component is eliminated completely in favor of a richer system of transformations with a "filtering effect" supplemented by surface filters. The former assumption, which is not uncommon, would be correct if everything else in the theory remained unchanged, specifically, the restrictive conditions on the base. But if the latter conditions are weakened—say, if the base is permitted to be an arbitrary context-free or even context-sensitive grammar, in the technical sense of these terms—then the conclusion evidently does not follow. It is appropriate to seek the most restrictive theory, but as noted in the preceding lecture, an empirically significant notion of "restrictiveness" will be one that restricts the class of potential grammars compatible with fixed data. Thus, a theory of the base constrained by some version of X-bar theory and a theory of the lexicon constrained in similar terms, supplemented by the general transformational rule "Move α," may well be more restrictive in the empirically significant sense of the term than a theory that permits a wider range of base structures and interpretive rules but no transformational component at all. The fallacious contrary assumption is, perhaps, motivated in part by mistaken considerations relating to weak generative capacity discussed in the preceding lecture.

I will keep to the assumption that D-structures and S-structures are distinct, related by application of the rule "Move α," and thus assume the structure of grammar already outlined: the base generates D-structures which become S-structures by application of the movement rule, the S-structures being assigned phonetic and logical form.

As already noted, surface structure—that is, the actual arrangement of a physical object into phrases—is not a reasonable candidate for semantic interpretation; it was this fact that led to the so-called "standard theory," which took base-generated "deep structures" to be the entities subject to semantic interpretation.[17] But the arguments for deep structure interpretation collapse under trace theory, and indeed in some respects S-structures seem more reasonable candidates for semantic interpretation than D-structures, as already noted. Actually the reasons for the latter conclusion are far stronger. Work of the past ten to fifteen years has shown, I think very persuasively, that deep structures are as inappropriate for semantic interpretation as are surface structures.[18] In fact, in the case of every transformational rule that merits serious consideration, it turns out to be the S-structure output rather than the D-structure input that is relevant for semantic interpretation, if there is any difference at all.[19] To cite only a few examples, consider the

rule of Prepositional Phrase-fronting, an application of "Move
α" (α = Prepositional Phrase) that forms the S-structure "In
France, I enjoyed myself," from "I enjoyed myself in France."
But now compare the two sentences: "I didn't have a good time
in France or England" (in neither) and "In France or England,
I didn't have a good time" (I don't recall which). The latter cannot mean that I had a good time in neither France nor England, as the former may. The reason is that properties of surface structure (actually, S-structure) determine the interaction of
negation and disjunction. For the same reason, the sentence
"they can't help either Tom or Bill" differs in its range of meaning from its passive, "either Tom or Bill can't be helped by
them." Or consider the rule of question-formation. The sentence "everyone saw pictures of five children" can be interpreted
to mean that for each person x, x saw pictures of five children
(maybe different ones for different choices of x). But the corresponding question, "which pictures of five children did everyone see" can only be understood as referring to specific pictures
of five children—i.e., with "everyone" limited to narrow scope.
Again, it seems that surface order (i.e., S-structure order) is
crucial.[20] Turning to a different sort of example, consider the
sentence "he will review the books that Bill wrote." Here we
understand the pronoun *he* to refer to someone other than Bill,
that is, we take this to be a case of intended non-coreference.
But in the corresponding question, "which books that Bill wrote
will he review," the reference of the pronoun is free; it may be
understood as referring to Bill. Again, S-structure is what is involved in the application of the relevant rules.

There are many similar examples. To my knowledge, the
facts generally support the conclusion that S-structure rather
than D-structure is submitted to semantic interpretation (though

certain properties of D-structure, specifically, the formal structures that underlie assignment of thematic relation, retain the
role they played in the standard theory, and nontrivial problems
remain concerning idioms). Perhaps one can construct some intricate system of rules that would permit the standard theory to
be maintained. But the simplest and most general rules by far
are those that apply to S-structure, so far as we know.

Note that it might be appropriate to make an effort to shore
up the standard theory in the face of the evidence against it if
there were some independent reason to do so. Some have
argued that this is indeed the case. Bever, Katz and Langendoen, for example, argue that "the standard theory takes the
strongest antiempiricist and antibehaviorist position," which, if
correct, would imply that some important issue is at stake. They
also assert that if properties of both deep and surface structure
are considered in semantic interpretation then we are permitting
"global rules"—i.e., rules that apply to pairs of phrase-markers
not contiguous in derivations—and thus radically increasing the
class of grammars available in principle over the standard
theory, a very unfortunate step.[21] But these statements are incorrect. The question of available grammars simply does not
arise, even if we take the rules of semantic interpretation to
apply to the pair (deep structure, surface structure), as in the
theories they have in mind. The standard theory permits a certain class of grammars; the alternative theory permits a different
class, not a superset of the first. It is not the case that the alternative theory makes more grammars available compatible with
fixed data.[22] Rather, the grammars made available simply differ
in a fixed respect—in fact, we can even think of them as the
very same formal objects, associated with a different rule of interpretation. As for the issue of empiricism and behaviorism,

even if it were somehow at stake this would not be relevant; our purpose, after all, is to find the truth, not to defend some doctrine. But no such question arises. If, for example, empiricist or behaviorist theories of learning are unable to account for the acquisition of grammars constructed in accordance with the standard theory, as Bever, Katz, Langendoen and I all agree, then they fail for exactly the same reasons to account for the acquisition of grammars that submit both D- and S-structures to semantic interpretation (or deep and surface structures), or only S-structures, where the surface structures and S-structures are determined by rules involving D-structures.[23] There are no consequences relating to available grammars or the adequacy of various conceptions of learning; choice between the standard theory and these alternatives is simply one of fact, and the facts support the conclusion that S-structure is the appropriate candidate for semantic interpretation, in our terms: mapping to LF.

Let us now return to the question of the existence of trace in mental representations: do movement rules in fact leave a phonetically unrealized category, as trace theory stipulates? I have already mentioned one reason for supposing this to be true: namely, it provides a quasi-quantificational structure for questions that seems quite appropriate for interpretation to logical form. I will return to this observation, which can be substantially strengthened, in a moment. But first I should mention that there is also syntactic and even phonetic evidence in support of the assumption that phonetically empty categories appear in mental representations at the level of S-structure. As for phonetic evidence, consider the phenomenon of contraction, as when we say, in normal speech, *wanna* instead of "want to" in such expressions as "I wanna go" ("I want to go"). There is a rule of colloquial English that says, in effect, that under a wide range of conditions that we need not consider here, the word *want* followed by *to* can be reduced to *wanna*. This is a rule that can easily be acquired by inspection. But it operates under curious constraints. Thus compare the sentences:

(4) (a) who do you wanna meet?
    (b) who do you wanna meet Bill?
    (c) who do you wanna visit?

The first, (4a), is grammatical. The second, (4b), is not; con-traction is blocked in this case and we must say, rather, "who do you want to meet Bill?" In the third case, (4c), the sentence is grammatical but must be interpreted as meaning: "for which person x do you want to visit x?" In contrast, without contrac-tion the sentence "who do you want to visit?" is ambiguous; it can have the meaning of (4c) or, alternatively, it can mean: "for which person x do you want x to visit."

There is a simple explanation for these facts in terms of trace theory. Note that the representations of the sentences (4a-c) at the level of S-structure are, respectively, (5a-c), where *t* is the trace of "who":

(5) (a) who do you want to meet *t*
    (b) who do you want *t* to meet Bill
    (c) who do you want to visit *t*

The unacceptable interpretation of (4c) would be (6):

(6) who do you want *t* to visit

In examples (5b) and (6) the rule of contraction is blocked by the intervening trace. To put it differently, the rule of contrac-tion that assigns to the expression *want* + *to* the phonetic form *wanna* does not apply unless *want* and *to* are contiguous, and to the mind's eye they are not in examples (5b) and (6), since they are separated by the Noun Phrase trace of *wh*-movement, which, though the mind does not know it at this point in mental computation, will ultimately have no phonetic realization.[24] The unacceptable sentences and interpretations are thus excluded for the same reason that prevents contraction of *want* and *to* in the sentence "John wants Bill to leave."

This observation is of some interest. Note that while the child could easily learn, by inspection, that *want* + *to* contracts to *wanna*, it is difficult to imagine that experience would establish that contraction cannot apply over a position from which an item has been moved. Relevant experience is surely lacking. By the argument from poverty of the stimulus, it is reasonable to conclude that the child's knowledge that the facts are as just reviewed derives from initial endowment. Trace theory suggests an answer as to what this factor may be: if it is true, as a matter of principle, that movement rules leave trace in mental representations, then contraction will be blocked as a matter of principle over a position from which the question word has been moved. Thus we have an argument in favor of abstract S-structures including trace, an argument that mental computations apply to representations that include categories that will turn out to be phonetically null and do not appear in surface structure.

There is a variety of syntactic evidence in support of the same conclusion. Much of it appears in literature that is readily accessible, so I will not review it here.[25] Instead, I would like to discuss some semantic evidence that has also appeared in the technical literature and to consider its further import. Consider the standard examples (7) and (8):

> (7) John betrayed the woman he loved
> (8) the woman he loved betrayed John

In both cases, the pronoun *he* can be taken to refer to John, as distinct, say, from the sentence "he betrayed the woman John loved," where it may not be so construed. Suppose now that we have a universal quantifier instead of *John* in the sentences (7), (8); thus (9) and (10), respectively:

(9) everyone betrayed the woman he loved
(10) the woman he loved betrayed everyone

The sentence (9) can be understood as meaning that for each person *x*, *x* betrayed the woman *x* loved. But the sentence (10) cannot be understood as meaning that for each person *x*, the woman *x* loved betrayed *x*. Rather we must assume that *he* in (10) refers to some person whose identity is fixed elsewhere.

Suppose we assume that one of the rules assigning LF-representations to S-structure is the quantifier rule mentioned in the preceding lecture (p. 125). Then the sentences (9) and (10) will be assigned the logical forms (11) and (12), respectively:

(11) for every person *x*, *x* betrayed the woman he loved
(12) for every person *x*, the woman he loved betrayed *x*

The pronoun *he* should now be interpretable as either coreferential to *x* or non-coreferential to *x*, exactly as in the case of (7), (8), where it is interpreted as either coreferential or non-coreferential to *John*.[26] But, as we have just seen, the bound variable *x* behaves differently from the name *John*: the coreferential interpretation is permitted in the case of (8), with *John* taken to be the antecedent of *he*, but not (12) with the variable *x* as antecedent of *he*. The fact that bound variables behave differently from names in this respect is not predictable on a priori grounds. It simply seems to be a fact about LF in natural language.

Now consider again the case of interrogative constructions. Returning to the sentences (7) and (8), suppose that we question *John*. We thus derive (13) and (14), respectively:

(13) who betrayed the woman he loved
(14) who did the woman he loved betray

Note that coreference in these interrogative constructions is understood in the same way as in the quantified expressions (9) and (10), not the expressions (7) and (8) with a name, *John*, in the questioned position. Thus if the answer to (13) and (14) is "it was John," we may understand the pronoun *he* in (13) to refer to John but not the pronoun *he* in (14); in (14) we understand *he* to refer to someone other than John, someone identified elsewhere in the discourse or context.

Why should *wh*-questions behave like quantified expressions. The answer is clear if we return to the notion of S-structure and LF that is developed in terms of trace theory. Thus, the logical forms corresponding to the S-structures of (13), (14) are (15) and (16), respectively:

(15) for which person x, x betrayed the woman he loved
(16) for which person x, the woman he loved betrayed x

Apart from choice of quantifier, (15) and (16) are identical to (11) and (12) respectively, so that the special property of variables that accounts for quantified expressions will carry over to *wh*-questions.[27]

Summarizing, we have evidence in support of the quantifier rule, as part of the mapping from S-structure to LF, and for the assumption that there really is a phonetically empty trace, understood as a bound variable, in S-structure. On these joint assumptions, we can explain why questions and quantified expressions behave alike with regard to coreference; a special property of bound variables accounts for both classes of expressions. Just as there is no a priori reason to suppose that bound variables should differ from names in the respect noted, so there is no a priori reason why the logical form of natural language should be based on the notation of quantifiers and variables. As is well-known, it is possible to analyze quantified expressions in a variable-free notation, and the same is true for interrogatives. Note that the quantifier in English appears phonetically in the position of the corresponding bound variable, whereas the interrogative expression appears in a different position in the phonetic string. Once again we see that surface structure is inappropriate for determining logical form, but S-structure is appropriate under trace theory; it provides directly for what appears to be the proper generalization.

The question has occasionally been raised whether the choice of notation for logical form—say, familiar quantifier-variable notation or a variable-free notation— could be an empirical issue. Thus suppose we have two systems of logic that are equivalent in expressive power. Does it matter which one we use to represent logical form? The obvious answer seems to be that it does not. To the extent that what I have been calling "logical form" enters into inference, for example, it will not matter whether we use a quantifier-variable notation or a variable-free system. Correspondingly, when a new approach to the analysis of quantifiers in natural language is proposed, it is natural to suppose that the issues that arise are not empirical ones. Barbara Partee has raised the question in the course of an exposition of Richard Montague's theory of quantifiers, which treats quantifier phrases such as *everyone* as similar to proper names. She comments: "Whether the unification of proper names and quantifier phrases is an important enough goal to merit the complications it adds is a difficult question; it is not readily apparent how to construe it as an empirical question." [28] She then suggests that though the issue does not seem to be an empirical one, nevertheless it does seem interesting from another point of view, namely, because if we accept this unification of proper names and quantifier phrases we have some support for the belief that semantic and syntactic rules are in one-one correspondence.[29]

As the preceding remarks indicate, we should not be too quick to dismiss the possibility that there is an empirical issue. Consider, for example, a comparable question that one might raise about phonetic form. There are competing theories of phonetic representation—different feature systems, features versus phones, various notions of suprasegmental representation, etc.—but though the alternatives might be equivalent in expressive power, no one supposes that no empirical issue arises in the choice among them, and there is a substantial literature concerning evidence relevant to such choice. The point is that whatever their expressive power, some of these systems of representations enter into rule systems that permit the formulation of significant principles and generalizations, while others do not. Explanations can sometimes be couched readily in one framework, but not another, a fact that bears directly on the truth of theories of rules and representations, at least if we continue to reject the bifurcation thesis and to maintain the normal assumptions of rational inquiry, as in the natural sciences. The same seems to be true of representations for logical form.

If the mapping from S-structure to phonetic or logical form were a "one-step" affair, that is, simply the arbitrary statement of some correspondence, it might indeed be true that no empirical issue arises in the choice of a system of representation. But if this mapping is "derivational," involving the successive application of various rules, empirical questions arise in both cases.[30] In the case of LF, there is evidence to support a classical interpretation of standard logical systems over proposals such as

Montague's "proper theory of quantifiers."[31] As in the case of phonology, the argument is indirect, framed in terms of explanatory power and significant generalization, but it is a substantive argument in both cases. Note that we also have a further consequence: namely, an argument against the view that syntactic rules relating to surface structure are in one-one correspondence to semantic rules. But there is, I believe, ample evidence in any event against this assumption, which Partee takes to be the central empirical thesis of Montague grammar.[32]

There is reason to believe, then, that the facts support the choice of familiar quantifier-variable notation over variable-free notation, just as they support the trace-theoretic analysis of movement rules over the theory that assigns no trace in S-structure. In short, empirical considerations provide evidence bearing on quite specific proposals as to the mental representations that appear at the level of S-structure and logical form, and in favor of certain assumptions about rules: the movement rule leaves trace and the quantifier rule is part of the mapping from S-structure to LF. That seems to be the way the mind works, if the preceding discussion is on the right track. None of this need be the case, but the evidence suggests that it is the case.

If these conclusions are correct, one might speculate that the familiar quantifier-variable notation would in some sense be more natural for humans than a variable-free notation for logic; it would be more readily understood, for example, in studying quantification theory and would be a more natural choice in the development of the theory. The reason would be that, in effect, the familiar notation is "read off of" the logical form that is the mental representation for natural language. The speculation seems to me not at all implausible.

There is additional evidence in support of the conclusions

just reached. Returning to the sentences (7) and (8), note that I was tacitly assuming that the main stress of the sentence (8) was on *betray*, not *John*; thus I was taking the sentence to be (8') rather than (8"), where capitals again indicate main stress:

(8') the woman he loved BETRAYED John
(8") the woman he loved betrayed JOHN

In fact, (8") behaves like (12) and (16), the expressions with quantifiers and question-words rather than names; in (8") we understand *he* to refer to someone other than John. This can be explained if we assume that one of the rules mapping S-structure into logical form is a rule of FOCUS, which converts (17) to (17') and converts (8") to (8"'):

(17) JOHN likes Bill
(17') the x, such that x likes Bill, is John
(8"') the x, such that the woman he loved betrayed x, is John

Now the logical form (8"') contains the embedded phrase "the woman he loved betrayed x," and the same principle that governs variables and pronouns will once again apply, giving the desired result.

This conclusion bears on a problem that arose in lecture 2. There, I discussed the question whether rules of grammar are involved in giving representations that provide the information relevant to the appropriateness of certain discourses involving such sentences as "it was DICKENS who wrote *Moby Dick*," so-called "cleft sentences." As noted there, this is an empirical question in principle, not to be settled by some a priori assumption as to the character of the mental representations generated by the internalized grammar. This discussion suggests that the rule of FOCUS may be involved in determining the LF-representation of cleft sentences, exactly as it is in the case of (17) and (8″). If so, then since the rule of FOCUS does appear to be part of the mapping from S-structure to LF for the reasons just reviewed, it follows that LF will include an indication of focus and presupposition in the sense relevant to determining the status of cleft sentences and the discourses in which they are appropriate. Suppose it were shown that the presupposition in question is "pragmatic" rather than "logical"; say, that it relates to rules of conversational implicature rather than inference. We would then conclude that LF provides representations relevant to pragmatic presupposition. One might therefore conclude that "logical form" is not an appropriate term for the representations of meaning given by the grammar, i.e., not an appropriate way to read the technical term "LF," but that is quite another matter.[33]

These remarks are, obviously, not intended to be in any sense definitive, but they do illustrate how empirical considerations can bear on fairly subtle questions concerning representations and rules, real questions of empirical fact, I am assuming.

In discussing sentences with quantifiers, wh-phrases and stress, with an embedded structure at the level of LF that contains a bound variable and a pronoun, I pointed out that whereas under some structural conditions the pronoun and the variable must be non-coreferential, in others the pronoun may be interpreted as either coreferential to the variable or non-coreferential to it, just as it may be interpreted as either coreferential to John or non-coreferential to John in the sentence "John betrayed the woman he loved" (=(7); see note 26). Actually, there is more to the matter. For reasons discussed at some length in the literature,[34] the proper interpretation of such sentences as (7) seems to be that the pronoun he is free in reference, rather like a multiply-denoting name that can take any person as its referent. There are structural conditions under which non-coreference (in fact, disjoint reference) is necessarily imposed. But the quantified expressions are slightly different. Consider again the sentence (9) with the logical form (11)

(9) everyone betrayed the woman he loved
(11) for every person x, x betrayed the woman he loved

We cannot say, in the case of (11), that the pronoun *he* is freely understood as referring to some arbitrary person, as in the case of "John betrayed the woman he loved" (=(7)), where *he* may freely refer to John or to someone else. That formulation would not permit the interpretation of (9) as in (11′)

(11′) for every person x, x betrayed the woman x loved

Nor can we say that for each particular choice of x, the pronoun *he* can refer freely to x or someone else. If that were the case, then the sentence (9) would be true if John betrayed the woman he himself loved, Tom betrayed the woman Bill loved, etc. In fact, (9) obviously permits exactly two interpretations: either (11′) or an interpretation in which the pronoun *he* is understood as in effect a name, referring to some person whose identity is fixed elsewhere, whatever the choice of x. To borrow a term from American Indian linguistics, the pronoun *he* within the domain of a quantifier must be marked either *proximate* or *obviative*, where a pronoun marked "proximate" *must* have an antecedent and a pronoun marked "obviative" *cannot* have an antecedent but must refer in the manner of a name. In some languages, Hopi for example, this distinction is morphologically marked and plays a central role in the grammar.[35] In English there is no morphological marking for obviation, but it seems to be the case that something similar nevertheless is found, at the level of LF. There are other conditions too, which I will not discuss here, under which we seem to find in English a process similar to obviation. By the standard argument from poverty of the stimulus, if obviation figures in Hopi, we conclude that it is one of the devices provided by universal grammar. There is some reason to believe that it figures in English and presumably in all languages at least in the interpretation of quantification, though with no overt indication in phonetic form that the pro cess is at work. We might express the principle by a reindexing rule that applies in the course of the mapping from S-structure to LF, assigning to the pronoun an index that is either the same as or different from that of a variable bound by a quantifier with scope extending over the pronoun in question, with the obvious interpretation.[36]

Notice that the questions I have been discussing relate closely to semantics, and crucially involve properties and elements that may have no physical realization in the language, though there may in some cases be phonetic reflexes (as in the case of contraction). But while these issues are closely linked to semantic considerations—questions of the relation between language and the world and of the structure of the conceptual system—they should be more narrowly understood as relating to the syntax of LF, a certain system of mental representation provided by the rules of grammar, analogous to representations of phonetic form that enter into determining a physical realization in terms of articulation. Many of the questions that are regarded as "semantic" can be understood, I think, as questions about the syntax of LF: the notation in which it appears, the properties of this notation and the rules that relate such representations to other elements of grammar, abstract S-structures if what I have said so far proves to be correct.

The discussion so far has centered on the hypothesis that phonetically unrealized categories appear in S-structure as a reflex of movement rules. There is, in fact, considerable evidence that such "empty elements" enter into representations at the S-structure level from a different source, a hypothesis that has further ramifications relating to some of the examples that I discussed earlier. To develop these points, I have to add some further assumptions about sentence structure. Let us assume that clauses come in two varieties, tensed and infinitival. Thus the sentence "for John to leave is a shame" contains the infinitival clause "for John to leave," whereas "that John left is a shame" contains the tensed clause "that John left." Suppose further that each clause contains a complementizer and a propositional content. The complementizer (COMP) of the infinitival clause is *for* and the complementizer of the tensed clause is *that*; the propositional contents are "John to leave" and "John left," respectively. In terms of X-bar theory, we have such structures as (18) at the level of D-structure:

(18)

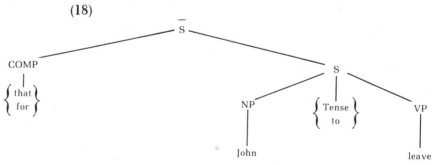

We can think of the COMP *that* as related to *Tense* and the COMP *for* to *to* by something like an "agreement rule."

Assume further that the rule of question-formation places the *wh*-word in the COMP position. Thus we have such structures as the following:

(19) it is unclear [s̄ [COMP what] [s he should do]]

Since clauses may be either tensed or infinitival, if rules apply freely (the simplest assumption), then the embedded S̄ in (19) could have been infinitival instead of tensed, as it is in (19). Thus corresponding to (19) we could have either of the structures (20):

(20) it is unclear [s̄ [COMP what] [s NP $\begin{Bmatrix} Tense \\ to \end{Bmatrix}$ VP]]

The embedded structure must be an S̄, since it undergoes the rules of *wh*-movement. It cannot be, for example, a verb phrase, since *wh*-words do not move to the front of verb phrases; we have no such forms as "John [VP what read]?" with the sense: "for which *x*, John read *x*"? Similarly, we would not want to say that some sentences can appear without subjects; that assumption would considerably complicate the rules of the base. Rather, the simplest theory of the base would state, as just indicated, that the propositional content of a clause S̄, namely S, is of the form NP α VP, where α is either Tense or *to*. And on the assumption that all rules of the syntax are optional—again, the simplest possible assumption—rules that analyze a Noun Phrase into a more explicit form, ultimately a phonetic form, may or may not apply, so that if they do not apply, the Noun Phrase simply remains empty.

Proceeding in this way, which seems to be minimal in terms of apparatus and assumptions, we conclude that any of the Noun Phrases in the embedded S in the sentence (20) may be empty; perhaps its subject, perhaps one of the Noun Phrases that may appear in its predicate VP.

Note that one of the Noun Phrases in the embedded S of (20) must be empty, hence missing in the surface structure; that is, one NP must be the trace of the question word *what* that was moved to the COMP position. In the sentence (19), for example, the direct object of the verb *do* is the trace of *what*. Now it is also a fact that one of the other Noun Phrases can be missing phonetically, in which case we understand it to be arbitrary in reference. Consider for example the sentence (21) derived from the S-structure (22), with *t* the trace of *who*:

> **(21)** it is unclear who to visit
> **(22)** it is unclear [s [COMP who] [s̄ NP to visit t]]

In this case the trace of *who* is the direct object of *visit*, and the subject of *visit* is a phonetically empty Noun Phrase. The meaning of the sentence is, roughly: "it is unclear for which person *x*, one is to visit *x*."

In the sentence (21), then, two Noun Phrases are phonetically missing, though both are present in the S-structure. One of them is the trace of movement of *who*. The other is simply generated in the D-structure but without lexical content; that is, the optional rules that expand the Noun Phrase and introduce lexical material simply do not apply, and a perfectly general principle interprets the empty Noun Phrase as arbitrary in reference.

Returning to the sentence (21), notice that it might also derive from the S-structure (23):

> **(23)** it is unclear [s̄ [COMP who] [s t to visit NP]]

In this case, the subject of *visit* is the trace of *who* and the object of *visit* is the empty base-generated Noun Phrase. The sentence, then, would mean: "it is unclear for which person x, x is to visit someone." That is a perfectly fine meaning, but it is not the meaning of the sentence (21). The question, then, is how we know that of the two missing Noun Phrases, the direct object must be the trace of *who* and the subject must be an empty Noun Phrase that is arbitrary in reference. Though the facts are obvious, the point is actually rather subtle. Somehow, we know how to interpret two Noun Phrases, each null, and to interpret them quite differently: one as a bound trace and the other as arbitrary in reference. The argument from poverty of the stimulus leads us to assume that some general principle of language is at work that has as a consequence that only the subject of the embedded clause can be interpreted as arbitrary.

Other examples permit us to extend the principle. Recall that clauses can be tensed or infinitival, but we see at once that in a tensed clause neither the subject nor any other noun phrase can be phonetically missing and understood as arbitrary in reference. The rules of the grammar will allow base-generation of empty Noun Phrases in either subject or object position in the embedded clause of sentence (24):

(24) it is unclear [who [NP found NP]]

If the subject is empty in D-structure, the object must be the trace of *who*; if the object is empty in D-structure, the subject must be the trace of *who*. But neither choice allows an interpretation of the sentence. We conclude, then, that no Noun Phrase in a tensed sentence can be interpreted as arbitrary in reference.

In summary, while the empty Noun Phrase that is bound as the trace of a *wh*-phrase can appear anywhere in a sentence, a base-generated empty Noun Phrase, understood in effect as a free variable, can appear only as the subject of an infinitive.

This observation suggests that we should seek some notion of "opacity." That is, much as modal operators or verbs of propositional attitude create an opaque domain in which a referring expression cannot be subject to existential generalization leaving a variable free within the domain, so some linguistic operators apparently create opaque domains in which an empty Noun Phrase functioning as a variable in logical form cannot be free. I will return to the formulation of the principle in a moment, merely noting so far that its consequences are that in a clause, only the subject of an infinitive is not in an opaque domain.

If what is at work here really is a principle of opacity, we should expect to find consequences of its application elsewhere. And, in fact, the configuration just noted appears quite widely. Let us return to the examples of reciprocals used earlier as illustration. Recall that the sentence (25) means that each of the candidates wanted the other to win, while sentence (26) is not well-formed with the meaning of "each of the candidates wanted me to vote for the other":

(25) the candidates wanted [s̄ each other to win]
(26) the candidates wanted [s̄ me to vote for each other]

In a tensed clause, the reciprocal phrase cannot appear even as subject:

(27) the candidates believed [each other would win]

In short, *each other* can appear only as the subject of an infinitive, the one position that is not in an opaque domain.

The phrase *each other* is variable-like in that it must be connected to an antecedent which, in effect, "binds it." Such an expression is called an "anaphor." Let us extend the term "anaphor" to cover empty Noun Phrases that may be thought of as free variables, arbitrarily denoting within a certain category. Then we see that an anaphor can be free in a clause only if it is the subject of an infinitive; all other domains in the clause are opaque. Since bound trace is not free, it can appear anywhere.

The opacity principle can be sharpened by noting that reciprocals can be embedded in Noun Phrases as well as clauses, as in the sentences of (28):

(28) (a) they like [$_{NP}$ each other's books]
     (b) they like [$_{NP}$ the pictures of each other]

But *each other* cannot be free in a Noun Phrase with a "subject," where we take the possessive Noun Phrase of a larger Noun Phrase to be its subject, as is natural on other grounds. Thus (29) is ungrammatical:

(29) they like [$_{NP}$ my pictures of each other]

This observation suggests the correct formulation of the principle of opacity. Suppose we say that in the structure (30) α *c-commands* . . . :

(30)

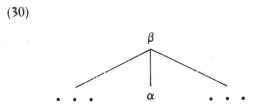

The notion c-command figures quite widely in the theory of anaphora, as has been shown elsewhere.[37] Then the opacity principle states:

(31) an anaphor α cannot be free in β (β = NP or $\bar{S}$) if α is the subject of Tense or is c-commanded by the subject of β

Actually, this formulation is still insufficiently general, but it can easily be extended to a number of other cases to which it applies.[38]

There are many other cases that illustrate the operation of the principle of opacity. To conclude these remarks, let's consider one case in which the principle interacts with the rule "Move α" in an interesting way.

Consider the sentence (32):

$$\qquad\qquad\quad \text{(a)} \qquad \text{(b)} \qquad \text{(c)}$$
(32) it is time [$_{\bar{s}}$ for [$_s$ John to give bones to the dog]]

The embedded $\bar{S}$ in (32) is a purposive clause. In this case, the embedded purposive clause has three Noun Phrases: *John, bones, the dog*. The rules of the base, applying freely, will permit an empty Noun Phrase to appear in any one of the Noun Phrase positions of the purposive clause, that is, in the positions labeled (a), (b) or (c) in (32). These possibilities are illustrated in the sentences of (33):

(33) (i) Mary came over [$_{\bar{s}}$ — to give bones to the dog]   ((a) = empty NP)[39]

   (ii)   Mary brought some bones over [$_{\bar{s}}$ for John to give — to the dog] ((b) = empty NP)

  (iii)   Mary brought a dog over [$_{\bar{s}}$ for John to give bones to —] ((c) = empty NP)

Since each of the positions (a), (b), (c) can be empty, the rules of the base, applying without constraint, will also allow any pair of these to be empty. The possibilities are illustrated in (34):[40]

(34) (i) Mary brought bones [$_\bar{s}$ — to give — to the dog] ((a), (b) = empty NP)

(ii) Mary bought a dog [$_\bar{s}$ — to give bones to —] ((a), (c) = empty NP)

(iii) The dog got bones [$_\bar{s}$ for John to give — to —] ((b), (c) = empty NP)

Evidently, only cases (i) and (ii) are grammatical.

It should also be possible for all three positions to be empty, as in (35):

(35) Mary bought the dog bones [$_s$ — to give — to —] ((a), (b), (c) = empty NP)

This is ungrammatical.

Thus of the various theoretically possible cases, each of which would be perfectly meaningful if grammatical, only cases (33) and (34i, ii) are realized. What is the explanation for these facts?

We have postulated the rule "Move α" and the principle of opacity governing anaphors in logical form. Actually, these independently-motivated principles predict the configuration of data just reviewed. The principle of opacity allows exactly two positions in which an anaphor may be free in $\bar{S}$, namely, the COMP position and the subject of an infinitive. The rule "Move α," as we have seen, can move an NP to COMP. It is obvious that no more than one element can be moved to COMP: we have such sentences as "I wonder who saw what" but not "I wonder who what saw." [41] It follows that at most two NP positions can be free in $\bar{S}$; the subject and an NP moved to COMP. Thus case (35) is excluded. As for (34), case (iii) is excluded because at most one of the NPs in positions (b) and (c) can be moved to

COMP; the other will be in an opaque domain. But all the other possibilities are allowed, with a free anaphor in subject position and a free anaphor moved to COMP.[42]

There are still further ramifications. Consider, for example, the sentence (36), which, by the opacity condition, must derive from the S-structure (37):

(36) Mary bought a dog to play with
(37) Mary bought a dog [NP_2 [NP_1 to play with t]]

In (37) t is the trace of the empty NP_2, which has been moved to COMP. We understand (36) to mean that Mary bought a dog for her to play with, not that Mary bought a dog for the dog to play with her. This is a rather subtle judgment; the two possibilities are virtually if not completely synonymous, yet we understand (36) to be associated with one interpretation though not the other. Thus we know something about LF that appears to go beyond synonymy (or virtual synonymy) in sharpness of discrimination among interpretations. Presumably, some general principle applies to determine these judgments. The principle in question might be a kind of "minimal distance principle." In (37), which is submitted to the rules of interpretation to yield LF, NP_2 is the "most prominent" (c-commanding) NP; thus it is the first one to be subject to interpretation, under natural principles. A natural interpretation of "minimal distance" would associate it with the NP that immediately c-commands it, namely *a dog*. This leaves only the possibility of associating NP_1 with *Mary*, giving the interpretation: "Mary bought a dog for her to play with the dog."[43] Consideration of other verbs in the main clause reveals that questions involving thematic relations arise, complicating the issue.[44] Again, the examples illustrate the subtlety and complexity of the judgments provided by what must be rather deep-seated principles of universal grammar, so it seems reasonable to conclude.

These examples provide additional confirmation for the rule "Move α" and the principle of opacity. The two principles interact, along with others, to predict a curious configuration of judgments concerning the interpretation of phonetically unrealized Noun Phrases. These judgments therefore provide evidence that grammars contain the rule "Move α," that LF is governed by the principle of opacity, and that the mental representations formed by the rules of our internalized grammar contain categories that are phonetically null but on a par with other categories that happen to be phonetically realized at a later point in the operation of rules. It is difficult, again, to imagine that each of us, or any of us, has learned these properties of purposive clauses from experience. There are no "regularities" or "conventions" governing such cases as these. Rather, it seems that abstract principles of the language faculty, part of our biological endowment, interact with materials provided by experience to yield quite precise judgments over a complex range of cases that lie far beyond experience. These principles thus play a fundamental part in determining our knowledge that sounds are paired with meanings in certain specific ways, along with much else.

The interaction of principles to yield certain properties of purposive clauses illustrates what we expect to find in a theory of universal grammar, though these illustrations barely begin to scratch the surface. I have said virtually nothing about the parameters left open in universal grammar that provide for the variety of languages. There are options for base ordering, for the scope and conditions of application of the rule "Move α,"[45] for what counts as an "anaphor," and much else. As we proceed to formulate unifying principles that interact to yield specific consequences and to identify the parameters and the choices they permit, we begin to approach a theory of the innate schematism that underlies systems of human language and that provides the answer, in this case, to our version of what might be called "Plato's problem": how can we know what in fact we do know.

As I have tried to show in earlier lectures, it makes sense to think of other cognitive systems on the model of the human language faculty, despite the fact that knowledge of language is not a "central case" of knowledge, and on the assumption of modularity, can be expected to involve principles different from those that enter into other cognitive systems. My own feeling is that a theory of mind should proceed by tentatively identifying such cognitive systems and submitting them to detailed study to determine their specific properties. Some such systems may be like language in that they are properly conceived in terms of grammar-like theories of rules and representations. It may turn out that in the domains where we speak of "knowledge of X" (knowledge of language, of music, of mathematics, of the behavior of objects, of social structure, of human characteristics, etc.), with the consequences of such knowledge in the form of expectations or knowing that such-and-such, there is a mentally-represented system of this nature which can be taken to be an object of knowledge, just as there is good reason, I believe, to think of what we know as a grammar when we speak loosely of "knowing a language." These cognitive systems serve as vehicles for the exercise of our various capacities and thus enter into our thought and action, as when we come to understand what is said to us, or what is happening around us, or what some other person is doing—say, reading a book, or pursuing a goal.[46] To identify these cognitive systems and to discover their properties and modes of interaction we must be willing to entertain fairly far-reaching idealization and to attribute internal structure, sometimes in the form of rules and representations, to the human mind, including substantial innate structure, which might take various forms: principles, rules, systems of representation, schemata, modes of functioning and integration, and so on. We must, in short, be willing to approach the study of mind much in the manner of the natural sciences.

In these lectures, I have been trying to make two basic points. First, a variety of objections of principle that have been raised to such an approach are not well-founded, while alternative approaches to similar problems that seek to avoid attribution of internal mental structures as vehicles for the exercise of cognitive capacities are fundamentally flawed. And second, in some domains of human knowledge it is possible to obtain nontrivial results by studying the rules and representations of cognitive systems. A framework of the sort I have been discussing seems to me natural and appropriate for the study of such products of the human mind as human language, or the study of the use of language. I would like to end by speculating that if the so-called "cognitive sciences" do develop in a serious and fruitful way, it will be within a framework of essentially this character.

Part II

5

On the Biological Basis of
Language Capacities

THE TITLE OF this chapter is, of course, taken from Eric Lenneberg's major study of language and biology (1967), now recognized as a classic in the field. He set himself the task of studying language as "an aspect of [man's] biological nature, to be studied in the same manner as, for instance, his anatomy."[1] The purpose of this study was "to reinstate the concept of the biological basis of language capacities and to make the specific assumptions so explicit that they may be subjected to empirical tests." Adopting this point of view, we may regard the language capacity virtually as we would a physical organ of the body and can investigate the principles of its organization, functioning, and development in the individual and the species. Personally, I feel that this is just the right way to approach the study of human language. I would like to make a few comments on the program that Lenneberg outlined and developed, concentrating on two theses that seem to me of particular significance.

Adapted from George A. Miller and Elizabeth Lenneberg, eds., *Psychology and Biology of Language and Thought: Essays in Honor of Eric Lenneberg* (New York: Academic Press, 1978). First published in R. W. Rieber, ed., *The Neuropsychology of Language* (New York: Plenum Press, 1976).

In his concluding discussion, Lenneberg presented two important observations on the nature of the inquiry into language and biology. He noted in the first place that

the rules that underlie syntax (which are the same for understanding and speaking) are of a very specific kind, and unless man or mechanical devices do their processing of incoming sentences in accordance with these rules, the logical, formal analysis of the input will be deficient, resulting in incorrect or random responses. When we say rules must have been built into the grammatical analyzer, we impute the existence of an apparatus with specific structural properties or, in other words, a specific internal organization.

He then observed that the fundamental question in the study of the biology of language is: "Just what is postulated to be innate in language behavior?" Evidently, "we must assume a biological matrix with specifiable characteristics that determines the outcome of any treatment to which the organism is subjected." The evidence, he argued, points "to great specificity of the underlying matrix." The "only thoroughly interesting problem" is to determine the range of possibilities that might be realized under given environmental conditions, this range evidently determined by the biological matrix. It is, he emphasized correctly, "entirely an empirical question"; there is no room for dogmatic preconceptions or a priori argument. Biology, he observed,

does no more than to discover how various forms are innately constituted, and this includes descriptions of a creature's reactions to environmental forces. Research into these reactions does not eventually free us from the postulation of innate features, but merely elucidates the exact nature of innate constitutions. The discovery and description of innate mechanisms is a thoroughly empirical procedure and is an integral part of modern scientific inquiry.

When I met Eric Lenneberg as a graduate student, just twenty-five years ago, these basic concerns were beginning to take shape in his mind. He wanted to see the study of language assimilated to the natural sciences, and he devoted his subsequent efforts to placing language in its biological matrix. From the point of view he was to adopt, the study of systems of grammar is concerned with the "specific internal organization" and "specific structural properties" of an "apparatus" to which we "impute existence" as one component in the system of cognitive structures developed in the course of individual growth. What many linguists call "universal grammar" may be regarded as a theory of innate mechanisms, an underlying biological matrix that provides a framework within which the growth of language proceeds. There is no reason for the linguist to refrain from imputing existence to this initial apparatus of mind as well. Proposed principles of universal grammar may be regarded as an abstract partial specification of the genetic program that enables the child to interpret certain events as linguistic experience and to construct a system of rules and principles on the basis of this experience.

To put the matter in somewhat different but essentially equivalent terms, we may suppose that there is a fixed, genetically determined initial state of the mind, common to the species with at most minor variation apart from pathology. The mind passes through a sequence of states under the boundary conditions set by experience, achieving finally a "steady state" at a relatively fixed age, a state that then changes only in marginal ways. The basic property of this initial state is that, given experience, it develops to the steady state. Correspondingly, the initial state of the mind might be regarded as a function, characteristic of the species, that maps experience into the steady state. Universal grammar is a partial characterization of this function, of this initial state. The grammar of a language that has grown in the mind is a partial characterization of the steady state attained.

So viewed, linguistics is the abstract study of certain mechanisms, their growth and maturation. We may impute existence to the postulated structures at the initial, intermediate, and steady states in just the same sense as we impute existence to a program that we believe to be somehow represented in a computer or that we postulate to account for the mental representation of a three-dimensional object in the visual field. Evidence bearing on empirical hypotheses such as these might derive from many and varied sources. Ultimately, we hope to find evidence concerning the physical mechanisms that realize the program; it is reasonable to expect that results obtained in the abstract study of the program and its operation should contribute significantly to this end (and, in principle, conversely; that is, information regarding the mechanisms might contribute to understanding of the program).

In the case of the study of language, the question is complicated in practice by the obvious fact that the system of language is only one of a number of cognitive systems that interact in the most intimate way in the actual use of language. When we speak or interpret what we hear, we bring to bear a vast set of background assumptions about the participants in the discourse, the subject matter under discussion, laws of nature, human institutions, and the like. Continuing to think of the system of grammatical rules as a kind of "mental organ," interacting with other mental organs with other functions and properties, we face a rather typical problem of natural science, namely, the problem of appropriate idealization and abstraction. In an effort to determine the nature of one of these interacting systems, we must abstract away from the contribution of others to the actual performance that can be observed. Steps taken in this direction are not without their hazards; they are also inescapable in rational inquiry. We therefore proceed to experiment with idealized systems, always bearing in mind the possibility that another approach might lead us closer to an understanding of the various systems that constitute the human mind.

There is much discussion in the literature of linguistics and psychology of the "psychological reality" of the linguist's constructions. I take it that the question at issue is whether it is legitimate to 'impute existence" to the "apparatus," the properties of which are characterized by particular grammars or by universal grammar (which is, of course, not a grammar but rather a system of conditions on the range of possible grammars for possible human languages). The discussion of "psychological reality" sometimes seems to me to be rather misleading. Perhaps I can explain my misgivings by an analogy.[2]

Consider the problem of determining the nature of the thermonuclear reactions that take place deep in the interior of the sun. Suppose that available technique permits astronomers to study only the light emitted at the outermost layers of the sun. On the basis of the information thereby attained, they construct a theory of the hidden thermonuclear reactions, postulating that light elements are fused into heavier ones, converting mass into energy, thus producing the sun's heat. Suppose that an astronomer presents such a theory, citing the evidence that supports it. Suppose now that someone were to approach this astronomer with the following contention: "True, you have presented a theory that explains the available evidence, but how do you know that the constructions of your theory have physical reality—in short, how do you know that your theory is true?"

The astronomer could respond only by repeating what he had already presented; here is the evidence available and here is the theory that I offer to explain it. The evidence derives from investigation of light emitted at the periphery. We might want to place a laboratory inside the sun to obtain more direct evidence, but being unable to do so, we must test and confirm our theory indirectly. One might argue that the evidence is inconclusive or that the theory is objectionable on some physical (or, conceivably, methodological) grounds. But it is senseless to ask for some other kind of justification for attributing physical reality to the constructions of the theory, apart from consideration of their adequacy in explaining the evidence and their conformity to the body of natural science as currently understood. There can be no other grounds for attributing physical reality to the scientist's constructions.

Suppose now that an ingenious experimenter hits upon a more direct method for studying events taking place in the interior of the sun, namely, study of the neutrinos that are released by the assumed thermonuclear reactions in the solar interior and that escape into space. Using this new evidence, he may substantiate the old theory or construct a better one. Has this more "direct" investigation of events in the interior of the sun now answered the original objections? Are we now entitled to attribute "a higher order of physical reality" to the constructions that were only postulated before? Not really. No empirical evidence can be conclusive. Again, we can only say that with our more direct and more conclusive evidence, we may now be more confident than before that the entities and events postulated are physically real—that the theoretical statements in which reference is made to these entities, processes, and so on are, in fact, true. But again, there is little sense to the contention that we still do not know that what is postulated is physically real, as if there were some further standard that might be achieved in some qualitatively different way. The enterprise in question is empirical science, not mathematics; at best, we can settle on one of indefinitely many possible theories that account for crucial evidence, attributing physical reality to whatever is postulated in that theory.

Our investigation of the apparatus of the language faculty, whether in its initial or final steady state, bears some similarity to the investigation of thermonuclear reactions in the solar interior that is limited to evidence provided by light emitted at the periphery. We observe what people say and do, how they react and respond, often in situations contrived so that this behavior will provide some evidence (we hope) concerning the operative mechanisms. We then try, as best we can, to devise a theory of some depth and significance with regard to these mechanisms, testing our theory by its success in providing explanations for selected phenomena. Challenged to show that the constructions postulated in that theory have "psychological reality," we can do no more than repeat the evidence and the proposed explanations that involve these constructions. Or, like the astronomer dissatisfied with study of light emissions from the periphery of the sun, we can search for more conclusive evidence, always aware that in empirical inquiry we can, at best, support a theory against substantive alternatives and empirical challenge; we cannot prove it to be true. It would be quite reasonable to argue against a claim for psychological reality—that is, truth of a certain theory—on the grounds that the evidence is weak and susceptible to explanation in different terms; needless to say, the evidence that supports the linguist's constructions is incomparably less satisfying than that available to the physicist. But in es-

sence the problems are the same, and the question of psychological reality is no more and no less sensible in principle than
the question of the physical reality of the physicist's theoretical
constructions.

The literature takes a rather different view. Certain types of
evidence are held to relate to psychological reality, specifically,
evidence deriving from studies of reaction time, recognition,
recall, etc. Other kinds of evidence are held to be of an entirely
different nature, specifically, evidence deriving from informant
judgments as to what sentences mean, whether they are well
formed, and so on. Theoretical explanations advanced to explain evidence of the latter sort, it is commonly argued, have no
claim to psychological reality, no matter how far-reaching, extensive, or persuasive the explanations may be, and no matter
how firmly founded the observations offered as evidence. To
merit the attribution of "psychological reality," the entities,
rules, processes, components, etc., postulated in these explanatory theories must be confronted with evidence of the former
category. If these theoretical constructions can be shown to play
a role in the study of reaction time, etc., then perhaps we may
attribute to them psychological reality. Note that what is apparently claimed is that there is some conceptual distinction between two kinds of theories, a distinction based on the nature of
the evidence advanced to support them, not on the reliability of
the evidence or the depth of the theories.

Let me illustrate with a concrete example, much simplified
for the purposes of exposition. Suppose that we are concerned
with the process of sentence-formation in colloquial English
and we note that while some questions are judged to be well
formed, others are not. Consider the sentence

(1) Violins are easy to play sonatas on.

This sentence might, for example, be the answer to the question

(2) What instruments are easy to play sonatas on?

But sentence (1) is not a possible answer to question (3):

(3) What kinds of music are violins easy to play on?

In fact, (3) is not a well-formed question at all. Corresponding to (1) we have such questions as

(4) What violins are easy to play sonatas on?

but not

(5) What sonatas are violins easy to play on?

The distinction between (4) and (5) has been repeatedly noted in recent discussion; let us assume that careful inquiry shows it to be well founded. Thus (5), like (3), is just not a well-formed question in colloquial English. The problem with (5) and (3) cannot be that the questioned term (*sonatas* in (1)) is too far towards the end of the sentence, or that it is within a verb phrase complement, or the like. Thus there is nothing wrong with question (6), which corresponds to sentence (7) as (5) corresponds to (1):

(6) What sonatas did John want Bill to play on the violin?
(7) John wanted Bill to play sonatas on the violin.

Evidently, (6) conforms to the rules of English grammar, as these are represented somehow in our minds, in a way in which (5) does not. Many facts of this sort have been noticed in the literature of linguistics. Clearly, they call for explanation. If an interesting explanation is forthcoming, then these observations will have been demonstrated to be significant for the insight they provide into mental representations, and the computations involving them.

Suppose now that someone were to advance the following explanation for the facts noted.[3] We know that *wh*-clauses are "islands" in English in the sense of Ross.[4] We say that a phrase is an "island" if it is immune to the application of rules that relate its parts to a position outside of the island. Thus to say that a *wh*-clause is an island is to say, in particular, that the rule of *wh*-movement that forms questions and relatives by moving such expressions as *who, what, what sonatas*, etc., to the left of a clause cannot be applied in general to a *wh*-expression within a *wh*-clause. For example, given the sentences of (8), we cannot form the corresponding questions of (9), questioning *the book:*

(8) (a) We wondered [to whom John gave the book].
(b) We found out [who wrote the book].
(c) We did [what you asked us to do about the book].

(9) (a) What book did we wonder to whom John gave?
(b) What book did we find out who wrote?
(c) What book did we do what you asked us to do about?

In sentences comparable to (8) but without the bracketed *wh*-clause, the phrase *the book* is accessible to the *wh*-movement rule for forming question; compare (9'):

(9') (a) What book did we say that John gave to Bill?
(b) What book did we find out that John wrote?
(c) What book did we ask you to tell Bill to do something about?

From such examples, we might conclude that expressions that lie within *wh*-clauses, such as those bracketed in (8), are not accessible to the rule of question-formation. More generally, *wh*-clauses are "islands," immune to such rules as *wh*-movement. The explanation for this and other island phenomena lies in still deeper properties of rules of grammar, I believe—specifically, the "locality principle" noted in lectures 3 and 4, above—but we may put this matter aside for now.

Returning to sentence (1), suppose that the expression *to play sonatas on* in (1) is the residue of a *wh*-clause in the mental computation by which (1) is formed—in particular, the same clause that appears as an infinitival relative in (10), analogous to the finite relative in (11):

(10) I found [$_{NP}$ a violin [$_s$ to play sonatas on]]⁵

(11) I found [$_{NP}$ a violin [$_s$ that you can play sonatas on]]

Suppose, in other words, that we postulate that there really is a *wh*-clause, perhaps the clause represented as in (12), at the stage of computation at which *wh*-movement applies to give ultimately the sentence (5):

(12) [$_s$ which for PRO to play sonatas on *t*]⁶

Then the rule of question-formation cannot apply to the phrase *sonatas*, just as it cannot apply to the phrase *the book* in (8), and for the same reason: application is blocked by the *wh*-clause island constraint, and ultimately, by the deeper properties of grammar from which this constraint derives.

We might find supporting evidence of varied sorts for the assumption that a *wh*-clause actually appears in mental representations in such cases. For example, there is good reason to believe that the structure of (13) is related to that of (1):

(13) this is an easy violin to play sonatas on

But in such structures as (13), the *wh*-word is sometimes overt, as in (14a):

(14) (a) he is an easy person to whom to speak about your problems
     (b) he is an easy person to speak about your problems to

These are analogous in structure to (15):

(15) (a) I met a person to whom to speak about my problems
     (b) I met a person to speak about my problems to

There is good reason to suppose that the examples of (15) are analogous, respectively, to those of (16):

(16) (a) I met a person to whom I spoke about my problems
     (b) I met a person whom I spoke about my problems to

The *wh*-phrase which is overt in (16b) is deleted, for reasons that need not concern us here, in (15b) and (14b). It remains overt in (14a), lending independent support to the assumption that it appears in the mental representation underlying (1), but is deleted, as in (15b) and (14b). Embedding these observations in a more general theory of English grammar, and universal grammar, we derive additional support for the analyses and explanations proposed for the earlier examples.

Tentatively accepting this explanation, we impute existence to certain mental representations and to the mental computations that apply in a specific way to these mental representations. In particular, we impute existence to a representation in which (12) appears as part of the structure underlying (5) at a particular stage of derivation, and to the mental computation that produces this derivation, and ultimately produces (5), identified now as ungrammatical because the computation violates the *wh*-island constraint when the rule of *wh*-movement applies to *sonatas* in (12). We attribute psychological reality to the postulated representations and mental computations. In short, we propose (tentatively, hesitantly, etc.) that our theory is true. Have we gone beyond the bounds of what is legitimate and proper, in so doing?

I think not. Granting the vast differences in the nature of the evidence, the depth and explanatory power of the postulated principles, etc., still the argument sketched seems to me analogous in relevant respects to that of the physicist postulating certain processes in the interior of the sun. Of course, there are differences; the physicist is actually postulating physical entities and processes, while we are keeping to abstract conditions that unknown mechanisms must meet. We might go on to suggest actual mechanisms, but we know that it would be pointless to do so in the present stage of our ignorance concerning the functioning of the brain. This, however, is not a relevant difference of principle. If we were able to investigate humans as we study other, defenseless organisms, we might very well proceed to inquire into the operative mechanisms by intrusive experimentation, by constructing controlled conditions for language growth, and so on, thus perhaps narrowing the gap between the language example and the astronomical example. The barriers to this direct investigation are ethical. We must be satisfied with quite indirect evidence, but no particular philosophical problems arise from this contingency, just as no such problems arise in the case of the astronomer limited to investigation of light emissions from the sun's periphery as compared with the astronomer studying neutrinos escaping from the solar interior.

There are many questions that may legitimately be raised about the hypothetical explanation that I have briefly outlined. Thus, one might ask how firm is the evidence, and how well supported independently are the principles on which the evidence is based? Let us examine these questions.

Consider first the question of the nature of the evidence. There is no reason why we cannot proceed to test and refine the initial judgments of well-formedness for colloquial English. For example, we might devise experimental tests of acceptability, and if these tests met appropriate empirical conditions, we might decide to rely on them to determine the adequacy of the judgments to which we have appealed here, recognizing, however, that "well-formedness" is a theoretical concept for which we cannot expect to find a precise set of necessary and sufficient operational criteria (a fact of no great moment in itself). Notice that it is a trivial point, though one often overlooked, that any test of acceptability must itself meet certain empirical conditions, just as an explanatory theory must meet such conditions.[7] Some linguists have been bemused by the fact that the conditions that test the test are themselves subject to doubt and revision, believing that they have discovered some hidden paradox or circularity of reasoning.[8] In fact, they have simply rediscovered the fact that linguistics is not mathematics but rather a branch of empirical inquiry. Even if we were to grant that there is some set of observation sentences that constitute the bedrock of inquiry and are immune to challenge, it nevertheless remains true that theory must be invoked to determine to what, if anything, these pure and perfect observations attest, and here there is no Cartesian ground of certainty. All of this is, or should be, obvious. Many argue that the problems of empirical uncertainty can be overcome by restricting attention to a corpus, and some (e.g., Ney) seem to believe that this has been the practice of traditional grammar. That is untrue. A corpus may contain examples of deviant or ungrammatical sentences, and any rational linguist will recognize the problem and try to assign to observed examples their proper status. Furthermore, any serious work on language uses "elicited" material, often "self-elicited," as, for example, in Jespersen's classic works and other work that deserves serious attention. And insofar as a corpus is used as a source of illustrative examples, we rely on the same intuitive judgments to select examples as we do in devising relevant examples with the aid of an informant (or ourselves). Restriction of grammatical analysis to a real corpus would be about as sensible as restriction of physics or biology to motion pictures of events happening about us in our normal lives.[9]

To consider what appears to be a more productive (as well as intellectually far more interesting) approach, we may turn to the second of the two questions raised above and try to put the principles used in the explanation to independent empirical test. One way to approach this question is by trying to explain the wh-clause island constraint itself in terms of deeper principles of grammar that have other consequences, thus opening the proposed explanation to a broader empirical challenge. Or, as already briefly indicated, we may try to find other evidence bearing on the postulated analysis of (1), with the underlying mental representation including (12) and the mental computation postulated.[10]

Suppose that both of these approaches prove eminently successful. Thus we establish the reliability of the judgments and give substantial independent evidence for the theoretical constructions, showing that the postulated principles explain many other facts of a similar nature, withstand empirical tests in English and other languages, etc. Would we then have provided evidence for the psychological reality of the mental representations and mental computations postulated? If I read the literature correctly, many linguists would still reject this conclusion, arguing that something else is needed to carry us over that qualitative barrier of principle that distinguishes purely hypothetical constructions from others to which we may properly attribute "psychological reality."

Suppose now that someone were to devise an experiment to test for the presence of a wh-clause in underlying representations—let us say, a recognition or recall experiment. Or let us really let down the bars of imagination and suppose that someone were to discover a certain pattern of electrical activity in the brain that correlated in clear cases with the presence of wh-clauses: relative clauses (finite and infinitival) and wh-questions (direct and indirect). Suppose that this pattern of electrical activity is observed when a person speaks or understands (1). Would we now have evidence for the psychological reality of the postulated mental representations?

We would now have a new kind of evidence, but I see no merit to the contention that this new evidence bears on psychological reality whereas the old evidence only relates to hypothetical constructions. The new evidence might or might not be more persuasive than the old; that would depend on its character and reliability, the degree to which the principles dealing with this evidence are tenable, intelligible, compelling, and so on. In the real world of actual research on language, it would be fair to say, I think, that principles based on evidence derived from informant judgment have proved to be deeper and more revealing than those based on evidence derived from experiments on processing and the like, although the future may be different in this regard. If we accept—as I do—Lenneberg's contention that the rules of grammar enter into the processing mechanisms, then evidence concerning production, recognition, recall, and language use in general can be expected (in principle) to have bearing on the investigation of rules of grammar, on what is sometimes called "grammatical competence" or "knowledge of language." But such evidence, where it is forthcoming, has no privileged character and does not bear on "psychological reality" in some unique way. Evidence is not subdivided into two categories: evidence that bears on reality and evidence that just confirms or refutes theories (about mental computation and mental representations, in this case). Some evidence may bear on process models that incorporate a characterization of grammatical competence, while other evidence seems to bear on competence more directly, in abstraction from conditions of language use. And, of course, one can try to use data in other ways. But just as a body of data does not come bearing its explanation on its sleeve, so it does not come marked "for confirming theories" or "for establishing reality."

It is not uncommon to draw a line separating the two disciplines, linguistics and psychology, in terms of the kinds of evidence they prefer to use and the specific focus of their attention. Thus, linguistics is taken to be the field that relies on informant judgments, elicited material, whatever limited use can be made of an actual corpus, and so on, to try to determine the nature of grammar and universal grammar. Its concern is competence, the system of rules and principles that we assume have, in some manner, been internally represented by the person who knows a language and that enable the speaker, in principle, to understand an arbitrary sentence and to produce a sentence expressing his thought; and its further concern is universal grammar, the principles that specify the range of possible human grammars. Psychology, in contrast, is concerned with performance, not competence; its concern is the processes of production, interpretation, and the like, which make use of the knowledge attained, and the processes by which transition takes place from the initial to the final state, that is, language acquisition.

To me, this distinction has always seemed quite senseless. Delineation of disciplines may be useful for administering universities or organizing professional societies, but apart from that, it is an undertaking of limited merit. A person who happens to be interested in underlying competence will naturally be delighted to exploit whatever understanding may be forthcoming about process models that incorporate one or another set of assumptions about linguistic knowledge. Furthermore, it seems evident that investigation of performance will rely, to whatever extent it can, on what is learned about the systems of knowledge that are put to use. The theory of particular and universal grammar, so far as I can see, can be sensibly regarded only as that aspect of theoretical psychology that is primarily concerned with the genetically determined program that specifies the range of possible grammars for human languages and the particular realizations of this schematism that arise under given conditions. One may perfectly well choose to study language and grammar with other purposes in mind and without concern for these questions, but any significant results obtained will nevertheless be a contribution to this branch of psychology. I take it that this is one major point that Lenneberg was putting forth in his work. It seems to me entirely correct.

Not everyone agrees, or so a literal reading might suggest. It is illuminating to see how opposing views are put in the literature. In chapter 1 of their text on cognitive psychology, Kintsch and associates[11] argue that the "strict separation" between competence and performance permits the linguist to deal with convenient abstractions, uninhibited by psychological reality, and it provides the psychologist with the face-tious argument that linguistic theories have nothing to do with pro-cesses anyway. As long as linguistic theory is strictly a competence theory, it is of no interest to the psychologist. Indeed I doubt that it should be of much interest to linguists either, but that is for them to decide.

These remarks, which are not untypical, reflect deep-seated confusions. The approach that Kintsch criticizes, as his refer-ences make clear, is the one outlined above: the approach based on the assumption that a person's knowledge of language can properly be represented as a system of rules of grammar, and that process models concerned with language use will incorpo-rate such representations of grammatical competence. On this assumption, which is of course not God-given but must be evaluated in terms of its empirical consequences, the goal of the investigator will be to determine the nature of the competence system that expresses what it is that the mature speaker knows, and to develop process models that show how this knowledge is put to use.

Kintsch asserts that study of the abstracted competence system is "uninhibited by psychological reality"; only processes have "reality." But plainly we can have no special insight into what is real apart from normal scientific practice. Adhering to these rea-sonable norms, we impute existence, subject to verification and test, to whatever structures and processes are postulated in the effort to explain significant facts. The enterprise is not "unin-hibited by psychological reality," but is rather concerned with specific aspects of psychological reality. Kintsch's psychologist has "no interest" in explanatory theories, no matter how far-reaching and well-confirmed, dealing with these aspects of knowledge of language and the basis for its acquisition (particular and universal grammar). In short, fundamental questions of cognitive psychology are to be excluded from the concern of the psychologist (or for Kintsch, the concern of anyone). Note that these positions are taken on purely a priori grounds, not on the basis of alleged empirical or conceptual inadequacies of the approach he rejects as compared with some alternative. It is difficult to imagine comparable dogmatism in the natural sciences.

Kintsch's psychologist not only declares his lack of interest in this central domain of human psychology; furthermore, he decides, a priori, that a characterization of the system of knowledge attained can be of no relevance for investigation of the process models to which he limits his attention. Note that this is what a literal reading of Kintsch's remarks implies. If the study of competence models along the lines he rejects (namely, those I have just outlined) were to bring to light a system embedded in processing models in the way that Lenneberg (and others) propose, then clearly results attained in this study would be of great relevance for the investigation of process models, but Kintsch excludes this possibility on a priori grounds. Again, such astonishing dogmatism about matters so poorly understood can hardly be imagined in the natural sciences. One might put forth a rational hypothesis that perhaps expresses what Kintsch has in mind. Namely, one might propose that once process models are developed we will find that all relevant facts are explained without any abstraction to a rule system that articulates the speaker-hearer's knowledge of his language. This thesis might prove correct. To reject it out of hand would be as irrational as Kintsch's dogmatic stand. But the dogmatic insistence that it must be correct and that alternatives must be discarded on a priori grounds, as a literal reading of Kintsch's remarks implies, is simply a reflection of the irrationality that has hampered investigation in the human sciences for many, many years.

Note that the "strict separation" between competence and performance that Kintsch deplores is a conceptual distinction; knowledge of language is distinguished from behavior (use of this knowledge). This conceptual distinction is surely quite "strict," though one might argue that a different conceptual framework would be preferable. In fact, Kintsch adopts throughout the conceptual distinction that he believes he rejects, where his discussion is coherent.[12] The main concern of his book is "the study of the properties" of a certain "level of representation in memory, both theoretically and empirically," namely, representation of a sentence "conceptually in terms of its meaning," which he takes to be a "propositional" representation. This is the study of a certain aspect of competence. Kintsch simply presupposes some system of rules that generates the representations he postulates, in particular cases. And like everyone else, Kintsch tries to gain some understanding of this "level of representation" through the study of performance and tries to show how it figures in process models. In short, while Kintsch believes that his approach "has no use at all for the competence-performance distinction," in fact, he invokes it in pretty much the conventional way. This is not surprising, given that no coherent alternative framework of concepts has been proposed in this domain, to my knowledge.

My comments so far have been directed to the first of the two conclusions cited from Lenneberg's study of the biology of language. Let me now turn to the second, namely his conclusion that "the discovery and description of innate mechanisms is a thoroughly empirical procedure and is an integral part of modern scientific inquiry." The study of innate mechanisms leads us to universal grammar, but also, of course, to investigation of the biologically determined principles that underlie language use, what has sometimes been called "pragmatic competence," and cognitive structures of other sorts that enter into the actual use of language.

In drawing his conclusions concerning the investigation of innate mechanisms, Lenneberg felt that it was necessary to emphasize the empirical nature of this research because "there was a time when 'innateness' was on the index of forbidden concepts," and "there are still many scientists who regard the postulation of anything innate as a clever parlor trick that alleviates the proponent from performing 'truly scientific' investigations," a position, he noted, that "is odd to say the least," but one that has had and in fact still retains quite a grip on the modern imagination.

It is easy to illustrate the persistence, to this day, of serious qualms concerning explanations that rely on postulated innate mechanisms, though I agree entirely with Lenneberg that these reservations are "odd to say the least." Of course, specific proposals may be open to all sorts of legitimate objections. But I am referring now rather to the commonly expressed belief that there is some objection in principle to such an approach. Such objections have been expressed in an extreme form by a number of philosophers. I have argued elsewhere that their objections are groundless, and will have nothing to say about this here.[13] Similar doctrines sometimes appear in the linguistic literature as well (see, for example, Peizer and Olmsted),[14] also, to my knowledge, without valid supporting argument.

Appeal to innate mechanisms is also regarded with great suspicion by many psychologists, and not—contrary to widespread belief—only by those who regard themselves as "behaviorists," whatever that designation may mean today, if anything. Consider, for example, the objections raised by Piaget and his colleagues. Piaget[15] argues that the postulated innate mechanisms are "biologically inexplicable" and that what can be explained on the assumption of fixed innate structures can be explained as "the 'necessary' results of constructions of sensorimotor intelligence." However, he offers no argument at all that the postulated mechanisms are any more "inexplicable" than mechanisms postulated to account for physical development; indeed, even the most radical "innatists" have suggested mechanisms that would add only a small increment to what any rational biologist would assume must be genetically determined. Piaget's complaint would be correct if he had said "biologically unexplained" instead of "biologically inexplicable," but then the same might be said about current ideas concerning development of physical organs of the body. As for Piaget's further claim that the facts for which an explanation has been offered in terms of a postulated genetically determined universal grammar can be explained as the "necessary" result of constructions of sensorimotor intelligence, I will only state the obvious: the literature contains no evidence or argument to support this remarkable factual claim, nor even any explanation of what sense it might have. Again, we see here an instance of the unfortunate but rather common insistence on dogmatic and unsupported factual doctrines in the human sciences.

The same doctrine is advanced by Piaget's colleagues. Consider, for example, the discussion of this point by Inhelder, Sinclair, and Bovet.[16] Citing Piaget, they put forth "the basic hypothesis of developmental constructivism," which "postulates that no human knowledge, with the obvious exception of the very elementary hereditary forms, is preformed in the structures of either the subject or the object." In particular, they reject the hypothesis that certain principles of language structure (and other cognitive structures) are "not only present at an extremely early age, but hereditary."[17] The postulated principles, they insist, are not "preformed" (i.e., governed by genetically determined factors) but rather arise through the child's activity, and are explained by "regulatory or autoregulatory mechanisms." These are, however, described in terms so vague that it is hard to know what is intended. Taking the hypothesis of "developmental constructivism" literally, they are claiming that such principles as the wh-island constraint, or the deeper principles from which it derives, must arise on the basis of the same kinds of principles that account for the child's early sensorimotor constructions and the like. While one cannot dismiss this contention out of hand, it seems a most astonishing claim.

The persistence of such empirical claims in the absence of any argument or even an intelligible formulation can perhaps be explained in terms of another doctrine of the Geneva school. Thus, Inhelder et al. "agree with Piaget" that the approach they attribute to neonativists "does not help to solve any problem; all it does is to transfer the question from the psychological to the biological level by formulating it in terms of biological development."[18] If this argument had any merit, it would apply as well to standard accounts of physical development. Suppose that someone postulates that binocular vision or the fact that we grow arms instead of wings is genetically determined. By the argument of the Geneva school, this assumption "does not help to solve any problem," but only transfers the question from the psychological to the biological level.

Plainly, no one would take this argument seriously, nor

would the Geneva psychologists advance it in the case of physical development. If the general structure of binocular vision is genetically determined, then naturally we must seek to explain its origin in terms of biological (evolutionary) development rather than in terms of learning. In short, we must "transfer the question [of development] from the psychological to the biological level." Exactly the same is true when we turn to cognitive structures or the (unknown) physical mechanisms that underlie them. If, say, we find extensive evidence that the principles that underlie the *wh*-island constraint belong to universal grammar and are available to the language learner without relevant experience, then it would only be rational to suppose that these mechanisms are genetically determined and to search for a further account in terms of biological development. The Geneva school doctrine seems to be that no matter how substantial the evidence in favor of such a thesis may be, and no matter how weak the argument for ontogenetic development, nevertheless we must maintain the thesis that the principles in question are derived by "regulatory or autoregulatory mechanisms" in accordance with the hypothesis of "developmental constructivism." At least, I see no other way to read their proposals, since the arguments they put forth are in no way empirical but rather purely a priori. All of this again simply constitutes another chapter in the history of dogmatism.

Notice that I do not suggest that the Piagetians cannot be correct in their contentions. Rather, I ask why they insist that they must be right, whatever the evidence seems to show, and why they propose arguments in the case of mental development of a sort that they would never accept in the case of physical growth of organs? Why, in short, must the normal procedures and assumptions of scientific inquiry—in particular, its open-mindedness—be abandoned, when we turn to cognitive structures and their development?

To mention one last case, consider the critique of "nativist" linguistics and psycholinguistics by the distinguished Russian neuropsychologist A. R. Luria.[19] He insists that the natural place to seek the origin of principles of universal grammar[20]— say, the principles that underlie the wh-island constraint, to make the discussion concrete—is "in the history of our society and in the active forms of man's relations with reality." Just how the principles of universal grammar might arise in this way, Luria does not tell us, even in the most vague and hypothetical way. Rather, like Piaget and others he offers a purely methodological argument. The assumption that certain principles of universal grammar are genetically determined, he asserts, "makes a postulate out of a problem and this in itself means that all further study in the area can lead us nowhere."

Once again, if this a priori argument were valid, then it would hold as well for the development of physical organs; that is, it would show that the hypothesis that the growth of arms rather than wings is genetically determined makes a postulate out of a problem and guarantees that further inquiry will lead us nowhere. Since Luria would obviously not accept this conclusion, we are left with only one way of interpreting his argument: cognitive development must, on a priori grounds, be fundamentally different from physical development in that it has no genetic component. It is an a priori truth that cognitive development is "decoupled" from biology in this basic respect. Luria goes on to make a series of empirical claims about what "we must" assume and where "we must look" for an account of the origin of linguistic universals: namely, "in the relations between the active subject and reality and not in the mind itself." Note that no argument is advanced to show that this *is* true, or even any hint of an argument. Rather, it *must* be true; argument is therefore superfluous. If, indeed, investigation shows that the *wh*-island constraint derives from principles of universal grammar and is available to the language learner without relevant experience, we must, nevertheless, insist that this constraint (or the underlying principles) is acquired by the child through "the active relationship between the subject and the world" or "active reflection on the objective world." Note that the reference to "the history of our society" is entirely beside the point, since however language has evolved, a given child must acquire it on the basis of the evidence available. What is most curious of all, perhaps, is that all of this is offered as the "genuinely scientific" approach, the "scientifically philosophical manner" of studying the question at hand. One can imagine how comparable dogmatism would be regarded in the natural sciences.

Perhaps these citations suffice to show that Lenneberg was quite right to take the trouble to emphasize that "the discovery and description of innate mechanisms is a thoroughly empirical procedure and is an integral part of modern scientific inquiry," and to insist that there is no room here for dogmatism or a priori doctrine. It is significant that this simple observation seems so difficult for many researchers to accept. Rather, the normal canons of scientific method and procedure have met with great resistance in the study of mind and cognition, and there has been a compulsion to adhere to a priori theses, whether they are those of associationism, S-R psychology, developmental constructivism, etc. The belief expressed by Luria, that "all patterns present in the human mind are simply a reflection of the interaction between the subject and the outside world," can be traced directly back to scholastic doctrine (though Luria's formulation suggests that he may have had some strange version of "Marxism" in mind), and is often attributed, probably erroneously, to Aristotle. It is interesting to ask why this doctrine is regarded as so sacrosanct. I think that a history of the study of these questions in the modern period will show that such doctrines have been proposed not as bold empirical hypotheses, to be developed and tested—but rather as necessary truths that it would somehow be dangerous to abandon, whatever inquiry may reveal. It seems evident that no science can advance unless it frees itself from intellectual shackles of this nature.

It is interesting to note, in this connection, that the approach that Lenneberg and others recommend—the approach often designated by its opponents as "nativism," though "open-mindedness" would seem a more accurate term—has not met with comparable objections from natural scientists, to my knowledge. Conclusions that have been tentatively advanced by "neonativists" seem to be regarded as unexceptionable in principle, though perhaps incorrect as formulated, by many biologists speculating on questions of language and mind.[21] Furthermore, assumptions similar to those of the "neonativist" psychologists and linguists are proposed without special comment by neurophysiologists quite regularly. To cite one case, in a review of research on vision two neurophysiologists formulate what they call the "principle of restricted potential" in the following terms:

By this we mean to emphasize that the developing nervous system is not a tabula rasa, free to reflect whatever individual experience dictates. Rather, the development of the nervous system is a process sharply constrained by a genetic program. At certain points, the genetic program permits a range of possible realizations, and individual experience acts only to specify the outcome within this range.[22]

In particular, they suggest, "there appears to be a small range within which individual experience operates to assure proper binocular fusion," though the general character of binocular vision in cat and monkey is genetically determined; and "there is some genetically determined range of possible orientation specificities for an individual neuron within which the actual orientation specificity is realized by experience." I have no independent judgment as to whether these suggestions are correct. My point, rather, is that no one would argue that by thus attributing some general restrictive principles to the genetic program they are violating some methodological canon, turning a problem into a postulate, aborting further inquiry, etc. Why then should we take a different stance when it is proposed that universal grammar, genetically determined, permits "a range of possible realizations" and individual experience acts only to specify the outcome—namely, as a particular grammar and performance system—within this range?

The answer is: we should not. Specific arguments with regard to native endowment should be assessed on their merits, without intrusion of a priori doctrine as to the nature of legitimate idealization, the structure of mind, the character of mental representations and mental computation, the role of history, society and experience, etc. There is, in short, no reason to adopt the common view that the human mind is unique among the systems known to us in the biological world in that, in its higher cognitive functions, it is unstructured apart from some minimal "hereditary forms" or "quality space."

One might be disinclined to suppose that a principle such as the wh-island constraint, assuming it to be a principle of universal grammar, is genetically programmed as such. Perhaps such a principle, if indeed it is genetically determined, arises from the interaction of other more basic properties of the language faculty. I think that this is in fact the case, as noted earlier. I have suggested elsewhere that the *wh*-island constraint follows from quite general properties of rule systems that have many other consequences as well. Suppose that we can show that these or other principles of comparable generality are well confirmed in human language and suffice to explain such principles as the *wh*-island constraint where they hold and, thus, to explain why the sentences described earlier are interpreted as they are. We might then ask whether these deeper principles are specific to the language faculty or apply to the operation of other "mental organs" as well. Thus, these deeper principles might result from some sort of organism-environment interaction, difficult as it is to imagine at present how this might come about, or more plausibly they might be characteristic of a broad class of cognitive processes, reflected in various ways in particular cognitive domains. Lenneberg has some interesting speculations along these lines. In discussing the general principles of organization of grammar, he suggests that phrase structure and transformational systems may be "simply special applications of general modes of organization, modes that are common to the organization of the behavior of all higher animals,"[23] though these systems must be "highly adapted biologically" in humans. It remains an open question, and an interesting one, to determine whether there really are significant analogies between the principles of mental representation and computation that seem to be well motivated in the study of language, and other mental operations, in other domains. Personally, I am rather skeptical; I see no interesting analogies in other cognitive domains, but so little is known that we can really say very little.

In this connection too, it seems to me that one must deplore the common tendency to insist that the mechanisms of language must be special cases of "generalized learning strategies" or general cognitive mechanisms of some sort. Perhaps this will prove true, but there is, for the moment, little reason to suppose that it is. I see nothing surprising in the conclusion, if it proves correct, that the principles of rule organization that underlie the wh-island constraint are special properties of the language faculty, just as distribution of orientation specificities is a special property of the visual cortex. Similarly, it would not come as a great surprise to find that, in some respects, the human auditory system is specifically adapted to speech or that general principles of semantic structure and organization derive from or are specifically related to the language faculty. At the level of cellular biology, we hope that there will be some account of the properties of all organs, physical and mental. There seems little reason to suppose, for the moment, that there are general principles of cognitive structure, or even of human cognition, expressible at some higher level, from which the particular properties of particular "mental organs," such as the language faculty, can be deduced, or even that there are illuminating analogies among these various systems. Of course, we do expect to find that some systems—say, the systems of memory—enter into a variety of cognitive processes, but that is another matter altogether.

There are many barriers to progress in the study of the biological basis for human language capacities, among them, the impossibility of direct experimentation on humans to answer the many questions that arise. In the case of some systems, such as the visual system, investigation of other higher animals helps to overcome this limitation, but the lack of significant analogues to the language faculty in other species, which, I suspect, will become clearer and better understood as research with symbolic systems in apes advances, appears to foreclose this option in the case of language. The abstract study of competence systems and the study of process models offers a great deal of promise, I believe, and can place significant conditions on the biological mechanisms that enter into the language capacities. Eric Lenneberg, in his very productive work, developed a range of other approaches that seem very promising, as have other researchers in several related disciplines. The study of the biological basis for human language capacities may prove to be one of the most exciting frontiers of science in coming years.

6

Language and Unconscious Knowledge

IF THE STUDY of human language is to be pursued in a serious way, it is necessary to undertake a series of abstractions and idealizations. Consider the concept "language" itself. The term is hardly clear; "language" is no well-defined concept of linguistic science. In colloquial usage we say that German is one language and Dutch another, but some dialects of German are more similar to Dutch dialects than to other, more remote dialects of German. We say that Chinese is a language with many dialects and that French, Italian, and Spanish are different languages. But the diversity of the Chinese "dialects" is roughly comparable to that of the Romance languages. A linguist knowing nothing of political boundaries or institutions would not distinguish "language" and "dialect" as we do in normal discourse. Nor would he have clear alternative concepts to propose, with anything like the same function.

Furthermore, even within the more restricted "languages"

The Edith Weigert Lecture, sponsored by the Forum on Psychiatry and the Humanities, Washington School of Psychiatry, November 19, 1976. From Joseph H. Smith, ed., *Psychoanalysis and Language*, Psychiatry and the Humanities, vol. 3, published by Yale University Press, copyright © 1978 by the Forum on Psychiatry and the Humanities of the Washington School of Psychiatry.

there may be considerable diversity. Two dialects of what we call a single language may be mutually incomprehensible. A single individual will generally command diverse modes of speech, in part associated with varying social conditions of discourse. No clear principles are known that determine the range and character of possible variation for a particular individual. Indeed, there is little reason to believe that such principles exist.

In the natural sciences, it is common to adopt what has sometimes been called "the Galilean style"—that is, to construct "abstract mathematical models of the universe to which at least the physicists give a higher degree of reality than they accord the ordinary world of sensations."[1] A comparable approach is particularly appropriate in the study of an organism whose behavior, we have every reason to believe, is determined by the interaction of numerous internal systems operating under conditions of great variety and complexity. Progress in such an inquiry is unlikely unless we are willing to entertain radical idealization, to construct abstract systems and to study their special properties, hoping to account for observed phenomena indirectly in terms of properties of the systems postulated and their interaction. Even when we speak of "an organism," we are engaged in idealization and abstraction. One might, after all, study an organism in the world from a very different point of view. Suppose we were to study the flow of nutrients or the oxygen-carbon dioxide cycle. Then the organism would disappear in a flux of chemical processes, losing its integrity as an individual placed in an environment. The "furniture of the world" does not come prepackaged in the form of individuals with properties, apart from human intervention: either the analysis provided by the cognitive systems that we might call "common sense understanding," or the more self-conscious idealizations of the scientist seeking to comprehend some aspect of physical or mental reality. Similarly, if we go on to study particular physical organs such as the eye or the heart, we abstract away from an intricate web of interconnections and adopt a point of view that is by no means a logically necessary one. Any serious study will, furthermore, abstract away from variation tentatively regarded as insignificant and from external interference dismissed as irrelevant at a given stage of inquiry. Such steps may eventually prove to have been misguided, but the only alternative is a form of natural history, tabulation and arrangement of facts, hardly a very serious pursuit however engaging the data.

There is no reason to abandon the general approach of the natural sciences when we turn to the study of human beings and society. Any serious approach to such topics will attempt, with whatever success, to adopt "the Galilean style." Political economy, with its far-reaching abstractions, is an obvious classic example, as, in the Marxian version, "individuals are dealt with only in so far as they are the personifications of economic categories, embodiments of particular class-relations and class interests,"[2] and capital is considered "not a thing, but rather a definite social production relation, belonging to a definite historical formation of society, which is manifested in a thing and lends this thing a specific social character";[3] and in general, economics is regarded in the final analysis as a study of class relations.

It should come as no surprise, then, that a significant notion of "language" as an object of rational inquiry can be developed only on the basis of rather far-reaching abstraction. How to proceed is a matter of controversy. My own view is this. We may imagine an ideal homogeneous speech community in which there is no variation in style or dialect. We may suppose further that knowledge of the language of this speech community is uniformly represented in the mind of each of its members, as one element in a system of cognitive structures. Let us refer to this representation of the knowledge of these ideal speaker-hearers as the grammar of the language. We must be careful to distinguish the grammar, regarded as a structure postulated in the mind, from the linguist's grammar, which is an explicit articulated theory that attempts to express precisely the rules and principles of the grammar in the mind of the ideal speaker-hearer. The linguist's grammar is a scientific theory, correct insofar as it corresponds to the internally represented grammar. (Exactly what is meant by the notion "corresponds" in the case of the abstract study of a physical system is a complex question, not unique to this enterprise.) It is common to use the term "grammar" with systematic ambiguity, letting the context determine whether it refers to the internalized grammar or to the linguist's theory. The practice is unobjectionable but may lead to confusion unless care is taken.

The grammar of the language determines the properties of each of the sentences of the language. For each sentence, the grammar determines aspects of its phonetic form, its meaning, and perhaps more. The language is the set of sentences that are described by the grammar. To introduce a technical term, we say that the grammar "generates" the sentences it describes and their structural descriptions; the grammar is said to "weakly generate" the sentences of the language and to "strongly generate" the structural descriptions of these sentences. When we speak of the linguist's grammar as a "generative grammar," we mean only that it is sufficiently explicit to determine how sentences of the language are in fact characterized by the grammar.[4]

The language generated by the grammar is infinite. Putting

aside irrelevant limitations of time, patience, and memory, people can in principle understand and use sentences of arbitrary length and complexity. Correspondingly, as these limitations are relaxed in practice, our ability to use language increases in scope—in principle, without bound. A sentence that is incomprehensible in speech may be intelligible if repeated several times or presented on the printed page, where memory limitations are less severe. But we do not have to extend our knowledge of language to be able to deal with repeated or written sentences that are far more complex than those of normal spoken discourse. Rather, the same knowledge can be applied with fewer extrinsic constraints.

To illustrate with a simple analogy, consider a person who knows arithmetic, who has mastered the concept of number. In principle, he is now capable of carrying out or determining the accuracy of any computation. Some computations he may not be able to carry out in his head. Paper and pencil are required to extend his memory. But the person does not have to learn something new to carry out a more complex computation, using paper and pencil. Rather, he uses the knowledge already represented in his mind, with access to more computing space than his short-term memory provides. Some computations may be too complex even for paper and pencil, but these limitations are independent of knowledge of arithmetic. They hold for other domains as well. Therefore a scientist interested in determining "arithmetical competence" would quite properly disregard these limitations, attributing them to independent components of the mind.

Although the language generated is infinite, the grammar itself is finite, represented in a finite brain. Thus, the rules of grammar must iterate in some manner to generate an infinite number of sentences, each with its specific sound, structure, and meaning. We make use of this "recursive" property of grammar constantly in ordinary life. We construct new sentences freely and use them on appropriate occasions, just as we comprehend the new sentences that we hear in novel circumstances, generally bringing much more than our knowledge of language to the performance of these creative acts. Though our language use is appropriate to situations, it is not controlled by stimulus conditions. Language serves as an instrument for free expression of thought, unbounded in scope, uncontrolled by stimulus conditions though appropriate to situations, available for use in whatever contingencies our thought processes can comprehend. This "creative aspect of language use" is a characteristic species property of humans. Descartes appealed to this property of language use as a criterion for the existence of "other minds."

It is important to bear in mind the fundamental conceptual distinction between generation of sentences by the grammar, on the one hand, and production and interpretation of sentences by the speaker, making use of the resources of the grammar and much else, on the other. The grammar, in whatever form its principles are represented in the mind and brain, simply characterizes the properties of sentences, much as the principles of arithmetic determine the properties of numbers. We have some understanding of the principles of grammar, but there is no promising approach to the normal creative use of language, or to other rule-governed human acts that are freely undertaken. The study of grammar raises problems that we have some hope of solving; the creative use of language is a mystery that eludes our intellectual grasp.

Proposals do exist with regard to the autonomy of normal behavior, but they do not seem to me to be very fruitful. Consider, for example, a formulation by David Rapaport.[5] In his view, the "ultimate nutriments" of the ego structures are drive stimuli, on the one hand, which "are the ultimate guarantee against stimulus slavery," and, on the other, external stimuli that "are the ultimate guarantees against drive slavery." "The balance of these mutually controlling factors does not depend on the outcome of their chance interactions, but is controlled by laws of the epigenetic sequence, termed autonomous ego development."[6] Ego structures and the motivations arising from them provide intrinsic nutriments apart from those arising from the evolutionary givens: (1) drives and (2) "apparatuses which prepare [the organism] for contact with its environment."[7] What is the status of the "nutriments" provided by autonomous ego structures? If autonomous ego development were taken to be determined by the "ultimate nutriments" provided by biologically given drives and external stimuli, we would have an unsatisfactory deterministic theory; if not, the homunculus still resides within, its choices unexplained.

The fact is that we simply have no reasonable grasp of the general problem of autonomy, as far as I can see. I mention this to distinguish the mystery posed by the creative aspect of language use from the difficult but still intelligible problems that arise in the investigation of the unbounded scope of grammar and human knowledge quite generally.

The grammar of a language, conceived as a system of rules that weakly generates the sentences of a language and strongly generates their structures, has a claim to that "higher degree of reality" that the physicist ascribes to his mathematical models of the universe. At an appropriate level of abstraction, we hope to find deep explanatory principles underlying the generation of sentences by grammars. The discovery of such principles, and that alone, will justify the idealizations adopted and indicate that we have captured an important element of the real structure of the organism. To account for the confused and disorderly phenomena of the "ordinary world of sensation," we will, in general, have to move from the idealizations to systems of greater complexity, considering variation of languages and grammars, the interaction of cognitive systems, and the use of language under specific conditions of human life.

We suppose, then, that the ideal speaker-hearer has a finite grammar, internally represented in some manner, generating a language that consists of an infinite number of sentences, each with its specific properties. He knows the language generated by the grammar. This knowledge of language encompasses a variety of properties of sentences. The grammar must deal with the physical form of a sentence and its meaning. Furthermore, the person who knows a language knows the conditions under which it is appropriate to use a sentence, knows what purposes can be furthered by appropriate use of a sentence under given social conditions. For purposes of inquiry and exposition, we may proceed to distinguish "grammatical competence" from "pragmatic competence," restricting the first to the knowledge of form and meaning and the second to knowledge of conditions and manner of appropriate use, in conformity with various purposes. Thus we may think of language as an instrument that can be put to use. The grammar of the language characterizes the instrument, determining intrinsic physical and semantic properties of every sentence. The grammar thus expresses grammatical competence. A system of rules and principles constituting pragmatic competence determines how the tool can effectively be put to use. Pragmatic competence may include what Paul Grice

has called a "logic of conversation." We might say that pragmatic competence places language in the institutional setting of
its use, relating intentions and purposes to the linguistic means
at hand.[8]

Linguistic knowledge, of course, extends beyond the level of
the sentence. We know how to construct and understand discourses of various sorts, and there are no doubt principles governing discourse structure. Furthermore, knowledge of language
is intimately related to other systems of knowledge and belief.
When we identify and name an object, we tacitly assume that it
will obey natural laws. It will not suddenly disappear, turn into
something else, or behave in some other "unnatural" way; if it
does, we might conclude that we have misidentified and mis-
named it. It is no easy matter to determine how our beliefs
about the world of objects relate to the assignment of meanings
to expressions. Indeed, it has often been argued that no principled distinction can be drawn

Theories of grammatical and pragmatic competence must
find their place in a theory of performance that takes into account the structure of memory, our mode of organizing experience, and so on. Actual investigation of language necessarily
deals with performance, with what someone does under specific
circumstances. We often attempt to devise modes of inquiry
that will reduce to a minimum factors that appear irrelevant to
intrinsic competence, so that the data of performance will bear
directly on competence, as the object of our inquiry. To the extent that we have an explicit theory of competence, we can attempt to devise performance models to show how this knowledge is put to use. If we knew only that language consists of
words, our performance models would necessarily be very primitive and of restricted interest; we could study the sequence of

linguistic signs and their formal and semantic properties, but nothing else. With a richer theory of competence that incorporates structures of greater depth and intricacy, we can proceed to more interesting performance models. Study of performance relies essentially on advances in understanding of competence. But since a competence theory must be incorporated in a performance model, evidence about the actual organization of behavior may prove crucial to advancing the theory of underlying competence. Study of performance and study of competence are mutually supportive. We must simply try to be clear about what we are doing in attempting to investigate something as complex and hidden as the human faculty of language and its exercise.

Ultimately, the study of language is a part of human biology. In the study of any organism or machine, we may distinguish between the abstract investigation of the principles by which it operates and the study of the physical realization of the processes and components postulated in the abstract investigation. Thus, the study of visual perception might lead to the hypothetical construction of certain abstract components—for example, feature detectors—that enter into this system. A further inquiry might reveal the physical mechanisms that meet the abstract conditions postulated. In studying some automaton, we might attempt to determine its program at an abstract level, then proceed to inquire into the circuitry or mechanical principles by which this abstract program is realized. We may say that the same program is represented in devices of very different design and constitution. In the study of humans, direct experimental inquiry into physical mechanisms is generally impossible because of the ethics of experimentation or simply the time span of feasible study. Therefore, the abstract level of inquiry must bear an inordinate burden. It is important to realize that there is no issue of principle here, no philosophical problem unique to this inquiry as a result of the limitations of feasible experiment. Similar problems would arise in the study of an inorganic device that for some reason we would not take apart.

We may speak of the abstract study of human intellectual capacities and their functioning as the study of mind, without thereby implying that there is a *res cogitans* as a "second substance" apart from body. We may also attempt to investigate the physical basis of mind insofar as this is possible.

How can we proceed to investigate the properties of language? To clarify the issue, we might think about the less controversial task of studying the physical structure of the body. A rational approach would be to select some reasonably self-contained physical system of the body—some bodily organ—and try to determine its nature. Having done this in a number of cases, we might proceed to a higher level of analysis and ask how organs interact, how they grow and develop, how they function in the life of the organism.

Consider the kinds of questions we might ask about an organ of the body—say the eye, or more broadly, the visual system regarded as an organ. We might organize our inquiry along the following lines:

(1) (a) function
(b) structure
(c) physical basis
(d) development in the individual
(e) evolutionary development

Thus we might ask (a) what the visual system does, what purpose it serves in human life. We seek further to determine (b) the principles in accordance with which it is organized and operates. Given some characterization of the structure of the visual system at this abstract level, we might try to establish (c) the physical mechanisms that meet the conditions of (b), asking how the structural principles and postulated elements are actually realized in the physical system of the brain. We want to know (d) how the system comes to assume its mature form, how nature and nurture interact in the growth of the organ—a question that can be raised at the abstract level of study of mind or with respect to the physical study of the brain. And finally, we might try to discover (e) how the genetically determined aspects of the organ, as established under (d), came to be as they are, for the species.

Pursuing these fundamental questions with regard to the visual system, we note that the organism begins in some genetically determined initial state common to the species with variations that we may ignore at the outset. It passes through a sequence of states until it attains a mature final state which then undergoes only marginal further change. This "steady state" is, it seems, attained at some relatively early stage in life. But though the organ of vision is essentially fixed in structure at that time, we may still "learn to see" in new ways throughout our lives, for example, by applying knowledge gained later in life or through exposure to some new form of visual representation in the arts, say, cubism. As the seventeenth-century British Platonist Ralph Cudworth expressed it:

a skillful and expert limner will observe many elegancies and curiosities of art, and be highly pleased with several strokes and shadows in a picture, where a common eye can discern nothing at all; and a musical artist hearing a consort of exact musicians playing some excellent composure of many parts, will be exceedingly ravished with many harmonical airs and touches, that a vulgar ear will be utterly insensible of.[9]

Classical rational psychology assumed that it was the mind, not the physical eye or ear, that was responsible for these more subtle accomplishments. Today, few would deny that some kind of physical change underlies, for example, the ability of the skilled and expert limner to perceive much that escapes the common eye, but it is reasonable to regard these achievements as based on an interaction of the organ of sight—the eye and visual cortex—with other components of the full cognitive system.

In recent years there has been exciting work on the nature and growth of the organ of vision, work that is highly suggestive for the study of cognitive structures such as language as well. Studies of the mammalian visual system have made some progress in determining the general structural principles of organization (1b) as well as their physical basis (1c), and in sorting out the genetically determined properties of the initial state (1d). A further task is to determine how the genetically determined initial state developed through evolution (1e), but this is evidently a problem of a very different order. It is here that questions of function (1a) arise in a significant way. No one supposes that children learn to have an eye capable of sight because it would be useful for this function to be fulfilled; the function of the eye is to see, but that observation is not a very interesting contribution to the study of ontogeny. Rather, it is in the context of (1e) that functional questions have their real interest, it would seem.

Suppose that we attempt to study language on the model of a bodily organ, raising the questions (1a)-(1e). Let us briefly consider these questions in turn.

What is the function of language? It is frequently alleged that the function of language is communication, that its "essential purpose" is to enable people to communicate with one another.

It is further alleged that only by attending to this essential purpose can we make any sense of the nature of language.

It is not easy to evaluate this contention. What does it mean
to say that language has an "essential purpose"? Suppose that in
the quiet of my study I think about a problem, using language,
and even write down what I think. Suppose that someone speaks
honestly, merely out of a sense of integrity, fully aware that his
audience will refuse to comprehend or even consider what he is
saying. Consider informal conversation conducted for the sole
purpose of maintaining casual friendly relations, with no particular concern as to its content. Are these examples of "communication"? If so, what do we mean by "communication" in
the absence of an audience, or with an audience assumed to be
completely unresponsive, or with no intention to convey information or modify belief or attitude?

It seems that either we must deprive the notion "communication" of all significance, or else we must reject the view
that the purpose of language is communication. While it is
quite commonly argued that the purpose of language is communication and that it is pointless to study language apart from
its communicative function, there is no formulation of this
belief, to my knowledge, from which any substantive proposals
follow. The same may be said of the idea that the essential purpose of language is to achieve certain instrumental ends, to satisfy needs, and so on. Surely language can be used for such purposes—or for others. It is difficult to say what "the purpose" of
language is, except, perhaps, the expression of thought, a rather
empty formulation. The functions of language are various. It is
unclear what might be meant by the statement that some of
them are "central" or "essential."

A more productive suggestion is that functional considerations determine the character of linguistic rules. Suppose it can be shown, for example, the some rule of English grammar facilitates a perceptual strategy for sentence analysis. Then we have the basis for a functional explanation for the linguistic rule. But several questions arise, quite apart from the matter of the source of the perceptual strategy. Is the linguistic rule a true universal? If so, then the functional analysis is relevant only on the evolutionary level; human languages *must* have this rule or one like it, by virtue of a species property. Suppose, on the contrary, that the linguistic rule is learned. We may still maintain the functional explanation, but it will now have to do with the evolution of English. That is, English developed in such a way as to accord with this principle. In either case, the functional explanation applies on the evolutionary level—either the evolution of the organism or of the language. The child does not acquire the rule by virtue of its function any more than he learns to have an eye because of the advantages of sight.

The second basic question (1b) is the one that deserves the most extensive discussion, but I will have little to say about it here. I cannot attempt to outline the answers that have been proposed to the question, What is the abstract structure of language? or the problems that arise along the way.[10] If work of recent years is anywhere near the mark, then a language is generated by a system of rules and principles that enter into complex mental computations to determine the form and meaning of sentences. These rules and principles are in large measure unconscious and beyond the reach of potential consciousness. Our perfect knowledge of the language we speak gives us no privileged access to these principles; we cannot hope to determine them by introspection or reflection, "from within," as it were. Correspondingly, there is no basis whatsoever for dogmatic stipulations as to the degree or quality of the complexity or abstractness that is "permitted" in a theory of language structure, just as such a priori doctrine would be out of place in the study of the visual system or any bodily organ.

The most intriguing of the studies of language structure are those that bear on linguistic universals, that is, principles that hold of language quite generally as a matter of biological (not logical) necessity. Given the richness and complexity of the system of grammar for a human language and the uniformity of its acquisition on the basis of limited and often degenerate evidence, there can be little doubt that highly restrictive universal principles must exist determining the general framework of each human language and perhaps much of its specific structure as well. To determine these principles is the deepest problem of contemporary linguistic study.

Let us consider again the model of the visual system. Recent work has led to the conclusion that "the development of the nervous system is a process sharply constrained by a genetic program. . . . the genetic program permits a range of possible realizations, and individual experience acts only to specify the outcome within this range."[11] For example, an individual neuron has a fixed orientation specificity, but the genetic program determines the range within which it can be fixed by experience. Similarly, the general properties of binocular vision are genetically determined but the precise control of matching inputs from the two eyes is fixed on the basis of visual experience. Comparable conclusions seem to hold in the case of human language. Here, too, it seems that biological endowment sharply constrains the course of language growth, or what is called, with somewhat misleading connotations, "language learning."

To account for the rapid transition to a uniform steady state on the basis of the limited experience available, we must postulate a genetically determined initial state that "permits a range of possible realizations," and furthermore, a fairly narrow range, with individual experience acting "only to specify the outcome within this range." There is good reason to suppose that across the human species the ability to acquire language is invariant within narrow limits, apart from pathology. We may assume that a fixed and highly restrictive initial state is a common human possession.

The child's initial state, it seems, must lay down the general principles of language structure in fair detail, providing a rich and intricate schematism that determines (1) the content of linguistic experience and (2) the specific language that develops under the boundary conditions given by this experience. If the initial restriction is sufficiently severe, it will be possible for the child to attain a system of great intricacy on the basis of limited data, data sufficient to rule out all possibilities but one or a few. Then he will know the language compatible with his limited experience, though there will be no relation of generalization, abstraction, induction, habit formation, or the like that relates the system attained at the final state to the data of experience. The relation between experience and knowledge will be quite abstract. The principles of language structure incorporated in the initial state express this relationship. Qualitative considerations suggest that this may be a reasonable approach to the fundamental question of development in the individual (1d). If so, the human language faculty is much like other organs known to biology.

We need not content ourselves with vague and metaphoric discussions of this sort. Rather, we can proceed to spell out in specific detail a schematism that characterizes the initial state. Call this schematism "universal grammar." We may think of universal grammar as, in effect, the genetic program, the schematism that permits the range of possible realizations that are the possible human languages. Each such possible realization is a possible final steady state, the grammar of a specific language. Universal grammar is a system that is genetically determined at the initial state, and is specified, sharpened, articulated, and refined under the conditions set by experience, to yield the particular grammars that are represented in the steady states attained. Looking at the question of growth of language ("language learning") in this way, we can see how it is possible for a person to know vastly more than he has experienced.

Once the steady state is attained, knowledge of language and skill in using language may still be refined, as in the case of learning to see. Wilhelm von Humboldt argued that the resources of a language can be enriched by a great thinker or writer, without any change in the grammar. An individual can expand his facility or the subtlety of his comprehension of the devices of language through his own creative activities or immersion in the cultural wealth of his society. But as in the case of the visual system, it seems quite appropriate to set this matter aside in abstracting the linguistic system as a separate object of study.

An approach of this sort contrasts with a familiar learning model, in accordance with which it is assumed that language is a system of habits and skills, acquired gradually through generalization, conditioning, induction, and abstraction. Linguistic knowledge, in this view, is a system of learned categories and patterns. This approach, too, can be made explicit in various ways, and in fact has been, in behavioral psychology and certain branches of structural linguistics.

Under either of these contrasting approaches, we assume a fixed, genetically determined state. The approaches differ in their conception of the nature of this initial state. One approach takes the initial state to be a rich system of principles, a restrictive schematism that specifies the range of possible grammars. The other takes it to be a system of procedures of segmentation, classification, generalization, and induction to be applied to the data of experience to yield a grammar. I have argued elsewhere that these two approaches can properly be described as rationalist and empiricist in character, respectively. One can, of course, consider mixed approaches of various sorts, but I think it is very useful to keep in mind these two general models, each with its possible variants, as points of reference.

One might ask whether there are not quite different models to explore in investigating the growth of language. Thus, it has been suggested by Piaget and his colleagues that an "interactionist" or "constructivist" theory is superior to either the empiricist or rationalist model.[12] In this theory, it is proposed that through interaction with the environment the child develops sensorimotor constructions which provide the basis for language, and as understanding and knowledge grow, new constructions are developed in some more or less uniform way. Thus, it is claimed, language at any stage merely reflects independent mental constructions that arise in the course of dealing with the environment, and at each stage the child develops new systems that reorganize his experience.

The studies conducted by the Geneva school have been extremely illuminating, but the interactionist-constructivist model itself is difficult to assess, because it remains at the level of metaphor. Allegedly, the child progresses through a fairly regular sequence of cognitive stages, but no mechanism or principle is proposed to explain why the child moves from a given stage to the next rather than to some quite different stage. It is difficult to imagine what answer could be provided, apart from recourse to some assumption concerning maturation to a genetically determined target stage, at each point. And when such an assumption is made precise, it seems that it will express genetically determined aspects of human belief and knowledge that are far more intricate than the "elementary hereditary forms" that the Geneva school is willing to contemplate. Furthermore, no suggestion has been offered as to how the specific principles of language structure that have been proposed might relate to constructions of sensorimotor intelligence. On consideration of the relevant principles, the prospects for any such association seem rather dim. Therefore, the Piagetian models do not seem to be a genuine alternative to those sketched above. The crucial questions remain unanswered, and no hint of an answer is offered. I know of no general principles advanced within developmental psychology that shed any real light on these questions.

The empiricist models are in accord with our normal way of discussing the development of language. Thus, we say that the child "learns language," not that language grows or matures. But we do not say that the embryo or the child learns to have arms rather than wings, or a visual system of a particular kind, or, say, mature sexual organs, to take a case of development that we assume to be genetically determined in essentials though it takes place well after birth. Furthermore, we are naturally impressed with the diversity among attested languages.

All of this is true but not very important. We say that the sun rises, but the fact—easy enough to explain in terms of common-sense experience—is of no interest to the physicist. It is entirely natural that in our normal lives we should be impressed with the diversity of language and the influence of experience on language acquisition. In normal life, there is no reason for us to pay attention to the uniformities among individuals and across cultures; these we can take for granted. What concerns us are the differences. For example, when we learn a foreign language, we concentrate on the respects in which this language differs from our own. A good teaching grammar or a standard traditional grammar will say little about general properties of language. Intended for the use of the intelligent reader, such grammars do not provide an analysis of the qualities of intelligence that the reader brings to bear on the information presented. The grammars discuss irregularities, but not deeper principles of universal grammar. These very general conditions on the form of language constitute part of the intelligence of the language learner; they form part of the schematism that is brought to bear in acquiring language, and therefore need receive no particular attention in our normal lives. In fact, we are quite unconscious of these elements of our knowledge of language, and cannot gain awareness of them through introspection.

For the scientist interested in the nature of language, it is the general principles that are of primary importance; the special properties of particular languages are of much less interest. For the normal person dealing with language in his daily life, precisely the opposite is true. The deeper principles, which are in any event far beyond the level of consciousness, are of no consequence, while the unpredictable irregularities must receive careful attention. It is no surprise that the commonsense view, focusing on irregularities and diversity, regards language as a learned and arbitrary phenomenon. Every frog, no doubt, considers his fellows to be a remarkably diverse and interesting crew; insofar as their behavior conforms to his own, it is only that this is the natural and obvious way to act, requiring no special attention.

In short, we can easily understand why empiricist models should seem compelling to a commonsense view, and why we should think of language as being "learned" rather than as growing in accordance with a fixed, genetically determined program, modified and filled out with specific detail through experience. The irregularities, which alone concern us in normal life, *are* learned. Similarly, the distribution of vertical and horizontal receptors in the visual system is fixed (learned) through experience, we learn how to do the high jump, and so forth. But we do not learn to have arms rather than wings, to walk or run rather than fly, to have binocular vision with analysis of stimuli in terms of linear contours, or to adhere to the principle that linguistic rules meet the various conditions of universal grammar. These requirements are elements of the genetically determined initial state, though of course they may only come into operation at a particular stage of maturation, much as sexual maturation—or, for that matter, death—though genetically determined, takes place only at a specific stage of life. And as in the case of physical structures of the body, the timing and precise character of the maturational development may themselves be influenced by environmental factors.

As the stages of development of other cognitive capacities come to be better understood, we may discover that quite generally the transition from one stage to the next is a matter of growth and maturation within bounds set by the genetic program, with some variation depending on nutritional level, social environment, accidental experience, and so on.

I have said nothing so far about the questions (1c) and (1e)—namely, the physical realization of the abstract structures of language and their evolutionary history. In fact, little is known about these questions, though the first, at least, may be open to serious investigation.

Can we expect to find, in other organisms, faculties closely analogous to the human language capacity? It is conceivable, but not very likely. That would constitute a kind of biological miracle, rather similar to the discovery, on some unexplored island, of a species of bird that had never thought to fly until instructed to do so through human intervention. Language must surely confer enormous selectional advantage. It is difficult to imagine that some other species, say the chimpanzee, has the capacity for language but has never thought to put it to use. Nor is there any evidence that this biological miracle has occurred. On the contrary, the interesting investigations of the capacity of the higher apes to acquire symbolic systems seem to me to support the traditional belief that even the most rudimentary properties of language lie well beyond the capacities of an otherwise intelligent ape.

The fundamental differences between human language and the systems taught to apes are clear at the most elementary level. Consider the five basic dimensions of inquiry suggested earlier, (1a)–(1e). From a functional point of view, human language is a system for free expression of thought, essentially independent of stimulus control, need-satisfaction, or instrumental purpose, hence, qualitatively different from the symbolic systems taught to apes. Structurally, human language is a system with recursive structure-dependent rules, operating on sequences organized in a hierarchy of phrases to generate a countable infinity of sentences. These basic properties are, so far as we know, unique to human language, and the same is true, *a fortiori*, of the more complex principles of universal grammar that characterize human language.

As far as the physical basis of human language is concerned, the very little that is known indicates that a crucial role is played by specific language centers in the dominant hemisphere that seem to have no direct analogue in other mammals. There is also evidence that humans with severe injury to the language centers of the brain and consequent irremediable language loss can readily acquire the systems designed for apes, supporting the natural assumption that these systems have only the most superficial resemblance to human language. As for development, language grows in the child through mere exposure to an unorganized linguistic environment, without training or even any particular language-specific care. Turning finally to the evolutionary level, though little is known, it seems clear that language is a fairly ancient human possession that developed long after the separation of humans from other primates.

Hence, along each dimension of inquiry, even the most superficial examination reveals fundamental properties that radically distinguish human language from other systems. This is not to suggest that studies of the intellectual capacities of apes are without interest. On the contrary, they are of considerable interest in themselves. One would assume that apes in the wild are capable of intellectual achievements specific to their lives and world that go well beyond the ability to acquire the symbolic systems artificially induced under laboratory conditions. Experiments in training apes to use symbolic systems are sure to further understanding of ape intelligence, and thus, indirectly, to teach us something more about the apparently quite different specific qualities of intelligence that underlie the use of language and other human achievements. We might discover that the unique human achievements in the linguistic domain result in part from organization of capacities that are individually present in some form in other organisms, though it is not unlikely that more than this is involved in the evolutionary development of a species capable of human language.

I have been suggesting that we pursue the study of mind— that is, the principles that underlie our thoughts and beliefs, perception and imagination, the organization of our actions, and the like—much as we investigate the body. We may conceive of the mind as a system of "mental organs," the language faculty being one. Each of these organs has its specific structure and function, determined in general outline by our genetic endowment, interacting in ways that are also biologically determined in large measure to provide the basis for our mental life. Interaction with the physical and social environment refines and articulates these systems as the mind matures in childhood and, in less fundamental respects, throughout life.

In considering such an approach to the structure of mind, we depart, as already noted, from beliefs that are deeply established in our intellectual tradition. I think it is fair to say that this tradition has been marked by a belief in the accessibility, uniformity, and simplicity of the mind, in a sense that I would now like to discuss.

In referring to "accessibility" of the structures of mind, I am thinking of the belief that its contents are in principle open to reflection and careful thought if only the barriers of dogma, superstition, or psychic disorder are removed. Classical rationalism held that the "natural light" of common sense suffices to lay bare the basic elements of our reasoning, thought, and understanding, though not necessarily the explanatory hypotheses of physical science.[13] Empiricist speculation shared much of this doctrine, and sought to show, by careful analysis, how our ideas could be resolved into their simple constituents by introspection. Vico's defense of the *Geisteswissenschaften* against the claims of scientific naturalism relied essentially on the principle that inner access to the products of our minds and our acts yields a degree of certainty unattainable in the natural sciences: the principles of what has "been made by men . . . are . . . to be found within the modifications of our own human mind,"[14] though how we determine these modifications of mind, in his view, is not very clear. Even Freud's evocation of the unconscious was not, I believe, accompanied by far-reaching questioning of the accessibility in principle of the products of mind.[15]

I do not mean to suggest that the principle of accessibility was articulated without qualification (cf. n. 15), but rather that it may be regarded as a kind of limit towards which much traditional thinking tended. Qualifications can be found, and in some cases they are severe. Thus, to Vico, "the clear and distinct idea of the mind, i.e., the Cartesian criterion, not only cannot be the criterion of other truths, but it cannot be the criterion of the mind itself; for while the mind apprehends itself, it does not make itself, and because it does not make itself, it is ignorant of the former mode by which it apprehends itself."[16] Or consider the notion of "mental chemistry" that developed within associationist psychology. Joseph Priestley, in the eighteenth century, wrote that "from the combination of ideas, and especially very dissimilar ones, there may result ideas which, to appearance, shall be so different from the parts of which they

really consist, that they shall no more be capable of being analyzed by mental reflection than the idea of white."[17] John
Stuart Mill developed a similar view:

The laws of the phenomena of mind are sometimes analogous to
mechanical, but sometimes also to chemical laws. When many impressions or ideas are operating in the mind together, there sometimes
takes place a process of a similar kind to chemical combination. When
impressions have been so often experienced in conjunction that each
of them calls up readily and instantaneously the ideas of the whole
group, these ideas sometimes *melt and coalesce* into one another, and
appear not several ideas but one.[18]

We cannot, then, discover the "elementary ideas" in which
our complex notions originate. "These, therefore, are cases of
mental chemistry, in which it is proper to say that the simple
ideas generate, rather than that they compose the complex
ones."[19] Where ideas are generated by mental chemistry, as distinct from association on a mechanical model, it is presumably
impossible to resolve them into their constituents by introspection.

More explicit rejection of accessibility appears in remarks by
C. G. Jung. He writes that "there is little hope of our ever being
able to reach even approximate consciousness of the self, since
however much we may make conscious there will always exist
an indeterminate and indeterminable amount of unconscious
material which belongs to the totality of the self." Jung's arche-
types are "empty and purely formal" structures; each is "a possibility of representation which is given *a priori*," "an irrepresen-
table, unconscious, pre-existent form that seems to be part of
the inherited structure of the psyche." It seems to him "proba-
ble that the real nature of the archetype is not capable of being
made conscious."[20] With regard to consciousness, he holds that

it is "a secondary phenomenon" both phylogenetically and ontogenetically: "the psyche of the child in its preconscious state is anything but a *tabula rasa*; it is already preformed in a recognizably individual way, and is moreover equipped with all specifically human instincts, as well as with the a priori foundations of the higher functions."[21] I take this to be an insistence on the inaccessibility to introspection of basic principles of the psyche, at least those that form part of its inherited structure, which, it should be stressed, is taken to comprise the a priori foundations of the higher mental functions, a conception that can be traced to Kant and his rationalist predecessors. It is worth noting, however, that Kant takes a clear contrary position on accessibility. Thus, in the *Critique of Pure Reason* he holds the following position: "All representations have a necessary relation to a *possible* empirical consciousness. For if they did not have this, and if it were altogether impossible to become conscious of them, this would practically amount to the admission of their non-existence."[22]

Despite such observations, which can no doubt be considerably extended, it still seems to me generally accurate to say that accessibility of the contents of the mind in principle is a fairly well-established doctrine that appears, in various forms, in diverse currents of our intellectual tradition. The study of language seems to me to suggest that it should be abandoned, even as a point of departure. There is no reason to suppose that we have any privileged access to the principles that enter into our knowledge and use of language, that determine the form and meaning of sentences or the conditions of their use, or that relate the "mental organ" of language to other cognitive systems.

The second doctrine I mentioned is the belief in the "uniformity" of the mind. Of course, it was traditionally assumed that the mind consists of separate faculties: "memory, imagination or fancy, understanding, affection, and will."[23] What I intend to signify in referring to the doctrine of uniformity of mind is the belief that the various cognitive structures develop in a uniform way—that is, that there are general principles of learning that underlie all of these systems, accounting for their development: "multipurpose learning strategies," as they are sometimes called, that apply "across the board." In contrast, it might be proposed that various "mental organs" develop in specific ways, each in accordance with the genetic program, much as bodily organs develop; and that multipurpose learning strategies are no more likely to exist than general principles of "growth of organs" that account for the shape, structure, and function of the kidney, the liver, the heart, the visual system, and so forth. Such principles may exist at the level of cellular biology, but there is no reason to anticipate a "higher level" theory of general organ growth. Rather, specific subcomponents of the genetic program, coming into operation as the organism matures, determine the specific properties of these systems. The same may well be true of the basic structures involved in our mental life.

The belief in uniformity, in this sense, is common to approaches as distinct as those of Piaget and Skinner, within psychology, and has been expressed by many contemporary philosophers in various forms. In Piaget's system, the early growth of language is modeled on prior "sensorimotor constructions," while later development is determined by general principles of "assimilation," "accommodation," and the like, that underlie other aspects of cognitive development as well. As already noted, these proposals seem to me too vague to be properly discussed. There seems little reason to suppose that the principles of grammar or universal grammar have any close analogue in other cognitive systems, though naturally one must keep an open mind about the matter. Furthermore, it would be in no way surprising if this were to prove to be the case, just as we do not expect the fundamental properties of the visual system to be reflected in language. Confident assertions to the contrary, which are prevalent in recent literature, seem to me rather dogmatic as well as without empirical support or plausible argument.

The belief in the "simplicity" of mental structures is related to the doctrine of uniformity. In the case of language, it is commonly argued by linguists and others that the principles of grammar cannot be "too complex" or "too abstract" but must reflect properties of sound and meaning, or must be directly determined in some manner by "functional considerations," aspects of language use. Evidently, there can be no a priori argument to this effect. To me, it seems that recent work tends to support a rather different view: that rules of syntax and phonology, at least, are organized in terms of "autonomous" principles of mental computation and do not reflect in any simple way the properties of the phonetic or semantic "substance" or contingencies of language use.

There are classical debates that bear on these questions. Consider, for example, the controversy over principles of geometry and the organization of perceptual space in early modern philosophy. Descartes and Cudworth believed the mind to be endowed with the principles of Euclidean geometry as an a priori property. We see a presented irregular figure as a (possibly distorted) triangle, straight line, circle, and so forth, because our minds produce these figures as "exemplars," just as "the intelligible essences of things" are produced by "the innate cognoscitive power." In Kant's phrase, objects conform to our "modes of cognition." To Hume, in contrast, nothing could be more certain than that we have no concept of "a perfect geometrical figure"[24] beyond what the senses convey:

As the ultimate standard of these figures is derived from nothing but the senses and imagination, it is absurd to talk of any perfection beyond what these faculties can judge of; since the true perfection of anything consists in its conformity to its standard.[25]

Thus, the first principles of geometry "are founded on the imagination and senses" and are far from certain; and our notions of regular figures are derived through experience. More generally, *"all our simple ideas in their first appearance, are derived from simple impressions, which are correspondent to them, and which they exactly represent"*[26] and our complex ideas are formed by union of these simple ideas on the basis of resemblance, contiguity, and causation (with unimportant exceptions, such as the missing colors). In these early debates, the questions of uniformity and simplicity arise in an interesting way, though as I have remarked, the principle of accessibility seems generally to be accepted, with some qualification.

Finally, let us consider briefly how language fits into the general system of cognitive structures. Surely the normal use of language requires access to other systems of knowledge and belief. We have already noted how difficult it is—if indeed it is possible in principle—to distinguish between semantic properties that are simply language-dependent and others that relate to our beliefs about the natural world. We use language against a background of shared beliefs about things and within the framework of a system of social institutions. The study of language use must be concerned with the place of language in a system of cognitive structures embodying pragmatic competence, as well as structures that relate to matters of fact and belief.

To gain further understanding of the general nature of the human mind, we should ask in what domains humans seem to develop complex intellectual structures in a more or less uniform way on the basis of restricted data. Wherever this is the case, we can reasonably suppose that a highly structured genetic program is responsible for the achievement, and we can thus hope to learn something significant about human nature by studying the systems attained. Language is an obvious area. It might be argued that the major intellectual interest of the study of language lies in the fact that it is a complex domain, particularly amenable to study, distinctively human, and associated in the most intimate way with every aspect of human life.

There are other topics that might be studied in a similar way. For example, humans have remarkable perceptual abilities in certain domains. Consider recognition of faces. A person can recognize an enormous number of human faces and can identify a presentation of a single face with various orientations. This is a remarkable feat that cannot be duplicated with other figures of comparable complexity. It might therefore be interesting to try to develop a "grammar of faces," or even a "universal grammar of faces," to explain these abilities. Perhaps, at some stage of maturation, some part of the brain develops an abstract theory of faces and a system of projection that allows it to determine how an arbitrary human face will appear in a given presentation. There is some evidence that face recognition is neurally represented in the right hemisphere and that this neural representation is delayed until past the time when language is fixed in the left hemisphere. Currently, these questions are being investigated. They might be profitably pursued along the general lines outlined above, much in the manner of investigation of the language faculty.

Are there other systems, more distinctively human in character, more enlightening as regards deeper and more fundamental characteristics of the human species? Perhaps so. Thus, one curious property of the human mind is our ability to develop certain forms of mathematical understanding—specifically, concerning the number system, abstract geometrical space, continuity, and related notions. It is hard to imagine that these capacities can be explained directly in terms of natural selection. It does not seem very likely that ability to solve problems in number theory was a factor in differential reproduction. Presumably, these capacities developed as a concomitant of others that did confer selectional advantage. However, this may be, it is certainly possible to inquire into the nature of these abilities and to try to discover the initial state of the mind that enables these abilities to develop as they do. Surely, these capacities lie at the core of the remarkable human ability to develop scientific knowledge in certain domains. The work of Piaget and his colleagues has been particularly suggestive in this regard.

These speculations raise further questions. Where complex intellectual structures are developed in an essentially uniform way on the basis of limited evidence, we have hopes of finding something significant about human nature, since it is natural to account for the fact on the basis of assumptions about the initial state of the mind; indeed, it is difficult to imagine an alternative, apart from sheer accident. In some cases, the empirical contingencies of human life may suffice to account for the general lines of development, but the extent to which it is necessary to postulate fixed capacities for organizing experience is often not fully appreciated.

The history of science suggests examples that might possibly be illuminating. Time after time, people have been able to construct remarkable explanatory theories on the basis of very limited evidence, often rejecting much of the available evidence on obscure intuitive grounds as they sought to construct theories that are deep and intelligible. Furthermore, although the creation of new theory is an achievement of the gifted few, it has been possible through most of the history of science for others, less talented, to comprehend and appreciate what has been accomplished. The theories that have been constructed, regarded as intelligible, and generally accepted as science has progressed have been vastly underdetermined by evidence. Intellectual structures of vast scope have been developed on the basis of limited and (until recently) fairly degenerate evidence. Applying the paradigm suggested earlier, we are led to inquire into the innate structures of mind that make this achievement possible.

What is the "science-forming capacity" that enables us to recognize certain proposed explanatory theories as intelligible and natural, while rejecting or simply not considering a vast array of others that are no less compatible with evidence? I do not speak here of the creative achievement, but rather of the appreciation of the achievement, a common human ability; the ability to recognize, with understanding and pleasure, that an intelligible explanatory theory has been produced. Some such science-forming capacity must be an innate property of mind. That is not to say that all potential scientific knowledge is "preformed" at birth. Rather, the human mind is endowed with some set of principles that can be put to work when certain questions are posed, a certain level of understanding has been achieved, and certain evidence is available, to select a narrow class of possible theories. Perhaps these principles, too, might fruitfully be regarded as a general schematism that characterizes the class of intelligible theories, thus permitting us to develop systems of belief and knowledge of great scope and power on limited evidence.

Evidently the scope and limits of knowledge are intimately related. Thus, if there are principles that make possible the acquisition of rich systems of knowledge and belief, then these very principles limit the class of accessible theories. Analogously, a rich set of principles of universal grammar permits us to attain our extensive knowledge of language on limited evidence, and by the same token, these principles exclude languages that violate the principles as inaccessible to the language faculty (some might be learned, with effort, application, and explicit formulation and testing of hypotheses, by means of other faculties of mind).

It is conceivable that we might discover the principles that underlie the construction of intelligible theories, thus arriving at a kind of "universal grammar" of scientific theories. And by analyzing these principles, we might determine certain properties of the class of accessible theories. We might then raise the following question: What is the relation between the class of humanly accessible theories and the class of true theories? It is possible that the intersection of these classes is quite small, that few true theories are accessible. There is no evolutionary argument to the contrary. Nor is there any reason to accept the traditional doctrine, as expressed by Descartes, that human reason is a "universal instrument which can serve for all contingencies." Rather, it is a specific biological system, with its potentialities and associated limitations. It may turn out to have been a lucky accident that the intersection is not null. There is no particular reason to suppose that the science-forming capacities of humans or their mathematical abilities permit them to conceive of theories approximating the truth in every (or any) domain, or to gain insight into the laws of nature. It might turn out, for example, that inquiry into what humans do and why lies beyond human competence, though a science of human nature could in principle be constructed by a biological organism with different qualities of mind. A pessimistic conclusion, some might feel, but not necessarily false.

Similar questions can be raised with regard to the arts. Certain conditions on the choice and arrangement of linguistic expressions characterize literary genres intelligible to humans, with aesthetic value for humans; others do not. Not every way of organizing sounds is a humanly accessible system of music. In these and many other domains, a certain range of possibilities has been explored to create structures of marvelous intricacy, while others are never considered, or if explored, lead to the production of work that does not conform to normal human capacities. Just why this should be so, we do not really know. Perhaps these questions are, nevertheless, amenable to inquiry modeled on the study of those few cognitive systems that have yielded at least a few of their secrets.

As Marshall Edelson has recently pointed out in some extremely interesting studies, Freud raised similar questions in his classic work. Edelson suggests that in making "explicit the operations by which a dream—a symptom, a joke, a myth, a work of art—is constructed," Freud made "one of his greatest contributions to psychoanalysis as a science of semiology."[27] A dream, in Freud's view, is "nothing other than a particular *form* of thinking" created by principles that he calls "the dream-work," which constitute "the essence of dreaming—the explanation of its particular nature." He posed the task "of investigating

the relations between the manifest content of dreams and the la-
tent dream-thoughts, and of tracing out the processes by which
the latter have been changed into the former. . . . the dream-
content seems like a transcript of the dream-thoughts into another mode of expression, whose characters and syntactic laws it
is our business to discover by comparing the original and the
translation."[28] It is tempting to draw an analogy here to rules of
grammar, which relate various levels of linguistic representation. One would not expect to find the same representations and
the same principles of "transcription" in such different "forms of
thinking" as dreams and normal use of language, but it is not at
all unreasonable, I think, to search for a more abstract relationship between the two systems, as Edelson does in pursuing
Freud's intriguing suggestions. I think he is quite right to
suggest this as a proper approach to "a science of semiology for
understanding works of the mind of man as apparently disparate
as poetry, music, metaphor, and the psychoanalyst's interpretation."[29]

Such a "science of semiology" may not lie very far beyond
the horizons of current inquiry. There has, of course, been very
distinguished and suggestive work in several of the domains that
might fall within a general theory of symbolic function, some of
it consciously related to ideas on the structure of human language,[30] and some attempts at a general synthesis.[31] One might
hope to relate this work to somewhat comparable studies on visual processing—for example, on the analytic systems involved
in identification of three-dimensional objects under various
conditions.[32] Perhaps it may be possible to sketch the bare outlines of a general cognitive psychology that will attempt to determine the structural properties of specific "mental organs" and
their modes of integration, and to propose biological universals

governing these systems, thus laying the foundations for a significant theory of human learning in various domains. Conceivably, the full range of questions on the nature of function, structure, physical basis, and development in the individual and the species may be open to investigation in coming years, for various components of the human mind. With the dramatic successes of the biological sciences in the past generation, it is perhaps not too much to hope that some of the classical questions concerning the nature of the human mind and its products may also be assimilated to the general body of natural science in the years that lie ahead.

Notes

1. Mind and Body

1. Quine identifies "mind" with "behavioural disposition, and *mostly* verbal." W. V. O. Quine, "Mind and Verbal Dispositions," in Samuel Guttenplan, ed., *Mind and Language* (London: Oxford University Press, 1975), p. 94. The "dispositional" approach to mind seems to me very wide of the mark, quite apart from the virtual identification of mind and language, for reasons I've discussed in detail elsewhere. See my *Reflections on Language* (New York: Pantheon, 1975), and references cited there.

2. Cf. *Reflections on Language*, ch. 1. A number of the points that I will briefly mention are discussed in more detail with specific references there.

3. For discussion of this matter see my paper "Knowledge of Language," in Keith Gunderson, ed., *Language, Mind, and Knowledge* (Minneapolis: University of Minnesota Press, 1975). See also Jonathan Rée's acute observation on the consequences of Descartes's broadened concept of thinking: Descartes put forth "the very significant thesis that human action and perception are more intellectual than they seem, in that they always involve thinking, ideas or mind; and hence that they are built on structures not wholly different from those involved in what the Platonistic theory would call intellectual knowledge." Rée, *Descartes* (New York: Pica Press, 1975), p. 98.

4. For some discussion of related notions, see Arthur C. Danto and Sidney Morgenbesser, "Character and Free Will," *Journal of Philosophy* (1957), 54: 502.

5. Compare, for example, two critical appraisals: "he has the [first-order] capacity to swim across the lake, but refuses to try"; "he has the [second-order] capacity to swim across the lake, but refuses to learn how." We might think of the second-order capacity of normal children still lacking appropriate experience to swim or speak Italian as first-order capacities to attain the mental or

physical state that would permit the exercise of the first-order capacities to swim or speak Italian. That is, as their minds and bodies are presently constituted, placed under appropriate external conditions they are able to (or for some cases just *will*) attain these states.

6. I have occasionally been surprised to read that I believe this. See, e.g., Emily Hahn, *Look Who's Talking!* (New York: Crowell, 1978), p. 136: "Like Descartes, as [Donald] Griffin says, Chomsky implies, if he doesn't assert outright, that animals are machines." Since the inadequacies of Cartesian mechanism have been familiar for centuries, it is difficult to see why anyone should assume that animals are Cartesian automata. Surely I do not.

7. See my *Language and Mind* (New York: Harcourt Brace Jovanovich, 1968; extended edition, 1972), p. 98, for further remarks. Page references below are to the 1972 edition.

8. *Principles of Philosophy*, Principle XLI, in Elizabeth S. Haldane and G. R. T. Ross, *The Philosophical Works of Descartes* (Dover, 1955), 1:235. Rée argues that the "main thesis" of Descartes's later philosophy is that "there are no mysteries which it is impossible for human beings to understand"—what he calls Descartes's "humanistic theory of knowledge" (pp. 145–46). He draws the conclusion from the assumption that Descartes's later philosophy placed no limits on inquiry into essences. The assumption is dubious (see, e.g., p. 23, below) and the conclusion in any event does not follow from it.

9. The Principle quoted is perhaps a bit ambiguous, however, as to whether we actually know the matter to be incomprehensible or rather might find that this is so. If the latter, then it is not stronger than what I have been saying, in this regard.

10. Cited in René Descartes, *Treatise of Man* Thomas Steele Hall, ed., (Cambridge: Harvard University Press, 1972), p. 104, note 150, from L. de La Forge, *Traitté de l'esprit de l'homme* (1661).

11. For further discussion, see my *For Reasons of State* (New York: Pantheon, 1973), ch. 9.

12. Cf. *Reflections on Language*, ch. 4, for some discussion. Also chapter 6, below.

13. Stephen Weinberg, "The Forces of Nature," *Bulletin* of the American Academy of Arts and Sciences (January 1976), 29(4):28–29.

14. It might be argued that the convergence is not mere chance, but results from evolutionary factors. This appears to have been Peirce's view, but it cannot be sustained. See my *Language and Mind*, p. 97.

15. For a detailed discussion, see Maurice Clavelin, *The Natural Philoso-*

phy of Galileo: Essays on the Origins and Formation of Classical Mechanics (Cambridge: MIT Press, 1974), part 2, ch. 5, pp. 224ff. For discussion of similar issues, see Imre Lakatos, "Falsification and the Methodology of Scientific Research Programmes," in I. Lakatos and A. Musgrave, eds., Criticism and the Growth of Knowledge (London: Cambridge University Press, 1970); for example, his discussion of Prout's law. For an intriguing study of related issues, see Paul Feyerabend, Against Method (Atlantic Highlands, N.J.: Humanities Press, 1975).

16. Richard Rorty, "Language, Philosophy, and 'the death of meaning'," the Machette Lecture, Brooklyn College, May 1977.

17. Jonathan Lear, "Going Native," Daedalus (Fall 1978), 177–78. See also Hilary Putnam, the John Locke Lectures, 1976, in Meaning and the Moral Sciences (London: Routledge & Kegan Paul, 1978), pp. 49–50.

18. Lear does assert that "Language is learned by public promptings and encouragements to respond to publicly observable circumstances," a factual claim that is not true in general so far as is known and would add nothing of substance to the argument if it were true.

19. Stephen Kosslyn, Image and Mind, forthcoming, and references cited there.

20. Putnam, p. 74. Putnam argues that if "we sometimes match pictures to the situations we are in," thus using mental images, there cannot be a theory of what we are doing at all, "even an 'unconscious' one," and that this conclusion holds more broadly for psychology. That seems a completely unwarranted conclusion. The passage is obscure, but this appears to be its import.

21. To avoid possible confusion, let me stress again that positing "interior mental objects" does not imply the existence of non-physical entities, as I am using these terms.

22. See W. V. O. Quine, "Methodological Reflections on Current Linguistic Theory," in Donald Davidson and Gilbert Harman, eds., Semantics of Natural Language (New York: Humanities Press, 1972).

23. Putnam, p. 49.

24. Cf. Reflections on Language, pp. 179–204.

25. Quine writes that "this indeterminacy of translation is unsuspected in mentalistic semantics," and he offers some reasons for this alleged fact. "Mind and Verbal Dispositions," p. 90. see also his "Reply to Chomsky," in D. Davidson and J. Hintikka, eds., Words and Objections: Essays on the Work of W. V. Quine (Dordrecht: Reidel, 1969). To my knowledge, the advocates of "mentalism" in semantics or elsewhere whom Quine seems to have in mind do not reject the thesis but regard it as obvious and unimportant. At

least this has always been my expressed view. Elsewhere, Quine has offered a significant critique of specific versions of mentalistic semantics. But this is a different matter entirely.

26. By the "indeterminacy thesis" I mean the thesis that whatever evidence we may accumulate in support of some hypothesis, there always exist alternative hypotheses inconsistent with ours but compatible with the evidence. The conclusion that there is, therefore, "no fact of the matter" is what seems entirely unwarranted, particularly if one is unwilling to draw the same conclusion for physics on the same grounds.

27. Putnam, p. 50, his emphasis. The reference to "equivalent descriptions" is misleading. Surely there are pairs of equivalent descriptions, but also, more to the point, there are sets of non-equivalent descriptions compatible with all available evidence, a fact which is commonly ignored only in the sense that it is too obvious to deserve comment.

28. Donald Hockney, "The Bifurcation of Scientific Theories and Indeterminacy of Translation," *Philosophy of Science* (1975), 42(4):411–27.

29. Putnam, pp. 70, 76. Actually, he says that "a certain version of scientism in the social sciences collapses right here." The content of the reservation is not clear.

30. Putnam's statement that we would need a "huge psychological theory," and several of the other comments quoted here, imply that such a theory is possible in principle, which is inconsistent with his conclusions cited above.

31. References from Putnam, pp. 64–65, 70–73.

32. *Ibid.*, p. 51.

33. With the qualification of note 27. In this injunction, Putnam appears to be rejecting the bifurcation thesis and placing physics and psychology (including linguistics) on a par. In both areas, theory is underdetermined by evidence; in neither does this fact lead to the conclusion that "there is no fact of the matter."

34. *Ibid.*, p. 41. Putnam happens to be talking about translation, specifically, but as the remark just quoted indicates, as well as the context throughout, the argument is held to apply generally to all of linguistics and presumably to psychological description as well.

35. Putnam perhaps thinks otherwise. He writes that it is the responsibility of "physicalists" to show that his "substantive metaphysical theory" of correctness in linguistics, cited above, is inadequate. This is again an illegitimate recourse to a bifurcation thesis unless he were to take the same attitude with regard to realism (or "physicalism") in the natural sciences. But he does not do so. In the case of the natural sciences, he sees the issues as relating to convergence in science and other such matters.

36. Putnam's discussion seems to assume this, though perhaps Quine would reject it, or deny that it has sense.

37. *Principles of Philosophy*, Principle CCIV, Haldane and Ross, p. 300; their interpolation.

38. *Aspects of the Theory of Syntax* (Cambridge: MIT Press,, 1965), p. 3.

39. Roy Edgley, "Innate ideas," in G. N. A. Vesey, ed., *Knowledge and Necessity*, Royal Institute of Philosophy Lectures, vol. 3, 1968–69, (London: Macmillan, 1970), p. 31.

40. I will return to a qualification of this comment in chapter 3.

41. Richmond Thomason, ed., *Formal Philosophy* (New Haven, Conn.: Yale University Press, 1974).

42. "Rules for the Direction of the Mind," Rule VIII, Haldane and Ross, p. 26.

43. "The Passions of the Soul," Article XLVII, *ibid.*, p. 353; "Meditation VI," *ibid.*, p. 196.

44. For a recent discussion, see Michael Williams, *Groundless Belief* (New Haven, Conn.: Yale University Press, 1977).

45. Arthur Schopenhauer, *On The Fourfold Root of the Principle of Sufficient Reason* (La Salle, Ill.: Open Court, 1974), p. 109.

46. V. H. Denenberg, J. Garbanati, G. Sherman, D. A. Yutzey, R. Kaplan, "Infantile Stimulation Induces Brain Lateralization in Rats," *Science* (September 1978), 201(22):1150–51.

47. Harry J. Jerison exploits this fact as one part of an argument that the exigencies of communication were not the primary factors responsible for the evolution of the language faculty. See his "Discussion Paper: The Paleoneurology of Language," in S. R. Harnad, H. D. Stéklis, and J. Lancaster, eds., *Origins and Evolution of Language and Speech*, New York Academy of Sciences, *Annals* (1976), 280. See also his "Paleoneurology and the Evolution of Mind," *Scientific American* (January 1976).

48. Charles Adam and Paul Tannery, eds., *Oeuvres de Descartes* (Paris, 1897 to 1913), 6:85. My translation.

49. "Reply to Objections V," in Haldane and Ross, 2:227–28.

50. See chapter 6, p. 247, below.

51. For discussion, see my *Cartesian Linguistics* (New York: Harper & Row, 1966), part 4; and *Reflections on Language*, ch. 1. One of the examples that Descartes uses is face recognition: ". . . when we look at a piece of paper on which little strokes have been drawn with ink to represent a man's face . . . the idea produced in us . . . is not so much that of the lines of the sketch as of the man. But this could not have happened unless the human face had been known to us by other means, and we had been more accus-

tomed to think of it than of these minute lines, which indeed we often fail to distinguish from each other when they are moved to a slightly greater distance away from us." See reference of note 49. Face recognition appears to be a "right hemisphere" task involving neural structures that mature rather late, perhaps about age ten or beyond. There has been considerable study of the task of recognizing objects on the basis of partial sketches. Performance tends to be impaired more by right hemisphere than left hemisphere lesions, and there are individual differences. Thus artists tend to do much better than others. Whether the differences result from experience or are innate, perhaps a factor in career choice, is unknown. On some cross-cultural and cross-group differences, see Andrea Lee Thompson, Joseph E. Bogen, John F. Marsh, "Cultural Hemisphericity: Evidence from Cognitive Tests," *International Journal of Neuroscience*, forthcoming, and references cited there.

Note that to sharpen the discussion, we should distinguish between the role of intrinsic structures in perception, on the one hand, and in the growth and development of cognitive structures, on the other. In each of these two distinct cases, we can discern applications of the argument from poverty of the stimulus.

52. Edgley, p. 9.

53. David Hume, A *Treatise of Human Nature*, Book I, Part IV, section 6; (London: Everyman's Library, J. M. Dent & Sons Ltd., 1911), 1:239–40.

54. Edgley, p. 10. I do not mean to suggest that Edgley disagrees. Thus he points out that even "a *tabula rasa* is not without structure; its structure is such that it receives information without adding to it" (p. 18). But I think he is wrong in thinking that Descartes's alternative is therefore "trivial" or "ludicrous." Rather, he has misidentified the issue, which is at heart an empirical one (in our terms) as to the nature of the mind's structure.

55. It is not to the point that Descartes thought of the argument as conclusive, since this was only true in the sense in which he regarded his conclusions about the physical world as necessarily true. On this matter, see Gerd Buchdahl, *Metaphysics and the Philosophy of Science* (Cambridge : MIT Press, 1969), ch. 3. See also Buchdahl's discussion of the concept of "innate ideas" in Cartesian philosophy. For a discussion of similar questions in the context of language acquisition, see my *Cartesian Linguistics*, part 4.

56. Note that I am assuming here one of the two interpretations of Descartes mentioned earlier, pp. 30–31.

57. See Otto Koehler, "The Ability of Birds to 'Count'," reprinted in J. R. Newman, ed., *The World of Mathematics*, New York: Simon and Schuster, 1956), 1, from the *Bulletin of Animal Behavior*, 9. Note that if it were discov-

ered that some other organism had something like "the number faculty," this would in any event not bear on the question of whether it is intrinsic to the human mind.

58. David H. Hubel, "Vision and the Brain," *Bulletin* of the American Academy of Arts and Sciences, (April 1978), 31(7):28.

59. Gina Bari Kolata, "Primate Neurobiology: Neurosurgery with Fetuses," *Science* (3 March 1978), 199:960–61, citing Edward Taub.

60. For a review of some relevant work, see Colin Blakemore, "Developmental Factors in the Formation of Feature Extracting Neurons," in F. O. Schmitt and F. G. Worden, eds., *The Neurosciences: Third Study Program*, (Cambridge: MIT Press, 1973), pp. 105–13.

61. See *Reflections on Language*, pp. 44f., 203, for discussion.

62. Similarly, in the case of growth of physical systems, there may be some principles of growth and development that are common across a considerable range, perhaps for reasons that lie ultimately in physics. The classic work of D'Arcy Thompson comes to mind. See *On Growth and Form*, J. T. Bonner, ed. (London: Cambridge University Press, 1961) or Benoit Mandelbrot's recent work on a variety of physical systems. Cf. Benoit Mandelbrot, *Fractals: Form, Chance and Dimension* (San Francisco: W. H. Freeman, 1977). It is wrong to suggest, as I do in chapter 6, that only at the level of cellular biology would we expect to find general principles governing organ growth. I am grateful to Joseph Bogen for pointing this out. For a more accurate statement, see *Language and Mind*, p. 97.

63. Jane H. Hill and Robert B. Most, Review of Hamad, Steklis and Lancaster, *Language* (September 1978), 54(3):651–52. The authors (an anthropological linguist and cognitive psychologist) note correctly that similar arguments are commonly offered by Piagetians. They assert that "there is no question that the kinds of behaviors which can be elicited from laboratory chimpanzees . . . become more understandable if language is seen as but one manifestation of cognitive development, and not as a 'separate organ'." This is a curious argument against modularity. Since advocates of modularity, at least those they mention, believe (correctly, to my knowledge) that recent work substantiates the familiar view that even the most elementary properties of human language (say, the use of recursive embedding to generate a discrete infinity of sentences) are beyond the capacities of apes, they would agree that no concept of "language faculty" will help to make the behavior of chimpanzees more understandable. (On this matter see John Limber, "Language in Child and Chimp?," *American Psychologist* [1977], 32:280–94; Herbert Terrace, "Is Problem Solving Language?" *Journal of the Experimental Analysis of Behav-*

ior, forthcoming; and my "Human Language and Other Semiotic Systems," *Semiotica,* forthcoming.) There are other confusions in the review that are typical of much recent literature, for example, the belief that one who concludes that apes lack the capacity for human language is committed to a "discontinuity theory" (whatever that is); as are, by the same logic, those who harbor the strange belief that humans can't fly and that the mammalian eye operates differently from the insect eye. Again, this notion is widespread. For example, a panel on human language and symbolic systems of apes at the February 1978 meetings of the American Association for the Advancement of Science (AAAS) was entitled: "Emergence of Language: Continuities and Discontinuities," on the implicit assumption that lack of homology between human language and ape symbol systems entails "discontinuities" in evolution. It would be equally reasonable to entitle a program devoted to the mammalian and insect eye: "Emergence of the Mammalian Visual System: Continuities and Discontinuities." Plainly, a separate course of evolution implies nothing about "discontinuity."

2. Structures, Capacities, and Conventions

1. Philip Kitcher, "The Nativist's Dilemma," *Philosophical Quarterly,* (January 1978).

2. Thus Kitcher argues that we are not "compelled" to look for an explanation in terms of internalized grammars, and therefore proposes that we account for examples of linguistic knowledge in terms of sets of dispositions that constitute abilities. There are several problems with his argument. First, he has not succeeded in establishing that an account in terms of dispositions is even a coherent alternative, let along preferable. A second problem is that if the alternative he rejects is even possibly correct, then it is also possibly correct that the consequences that follow from adopting it are valid—in this case, that there is innate knowledge of rules and principles. Kitcher is, presumably, not simply arguing that this conclusion is incorrect in fact, but that it could not be correct. Therefore his argument is not of the right form to establish his conclusion, even if we were to accept it.

Kitcher argues that his "dispositional approach" can be "articulated into a more detailed explanation" involving mental structures, modelled on the alternative he wants to reject. He writes that "Chomsky and Katz will view the speaker as passing through a sequence of states, each of which is a state of knowledge that a particular structure is generated by the grammar; they will

suppose that the states are linked by inferential processes and that they culmi-
nate in a state of linguistic knowledge, which is then expressed in the speaker's
utterance. The rival account sees the speaker as undergoing a sequence of
states which are linked causally; this sequence culminates in a state of knowledge, expressed in the speaker's utterance." These "causal links" are to be
expressed in dispositional terms (the speaker's linguistic ability is "a set of . . .
dispositions to pass from one type of psychological state to another type of psychological state"). This account is rife with problems. To begin with, Kitcher
mistakes a proposed account of the structure of a system of knowledge for a
theory of the speaker's performance, furthermore, a theory that there is not the
slightest reason to accept, indeed, that is barely coherent (with serial processing involving "inferential" links between "states of knowledge"). Turning to
Kitcher's "rival account," note that it does not deal with the question to which
the alternative is directed; namely, what is the nature of the structure of
knowledge that enters into the capacity to use language? Rather, he presents a
rival to the completely implausible performance theory that he has constructed. His account is even more implausible than its rival, since "inferential
links" are replaced in his serial production model with "causal links" somehow
dispositionally analyzed, a step that leads into a familiar hornet's nest of difficulties relating to indeterminate action. It is difficult to extract any dilemma
for the nativist from this discussion.

3. Ludwig Wittgenstein, Zettel, G. E. M. Anscombe and G. H. von
Wright, eds. (Berkeley and Los Angeles: University of California Press, 1967),
608, 609, p. 106e. I am indebted to Anthony Kenny for bringing this passage
to my attention, and also for discussion that has helped me clarify my rather
different view of the matter. See his "Origin of the Soul" in A. J. P. Kenny,
H. C. Longuet-Higgins, J. R. Lucas, and C. H. Waddington, The Development of Mind: the Gifford Lectures 1972–73 (Edinburgh: Edinburgh University Press, 1973), for a sophisticated version of the idea that I want to reject.
Kenny defines "mind" as a second-order capacity to develop such "capacities"
as "knowledge of English," whereas I would like to say, from a different
perspective, that if regarded as a "capacity" at all, the human mind (not mind)
should be thought of as a capacity to construct certain mental structures, such
as the one which constitutes knowledge of English. For additional remarks,
see Reflections on Language, pp. 22f.

4. On this matter, see my "Some Empirical Assumptions in Modern Philosophy of Language," in S. Morgenbesser, P. Suppes and M. White, Philosophy, Science, and Method: Essays in Honor of Ernest Nagel (New York: St.

Martin's Press, 1969); and "Knowledge of Language," in K. Gunderson, ed., *Language, Mind, and Knowledge* (Minneapolis: University of Minnesota Press, 1975).

5. For discussion of similar issues, see *Reflections on Language*, ch. 1, p. 230, note 18, and references cited there.

6. See the references of chapter 1, note 3.

7. See Peter Bryant, *Perception and Understanding in Young Children: An Experimental Approach* (New York: Basic Books, 1974).

8. In this case, possession of knowledge is reflected in behavior, but we would hardly want to say that the child's knowledge consists in his capacity to distinguish normal speech from speech with noncontent elements randomly interspersed.

9. See Julius Moravcsik, "Aitia as Generative Factor in Aristotle's Philosophy," *Dialogue*, 1975; "How Do Words Get Their Meanings," Yehoshua Bar-Hillel lecture (Jerusalem, December 1977), forthcoming.

10. For discussion of the similarity, and of why I think the modern versions are seriously misleading, see *Reflections on Language*, ch. 2, pp. 46f. and notes.

11. One must, of course, be extremely cautious in inferring that a certain system (cognitive or other) is functioning at an early stage of development merely on the grounds that some elements that will later enter into it can be observed. It might be, for example, that the bulk of the work on child language acquisition, which is limited to very early stages, is not really studying language at all, in a serious sense of the term. Much has been made of the fact that symbol systems taught to apes resemble in some ways the very earliest stages of "language acquisition," from which it is concluded that the apes are showing incipient human language behavior, a conclusion which is about as forceful as the comparable claim that children are revealing the early stages of bird flight when they move their arms. In fact, the analogy probably grants too much, in that there might indeed be some similarity in musculature or even evolutionary history in the latter case. On the matter of "discontinuity," see chapter 1, note 63.

12. See Maureen Dennis and Harry A. Whitaker, "Language Acquisition Following Hemidecortication: Linguistic Superiority of the Left over Right Hemisphere," *Brain and Language* (1976), 3:404–33; Dennis, "Language Acquisition in a Single Hemisphere: Semantic Organization" (and further references cited there), in *Biological Studies of Mental Processes*, David Caplan, ed. (Cambridge: MIT Press, forthcoming). Norman Geschwind has pointed out that one must be careful in drawing conclusions concerning the inherent

properties of the two hemispheres from such cases, since cortical development in the subjects in question was not normal to begin with.

13. I am indebted to Susan Curtiss for a very interesting discussion of her work with the young women in question. See her book *Genie: A Psycholinguistic Study of a Modern-Day "Wild Child"* (New York: Academic Press, 1977).

14. See, for example, E. S. Savage-Rumbaugh, D. M. Rumbaugh and S. Boysen, "Symbolic Communication between Two Chimpanzees," *Science* (August 18, 1978), 201: 641–42.

15. See A. Velletri-Glass, M. Gazzaniga, and D. Premack, "Artificial Language Training in Global Aphasics," *Neuropsychologia* (1973), 11:95–104; II. Gardner, E. Zurif, T. Berry, and E. Baker, "Visual Communication in Aphasia," *Neuropsychologia* (1976), 14:275–292; L. Davis, and H. Gardner, "Strategies of Mastering a Visual Communication System in Aphasia," in S. R. Harnad, H. D. Steklis and J. Lancaster, eds., *Origins and Evolution of Language and Speech*, New York Academy of Sciences, *Annals* (1976), 280.

16. Arthur Schopenhauer, *On the Fourfold Root of the Principle of Sufficient Reason* (La Salle, Ill.: Open Court, 1974), p. 163.

17. See, for example, his paper "Foundations of Philosophical Pragmatics," in *Basic Problems in Methodology and Linguistics: Logic, Methodology and Philosophy of Science 5*, R. E. Butts and J. Hintikka, eds (Dordrecht: Reidel, 1977), pp. 225–242.

18. See Marion Blank, Myron Gessner and Anita Esposito, "Language Without Communication: A Case Study," mimeographed (Piscataway, N.J.: Department of Psychiatry, Rutgers Medical School, 1978).

19. For discussion of views of Strawson, Grice and Searle on these issues, see my *Reflections on Language*, ch. 2, and my paper "A Naturalistic Approach to Language and Cognition," American Psychoanalytic Association, December 1978, to appear in a collection of essays edited by Julius Moravcsik and Daniel Osherson.

20. For an enlightening account of recent research, see Jacques Mehler and Josiane Bertoncini, "Infants' Perception of Speech and Other Acoustic Stimuli," in John Morton and John Marshall, eds., *Psycholinguistic Series 2*, (Cambridge: MIT Press, 1979).

21. For discussion of these issues, see my "On the Nature of Language," in *Essays on Form and Interpretation* (Amsterdam: Elsevier North-Holland, 1977); reprinted from Harnad et al., eds. On a related issue discussed there, see Ray Jackendoff, "How to Keep Ninety from Rising," *Linguistic Inquiry*, forthcoming.

22. I use capitals to indicate the position of heavy stress.

23. Consider, e.g., Jerrold J. Katz's concerns, as in his *Semantic Theory* (New York: Harper & Row, 1972).

24. See lecture 4, pp. 166f. Dennis presents evidence that representation of focus and presupposition is a left hemisphere function, along with the computational aspects of language and aspects of word meaning that involve grammatical structure, whereas referential aspects of meaning are not specialized in this manner. See note 12, above.

25. This statement is incorrect if we understand "inductive grounding" so loosely that any element of experience (shaping or triggering) that enters into the attainment of a system of knowledge counts as "inductive grounding" for the latter, thus depriving the concept of "grounding" or the "theory of induction" of any real substance. For some discussion of the point, see the critique of Jonathan Cohen's notions of "inductive logic" and "the technique of eliminative induction" in *Reflections on Language*, pp. 204ff.

26. François Jacob, "Darwinism Reconsidered," *Le Monde* (September 6–8, 1977); translated in *Atlas* (January 1978). See also his "Evolution and Tinkering," *Science* (June 10, 1977), 196(4295):1161–66.

27. There has been much discussion about whether the terms "empiricism" and "rationalism" are properly used in this connection; I think they are, with the qualifications that have been explicit from the start, for reasons discussed in detail elsewhere. For one example, see the discussion of John Searle's critique in *Reflections on Language*, pp. 214ff., which shows, I believe, that Searle is wrong about the texts. Searle is unconvinced. In a lengthy review-article on *Reflections on Language* ("The Rules of the Language Game," *Times Literary Supplement*, September 10, 1976) he gives the following reason: "I used to think that Chomsky's misuse of the terms 'Empiricism' and 'Rationalism' (and make no mistake: it is a misuse. I checked several standard histories and encyclopedias of philosophy to see if their definition of these terms matched my definition. Without exception they did) did not really matter." This will hardly do. Plainly, whatever Searle may have found in the books he consulted, what is at stake is what appears in the work of Descartes, Hume, Leibniz, and others whose work we were discussing, and about this, he was simply mistaken, as he was in his account of what I had written.

Searle goes on to explain why he thinks that this alleged "misuse" does matter, attributing to me certain views about philosophy and ideology that are so far removed from anything I believe or expressed that comment is unnecessary. Quite apart from the misrepresentation, Searle ends up with some positions of his own that are quite remarkable, as noted by Harry Bracken, "Philosophy and Racism," *Philosophia* (November 1978), 8(2–3):241–60.

For some further discussion of the historical accuracy of the terms, see David E. Cooper, "Innateness: Old and New," *Philosophical Review* (1972), 81:465–83; and N. Chomsky and J. J. Katz, "On Innateness: A Reply to Cooper," *Philosophical Review* (1975), 84:70–87.

28. Stephen P. Stich, "Empiricism, Innateness, and Linguistic Universals," *Philosophical Studies* (1978), 33:273–85. I believe that Stich attaches too much weight to an argument based on possible common origin, for reasons discussed in *Language and Mind*, p. 86. He argues further that the strategy of opting for a grammar of a particular language that conforms to a theory of universal grammar that also yields "the best grammars" for other languages "has great potential for generating specious universals." There is a potential, though I don't agree that it is great, but it is an unavoidable contingency of rational inquiry. The goal is a theory that will explain the facts from all languages, and will go beyond this to offer a hypothesis about "possible human languages." There is no way to avoid the problem that Stich notes, exactly as there is no way of avoiding it, say, in the study of the biochemistry of life. Stich correctly points out that there are experiments that are properly excluded on ethical grounds that would have considerable force (though again, no type or amount of evidence can avoid the possibility of such theoretical error), e.g., raising children in contrived environments.

29. I have mentioned several times the curious argument that if some point is not conclusively established, then it lacks grounds entirely. To mention another example, Rée denies that Descartes presented "a serious argument" for his belief that animals lack the capacity for language on the sole grounds that Descartes "admits that this is not a *proof* that animals do not think" *Descartes* (New York: Pica Press, 1975), p. 185, note 11.

30. I will return to some criticism of this usage that does not seem to me well-founded in the next lecture. See pp. 101f., below.

31. J. A. Foster, "Meaning and Truth Theory," in Gareth Evans and John McDowell, eds., *Truth and Meaning* (London: Oxford University Press, 1976), p. 2.

32. See chapter 1, pp. 16f.

33. See chapter 5, pp. 189f., for further discussion of the analogy.

34. In J. F. M. Hunter, *Essays after Wittgenstein* (Toronto: University of Toronto Press, 1973).

35. On this matter, see C. Graves, J. J. Katz, et al., "Tacit Knowledge," *Journal of Philosophy* (1973), 70:318–30.

36. Again, the fallacy mentioned repeatedly above.

37. See *Reflections on Language*, ch. 2. There is additional work and argument on this topic that is certainly worth discussion, but I will not go into

it here. I see no reason to modify any of the conclusions reached in the cited reference. See reference of note 19, above.

38. David Lewis, "Languages and Language," in Gunderson, ed.

39. For some recent discussion, see Fred Katz and Jerrold Katz, "Is Necessity the Mother of Intension?" *The Philosophical Review* (January 1977), 86:70–96; Leonard Linsky, "Believing and Necessity," *Proceedings and Addresses of the American Philosophical Association* (1977), 50:526–30. See also reference of note 10.

40. Two grammars are said to be "weakly equivalent" if they generate the same language. See the next note.

41. Quine calls two grammars "extensionally equivalent" if they generate the same language. This is an unfortunate terminology, since a grammar, i.e., a certain set of rules, generates not only a language but also an infinite set of structural descriptions, and in fact much else (e.g., a set of rhyming pairs). A familiar and preferable terminology, widely used in the technical literature, is that a grammar "weakly generates" a language and "strongly generates" a set of structural descriptions. In the next chapter, I will turn to the question of whether we need require that a grammar weakly generate a language at all, concluding that though this is presumably the case in fact, there is no conceptual requirement to this effect.

42. Here some care is necessary. If by a "grammar" we mean simply a system of rules that generates an infinite set of expressions in some alphabet or an infinite set of sound-meaning pairings, then for any such set ("a language") there will be infinitely many grammars. If by a "grammar," however, we mean one of the systems provided by a given linguistic theory, then for some languages there may be no grammars at all, and for others there may be only finitely many (or perhaps only one) grammar. It is entirely possible that the correct linguistic theory provides only finitely many grammars for possible human languages (and no grammars for infinitely many languages), and even that the correct linguistic theory provides no grammars for the systems loosely called "languages," for reasons already briefly noted, and for other reasons to which I will return in the next lecture. In more realistic terms, the correct linguistic theory—the theory that gives a correct account of the innate language faculty—may provide only finitely many grammars (or perhaps only one grammar) associated by the principles of language development with a collection of data sufficient for language acquisition.

3. Knowledge of Grammar

1. As I have mentioned, it seems to me that this quite common view can only be maintained if we simply do not consider the properties of the cognitive systems that are developed in the mind, apart from their most superficial characteristics. For some discussion of this point, in connection with Piagetian claims, see my paper "On Cognitive Structures and Their Development," paper from a conference sponsored by The Royaumont Center for A Science of Man, Paris, October 1975; Proceedings to be published by Harvard University Press, Cambridge. Quite apart from the problem of reconciling the belief in general purpose mechanisms of Piagetian or other varieties with the properties of various cognitive systems, it would seem that the growing knowledge of specialization of particular areas of the brain for particular cognitive tasks and their distinct developmental patterns, would render such positions rather implausible. But this discussion is really beside the point in more fundamental respects in that it deals with the adequacy of proposals that really have yet to be formulated in a meaningful way, though they are widely advocated.

2. Cf. Alvin I. Goldman, "A Causal Theory of Knowing," *Journal of Philosophy* (June 22, 1967), 64(12). On the Gettier problems, see Edmund Gettier, "Is Justified True Belief Knowledge?" *Analysis* (June 1963), 23(6):121–123; and for discussion, Roderick Chisholm, *Theory of Knowledge* 2nd ed., (Englewood Cliffs, N.J.: Prentice-Hall, 1977), and many other sources.

3. Arthur Danto, "Semantical Vehicles, Understanding, and Innate Ideas," in S. Hook, ed., *Language and Philosophy* (New York: New York University Press, 1969), p. 128. Danto suggests an affinity between my view of innate ideas and that of Locke. In a general way, I do not object, and have in fact made a similar point myself, following Leibniz; cf. my *Aspects of the Theory of Syntax* (Cambridge: MIT Press, 1965), p. 49. There are a number of references in the literature to the alleged fact that I have firmly rejected a Lockean approach and also seriously misinterpreted Locke. The assumption is probably based on some reviews and commentary so fanciful that I have not felt it necessary to comment on them (but cf. *Reflections on Language*, p. 218). The fact is that I could hardly have misinterpreted Locke since I have not discussed him at all, apart from marginal and to my knowledge unchallenged references, and have nowhere rejected (nor accepted) a Lockean approach to problems of language, contrary to what is widely assumed.

4. My emphasis, John Fisher, "Knowledge of Rules," *Review of Metaphysics* (December, 1974), 28(2), a thoughtful discussion of questions at issue here.

5. *Ibid.* Fisher suggests that I have failed to distinguish adequately between knowledge and belief or to distinguish the linguist's explicit knowledge from the speaker's implicit knowledge. I am not convinced that this is true; for example, he misinterprets my discussion of a "parallel" as a claim of "identity," and there are other misconstruals. But putting aside textual questions, his own conclusions seem to me generally persuasive.

6. I am here talking for the most part about possibilities, not known facts. The questions have not been very systematically explored, to my knowledge. I am concerned here with what would count as knowledge, with the possibility of innate knowledge, for example. It is a different question whether the possibilities are realized. I suspect that they are, but it would be premature to make such a claim.

7. Chapter 1, note 39.

8. It is obvious without comment that none of this bears on central concerns of this tradition, e.g., questions of skeptical doubt.

9. Roy Edgley, "Innate ideas," in G. N. A. Vesey, ed., *Knowledge and Necessity*, Royal Institute of Philosophy Lectures, vol. 3, 1968–69 (London: Macmillan, 1970), p. 28f.

10. *Ibid.*, p. 33. This argument does not seem consistent with his principle that a knowledge claim is based on the reasons for certainty *that one has*, i.e., the actual reasons, not those one might adduce to show that the knowledge is grounded (recall his crucial distinction between one's *having* reasons and there *being* reasons, stateable or not by the person in question). Were the child both a language learner and scientist, he could (as scientist) present justifying evidence that would not constitute his reasons for certainty (as child). There is a tension here between what are sometimes called "genetic" and "analytic" accounts of knowledge. For some discussion, see Michael Williams, *Groundless Belief* (New Haven, Conn.: Yale University Press, 1977), particularly pp. 97–98; Edgley's discussion in terms of the reasons that one has for certainty is, in this sense, genetic.

11. Cited in the introduction to S. Morgenbesser, ed., *Dewey and his Critics, Journal of Philosophy*, 1977, xii.

12. Alvin I. Goldman, "Innate knowledge," in Stephen S. Stich, ed., *Innate Ideas*, (Berkeley and Los Angeles: University of California Press, 1975). For modification and further development of his views, see his paper "Discrimination and perceptual knowledge," *Journal of Philosophy*, November 18, 1976, 771–91.

13. For discussion of their views, see *Reflections on Language*, chap. 2 and 4.

14. Williams, p. 32n.

15. Keith S. Donnellan, Review of Gunderson, ed., *Language, Mind, and Knowledge* (Minneapolis: University of Minnesota Press, 1975), *Language* (1977), 53(3):720.

16. See, for example, *Reflections on Language*, pp. 222–23; "Linguistics and Philosophy," in Hook, ed., (reprinted in the extended edition of *Language and Mind*, 1972), p. 87, and also subsequent discussions there.

17. Edward Sapir, "The psychological reality of the phoneme," reprinted in English translation in D. G. Mandelbaum, ed., *Selected Writings of Edward Sapir*, (Berkeley and Los Angeles: University of California Press, 1949), from *Journal de psychologie normale et pathologique*, 1933.

I should emphasize that this reconstruction is unfair to Sapir, who used the perceptual evidence, quite properly, as additional confirmation for the psychological reality of the phonological analysis he postulated on grounds of "linguistic evidence," showing that the perceptual judgments could be explained on the basis of this analysis. This procedure is entirely proper. My reconstruction rephrases Sapir's procedure in terms of subsequent misunderstandings.

18. For example, in W. Freeman Twaddell, *On Defining the Phoneme*, *Language Monograph* no. 16, 1935.

19. "Debate" is not exactly the right word, since virtually everyone was lined up on the same side the wrong side, I am suggesting

20. For some examples, see chapter 5, below.

21. Michael Dummett, "What is a Theory of Meaning? (2)," in Gareth Evans and John McDowell, eds., *Truth and Meaning* (London: Oxford University Press, 1976), pp. 70–71.

22. *Ibid.*, pp. 71–72.

23. See p. 13, above.

24. Dummett, pp. 69, 82, 92.

25. *Ibid.*, pp. 89, 99.

26. *Ibid.*, p. 81.

27. *Ibid.*, p. 101.

28. *Ibid.*, pp. 81–82.

29. *Ibid.*, p. 88.

30. *Ibid.*, p. 111.

31. *Ibid.*, pp. 114, 132.

32. From which it would not follow, clearly, that the core notion of the theory of meaning, in Dummett's sense, should be the notion truth.

33. Dummett, p. 122.

34. "What is a Theory of Meaning?," Part 1, in Samuel Guttenplan, ed., *Mind and Language* (London: Oxford University Press, 1975), pp. 134–135.

35. In the real world of nonhomogeneous speech communities, each individual, furthermore, evidently commands a system of a different sort, perhaps best thought of in some cases as a set of similar grammars for different circumstances, or perhaps in some other way.

36. "What is a Theory of Meaning?" Part 2, p. 71.

37. More precisely, I have suggested that what we should consider, in the "Galilean style," is an idealized version of this notion; that is, the grammar that would be represented in the mind of an ideal speaker-hearer in a homogeneous speech community and the property (assumed, under a further idealization, to be a shared property of humans) that would enable such a system to arise in the mind in a homogeneous speech community. This idealized framework, I have suggested, leads us to the real property of the mind that provides the basis for an inquiry into the mixed and perhaps inconsistent systems that are in fact represented in individual minds, and the even more complex notion of "language" as something socially shared.

38. One of them, the argument that Levelt presents about unlearnability, might be interpreted as an argument that languages are necessarily recursive, since they are learned. But Levelt, as we see directly, does not seem to interpret it in this way, and since the argument is without force in any event, we can perhaps drop the question.

39. Perhaps Dummett's intuitionism would lead him to conclude that the language must be recursive. It is difficult to see what might be made of such a claim. It surely does not seem impossible a priori that a person can have the mental representation, ultimately the physical coding, of some nonrecursive set. Surely, it is not only possible but even true.

40. Hilary Putnam, "Some Issues in the Theory of Grammar," *Proceedings of Symposia in Applied Mathematics* (1961), 12, American Mathematical Society, reprinted in Putnam's collected *Philosophical Papers*, vol. 2, *Mind, Language and Reality* (London: Cambridge University Press, 1975), pp. 85–106. See section 5, pp. 102f.

41. W. J. M. Levelt, *Formal Grammars in Linguistics and Psycholinguistics*, vol. 2, *Applications in Linguistic Theory* (The Hague: Mouton, 1974), pp. 39–41. I am indebted to Howard Lasnik for calling my attention to this reference and for helpful comments. See his paper "A Note on Learnability and Theory Construction in Linguistics," mimeographed, University of California, Irvine, December 1978.

42. Note that arithmetic is learnable (though not in Levelt's technical sense

of the word), though we might want to say that it is elicited rather than taught or learned. For a very interesting study of learnability, see Kenneth Wexler and Peter W. Culicover, *Formal Principles of Language Acquisition* (Cambridge: MIT Press, forthcoming). Note that it is not necessary that human languages constitute a learnable set in their sense; hence it would be an interesting empirical discovery if this proves to be so.

43. Perhaps an infinite set, though this is not clear, and would be denied on certain current theories of universal grammar. See chapter 4, note 7.

44. As has often been noted, under the assumption of modularity the language faculty does not exhaust the capacities of the mind. Some languages might be "learnable" through the exercise of other faculties—as a puzzle, through scientific inquiry, etc.—though not learnable under the conditions that suffice for acquisition of knowledge of language by exercise of the language faculty. For discussion of some fallacies in the literature in this connection, see *Reflections on Language*, pp. 209–10.

45. See, for example, *Aspects of the Theory of Syntax*, pp. 61–62.

46. Note that in this case the class of human languages would not be "learnable" in the sense of Wexler and Culicover.

47. Stanley Peters, "On restricting deletion transformations," in M. Gross, M. Halle and M.-P. Schützenberger, eds., *The Formal Analysis of Natural Language* (The Hague: Mouton, 1973); Stanley Peters and Robert Ritchie, "On the Generative Power of Transformational Grammars," *Information Sciences* (1973), 6. The common misunderstanding is the belief that their proof that transformational grammars without some such condition as the survivor property generate all recursively enumerable sets demonstrates that "anything goes." Obviously that is untrue, as pointed out, for example, in the reference of note 45. See also Thomas Wasow, "On Constraining the Class of Transformational Languages," *Synthese*, (1978), 39:81–104.

48. We might then want to say that recursiveness is a necessary (i.e., deducible) property of human language, regarded as a biological system with fixed properties (say, the survivor property). This would amount to saying that it is a biologically necessary property of human languages.

49. For discussion of this possibility, see my paper "Questions of Form and Interpretation," reprinted in *Essays on Form and Interpretation* (Amsterdam: Elsevier North-Holland, 1977).

50. Jaakko Hintikka, "Quantifiers in Natural Languages: Some Logical Problems 2," *Linguistics and Philosophy* (1977), 1:153–72.

51. Cf. Robert C. May, *The Grammar of Quantification*, MIT Ph.D. dissertation (1977).

52. In fact, the thesis cannot be correct as it stands, as we see by considering sentences of the form "if X-any-Y, then *p*," where *p* is a tautology, so that replacement of *any* by *every* gives a logically equivalent expression. I am indebted to Lauri Carlson for this observation. The "syntactic" alternative in the text does not face this difficulty. Hintikka in fact expresses doubt as to whether logical equivalence can be identified with synonymy, surely correctly, but it remains to be seen whether the thesis can be formulated in some other terms to avoid the problem. The effort seems pointless, unless there is some reason to depart from the purely syntactic reanalysis just suggested.

53. See my "Questions of form and interpretation" for discussion of these issues.

54. What is at stake is not very clear. It is well known that a generative grammar will not generate the set of sentences that a speaker-hearer will regard as acceptable; indeed, it is virtually a criterion of adequacy that it should not, since so many different factors enter into such judgments. Furthermore, it is not at all clear, in many cases, whether deviance should be regarded as "semantic" or "syntactic," or whether there is a clear demarcation (from which it is sometimes argued that there is no difference between semantic and syntactic concepts at all, a conclusion that is surely unwarranted by the argument and seems hardly reasonable; see chapter 4, note 29). See my *Aspects of the Theory of Syntax* (Cambridge: MIT Press, 1965), ch. 4. Were Hintikka's argument to hold, we would have to make a decision as to the term "syntactically well-formed," and it is not clear that there is much import to any decision we would make.

55. For references and further discussion of traditional views with regard to accessibility to consciousness, see chapter 6, below.

56. Searle, *Times Literary Supplement,* September 10, 1976. Searle assumes that if rules "do more than describe what happens" then they must be accessible to consciousness. Evidently, these possibilities are not exhaustive; they leave out exactly the case under discussion in the book he was reviewing.

57. Steven Davis, *Philosophy and Language,* (Indianapolis: Bobbs-Merrill, 1976), pp. 78–80.

58. The point is also discussed in some detail in *Reflections on Language,* ch. 4.

59. D. C. Dennett, "Why the Law of Effect Will Not Go Away," *Journal of the Theory of Social Behaviour* (1975), 5(2), citing Herbert Simon, in the latter quote. Reprinted in D. C. Dennett, *Brainstorms,* Bradford, 1978.

60. Niels Kaj Jerne, "Antibodies and Learning: Selection versus Instruction," in G. C. Quarton, T. Melnechuk and F. O. Schmitt, eds., *The Neuro-*

sciences: A Study Program (New York: Rockefeller University Press, pp. 200–05. Note that Jerne's alternatives are not exhaustive. One can, for example, imagine processes that combine elements of selection and instruction in his sense, and abduction does not fall within either category.

61. One might think of the change in this case as *in accord with* certain principles rather than as based on internal representation of these principles, as in some of the examples already discussed; thus as analogous to the noncognizing missile that acts in accord with laws governing the orbit of the moon rather than the cognizing missile that computes its trajectory by reference to a representation of these laws. In contrast, a non-Darwinian theory that explained the change by attributing to the moths calculations concerning the changing color of the wall, some principles concerning the birds, control over modification of their own color, etc., would be analogous to the cognizing missile which makes use of internal representations.

62. For further discussion of these matters, see *Reflections on Language*, ch. 1, 4; and chapter 6, below.

63. There is, in fact, evidence that voluntary action is necessary for perceptual systems to function in their normal way. This has been demonstrated in the case of accommodation to distorted environments by the work of Richard Held and others. Piaget has emphasized similar factors in his studies.

64. On this matter, see Julius Moravcsik, "Understanding," *Dialectica* (1979).

4. Some Elements of Grammar

1. For general discussion of the theory of representations and rules that I have in mind, see my *Logical Structure of Linguistic Theory* New York; (Plenum, 1975; actually written in 1955–56; the 1975 introduction gives some of the background). For a much improved version of the theory of phrase structure representation and transformational mapping developed there, see Howard Lasnik and Joseph J. Kupin, "A Restrictive Theory of Transformational Grammar," *Theoretical Linguistics*, (1977), 4(3):173–96. This approach allows for phrase-markers not represented in familiar tree-diagrams, and in particular, for an approach to coordinated structures that retains some of the properties of what were called "generalized transformations" in work of the 1950s, an approach that deserves serious consideration, I believe.

2. Possibly fewer; it might be argued that "to do" or even "is it easy" are words.

3. I use the device of labeled bracketing in the conventional way: paired

brackets enclose a phrase of the category indicated by the label of the leftmost bracket. Note that the representation given in (2) offers one of two possible interpretations of the sentence, associating *today* with *is* rather than *do* and thus resolving an ambiguity. The base structure should be further ramified. Note that the NP in the most deeply-embedded S is lexically unspecified, a matter to which I will return.

4. On this topic, see Ray Jackendoff, $\overline{X}$ *Syntax: A Study of Phrase Structure, Linguistic Inquiry Monograph 2,* (Cambridge; MIT Press, 1977), and references cited there; see also several papers in P. Culicover, T. Wasow and A. Akmajian, eds., *Formal Syntax* (New York: Academic Press, 1977) among many other contributions.

5. On the topics discussed here, see my *Reflections on Language* (New York: Pantheon, 1975), ch. 3; and several papers in my *Essays on Form and Interpretation.* Also papers in Culicover, Wasow, and Akmajian, eds., and also "Recent Transformational Studies in European Languages," *Linguistic Inquiry Monograph 3,* S. J. Keyser, ed., (Cambridge: MIT Press 1978); and much additional work that carries the study of these questions beyond the point that I can discuss here. For some more informal discussion of some of the questions that arise below, see Noam Chomsky and Mitsou Ronat, *Language and Responsibility* (New York: Pantheon, 1979).

6. Think of *e* as the identity element of the system of representation, regarded as a concatenation algebra with further structure. See *Logical Structure of Linguistic Theory* and my paper "On *wh*-movement" in Culicover, Wasow and Akmajian, eds., for further discussion. Again, details are omitted.

7. If a picture of this sort is correct in essence, then it is easy to imagine ways to fill in the various gaps in such a way as to yield the conclusion that there are only a finite number of possible grammars.

8. I say "would arise" rather than "did arise" because in fact, phrase structure grammars and transformational grammars were developed as models of generative grammar at the same time and in complementary fashion. That is, phrase structure grammars were devised (on the rough model of constituent analysis procedures in structural linguistics) for two basic purposes: one, because of their appropriateness for the theory of the base; two, as part of a negative argument showing their inadequacy, hence the necessity for rules of a transformational character. Actually, the earliest generative grammar in the modern sense of the word was neither a phrase structure nor a transformational grammar but rather a system somewhat like a phrase structure grammar but with indices to express properties that are not properly indicated in phrase structure rules; see my *Morphophonemics of Modern Hebrew,* 1949–51 (New

York: Garland, 1979). See the 1975 introduction to *Logical Structure of Linguistic Theory* for further discussion of the backgrounds.

9. See my paper "Conditions on Transformations," written in 1970, in *Essays on Form and Interpretation*, section 17; also the final remarks in "Conditions on Rules of Grammar," in the same volume. For a penetrating discussion of the issues, see Jan Koster, *Locality Principles in Syntax* (Dordrecht: Foris Publications, 1978).

10. One might nevertheless argue that full lexical insertion, including phonological and morphological properties of words, takes place at the level of S-structure, along lines that have been suggested by Carlos Otero, "The Dictionary in a Generative Grammar," mimeographed paper, UCLA, Los Angeles, 1976; and Hans den Besten, "Surface Lexicalization and Trace Theory," in H. van Riemsdijk, ed., *Green Ideas Blown Up*, University of Amsterdam, Publikaties van het Instituut voor Algemene Taalwetenschap, no. 13, 1976.

11. If phrase structure representations are taken to be sets of strings in the sense of the remarks on p. 143 and note 1, then an idiom rule simply adds a string to the phrase-marker. See Lasnik and Kupin.

12. For further discussion of this matter, see my *Studies on Semantics in Generative Grammar*, ch. 3 (The Hague: Mouton, 1972), and "The Amherst Lectures," lectures given at the 1974 Linguistic Institute, University of Massachusetts, Amherst, June 1974; Université de Paris VII, Département de recherches linguistiques.

13. There may be principled reasons for the distinction among idioms in this regard, in part at least, in which case it need not be specified by the idiom rule. Cf. Robert Fiengo, *Semantic Conditions on Surface Structure*, MIT Ph.D. dissertation (1974).

14. In the case of idioms, we naturally expect and indeed find some variation in judgment, and probably recourse to analogic processes of a poorly understood sort. But however judgments may vary with regard to specific items, there is, it seems, a fixed and important asymmetry: there are idioms that are taken as grammatical under movement but not in such structures as "NP is easy to V—," but not conversely. Correspondingly, there is good empirical motivation, I believe, for regarding passive and raising-to-subject as involving the rule "Move NP" (an instance of "Move α"), while rejecting a rule that forms "John is easy to please" by movement from "—is easy to please John." See "On *wh*-movement" and references cited there for discussion. The point is debated, but I think that these conclusions are correct. Note that a similar distinction holds, as would be expected on the assumptions just put forth, for existentials. Thus the two sentences "it is hard to believe John to be a fool"

and "it is hard to believe there to be unicorns in the garden" are parallel in structure, but "John is hard to believe to be a fool" is quite different in status from "there are hard to believe to be unicorns in the garden," even though "there" can be raised, as in "there seem to be unicorns in the garden."

To spell out the argument further, suppose that instead of postulating a movement rule to account for "John seems to be regarded as a fool" and an interpretive rule for "John is hard to believe to be a fool" (as the range of syntactic evidence suggests), we were to base-generate the two S-structures and postulate two different kinds of interpretive rule (in the former case, an interpretive rule with essentially the properties of cyclic movement rules). Then the question would arise: why is the idiomatic interpretation associated with the interpretive rule that has the property of the movement rules, rather than with both, or neither, or only the other kind of interpretive rule? This property follows at once from the assumption that idioms are specified at an independent D-structure level.

15. Consider, for example, the two sentences "they expected that pictures of each other would be on sale," "who did they expect that pictures of would be on sale." The latter is ungrammatical, the former grammatical. The distinction might be explained on the assumption that movement rules meet a strong "locality condition" (called "subjacency" in the references cited) that does not apply to rules of interpretation such as the rule that finds the antecedent for *each other* in the grammatical example. There is, I believe, some evidence to support this view; see the references cited above. If S-structures are generated directly, we will have two types of interpretive rule, one which has the properties of movement rules. If indeed we find rules of these two types, it becomes quite unclear whether the alternative of generating S-structures directly is a substantive alternative to a theory that involves movement rules. For a different approach to these questions, see Koster.

16. Thus I disagree with the conclusion of Langendoen, among others, that one of these two answers (namely, direct base-generation of S-structures) "will be a significant departure not only from [the standard theory] and [the extended standard theory], but also from the entire grammatical tradition . . . in which the distinction between deep and surface structure in syntax is taken to be fundamental." D. Terence Langendoen, "Review of *Essays on Form and Interpretation*," *Journal of Philosophy* (1978), 270–79. What he overlooks is the abstract character of S-structure and the fact that base-generation of S-structure adds new interpretive rules that have much the character of transformational rules. Note further that under either of these two alternatives, the

mapping from S-structure to surface structure involves many of the rules that have been regarded as part of the transformational component in earlier work: e.g., deletion rules, stylistic rules of various sorts, and possibly others; the proper way to partition these remains a debated question. Similarly, the mapping from S-structure to LF appears to involve transformational movement rules; e.g., the quantifier rule discussed earlier or the rule for embedded *wh*-phrases discussed in my paper "Conditions on Transformations."

Once again, the real issues have been confused by variations in terminology over the years. Thus, what I have here been calling "S-structure" is called "surface structure" in the book that Langendoen is reviewing and other work of the period, though the concept is quite different from the notion of "surface structure" that appeared in earlier work, and that I am using again here.

17. For a fairly recent exposition, see Jerrold J. Katz, *Semantic Theory* (New York: Harper & Row, 1972).

18. I borrow here from work of Ray Dougherty, Paul Postal and others. There is a substantial literature since the mid-1960s in support of the conclusion reiterated here. See the sources cited in notes 4 and 5 for further references.

19. Note that if we adopt the alternative just discussed and assume base-generated S-structures, the question dissolves. In fact, the only way to save the standard theory is to render it near-vacuous, so it appears.

20. The same seems true of other question-phrases, e.g., "how many pictures of five children did everyone see" as compared with "everyone saw several pictures of five children." These examples involve sufficiently many factors so that other directions might be pursued for explaining the distinction; perhaps questions of definiteness, in some cases at least.

21. Thomas G. Bever, Jerrold J. Katz, D. Terence Langendoen, *An Integrated Theory of Linguistic Ability* (New York: Crowell, 1976), introduction. See also the paper by Katz in the same volume: "Global Rules and Surface Structure Interpretation."

Others also seem to think that some fundamental issue is at stake. Thus Searle, *Times Literary Supplement*, Sept. 10, 1976, writes that what I am here calling "S-structure interpretation" (as presented in the same form though with different terminology in *Reflections on Language*) "confirms a retreat from positions for which Chomsky was once famous," namely D-structure interpretation. The question is why this is a "retreat" rather than an "advance," or simply a change. The answer can only be that some important position must have been abandoned; what it might be, Searle does not indicate. But that is a serious misunderstanding, perhaps relating to some confusion over misleading connotations of the word "deep" and "surface" discussed in *Reflections on Language*, pp. 82f.

22. The contrary claim is made by Bever, Katz and Langendoen and reiterated several times by Katz in his contribution to the volume just cited, but no argument is offered. There are good arguments against globality, to which Katz refers, but they simply do not apply in this case, since the so-called "extended standard theory," which takes into account both deep and surface structures for semantic interpretation, provides no further latitude beyond the standard theory, as inspection of these theories shows. Perhaps the term "extended standard theory" (EST) has been misleading; the change from the standard theory to EST is a revision, not an extension in the sense that Katz, et al., seem to have in mind. For the same reason, his remarks about what he calls "the revised extended standard theory" are beside the point.

23. This remains true if we consider a version of EST that maps paired deep and surface structure to semantic representation, or if we take only abstract S-structures to undergo this mapping, or if interpretive rules of a transformational character relate abstract base-generated S-structure to logical form. Bever, Katz and Langendoen again offer no argument for their belief to the contrary.

24. There has been much discussion of this issue in the past several years, which I will not review here. One question of some interest, first raised by Elisabeth O. Selkirk, *The Phrase Phonology of English and French*, MIT Ph.D. dissertation (1972), is whether the trace of wh-movement blocks contraction while others do not. Suppose that this turns out to be true. There is good reason to believe that the trace of *wh*-movement differs from the trace of NP-movement in other respects, and both types of movement differ in important ways from movement of V and other categories. Specifically the trace of *wh*-movement corresponds to a variable bound by a quasi-quantifier in logical form, which is not the case for other traces. A number of ways to express this difference have been proposed. See, among others, David Lightfoot, "On Traces and Conditions on Rules," in Culicover, Wasow and Akmajian, eds. Within the framework of my "On Binding" (MIT, January 1978; forthcoming in *Linguistic Inquiry*), the trace of *wh*-movement is marked for abstract Case whereas the trace left by other applications of the rule "Move α" is not, for reasons relating to the quantifier-variable structure in LF. Since the distinction is marked in S-structure, in this framework, it is available for the phonological rules. It might be, for example, that trace without Case is optionally deleted by convention prior to contraction. What is at stake is the precise char-

acterization of "contiguity," not the validity of the explanation for the facts in terms of trace theory. The question is interesting, but not really relevant here.

25. See the references of note 5 and many papers in the technical literature, among them Robert Fiengo, "On Trace Theory," *Linguistic Inquiry*, (Winter 1977), 8(1), and N. Chomsky and H. Lasnik, "Filters and Control," *Linguistic Inquiry* (Summer 1977), 8(3). Much of this "syntactic" evidence has to do with what I have been calling "the syntax of LF," if the approach in "On Binding" is correct.

26. I will speak freely of "coreference" and "non-coreference," but, as is obvious, what must be understood is something like "intended coreference" and "intended non-coreference." Grammar can tell us nothing about actual reference; e.g., it cannot guarantee that there is more than one object in the world, so that non-coreference is even possible. We may think of the term "coreference" here as referring to a syntactic association of two NPs that is a factor in their ultimate interpretation.

27. For discussion of this special property and related matters, see my *Essays on Form and Interpretation*, ch. 4, and for discussion of some simpler examples, *Reflections on Language*, ch. 3. See these sources for reference to earlier work by Paul Postal and Thomas Wasow that provided the basis for the reanalysis proposed in this discussion. For a substantial improvement over the theory presented in these sources, see James Higginbotham, "Pronouns and Bound Variables," in R. Vago, ed., *NELS IX*, CUNYForum, vol. 5–6, City University of New York, forthcoming.

28. Barbara Partee, "Montague Grammar and Transformational Grammar," *Linguistic Inquiry*, (Spring 1975), 6:203–300. See also her paper, "Some Transformational Extensions of Montague Grammar," in Robert Rodman, ed., *Papers in Montague Grammar*, Occasional Papers in Linguistics, no. 2 UCLA, Los Angeles (September 1972).

29. What Partee's attitude is towards this issue is unclear to me. In the work cited in note 28, she writes that "the principle of a one-one correspondence between syntactic and semantic rules" imposes so strong a constraint on grammar "that I think it is a serious open question whether natural languages can be so described." She presents a version of this principle as a "fundamental assumption in Montague's approach" (which she is elaborating) and argues that it leads to the solution of problems that remain open under other approaches. It is difficult to see how this principle can impose a strong empirical constraint, or any kind of constraint, unless it is possible to make at least some pre-theoretic distinction between syntactic and semantic rules, or at least between some notions of syntax and semantics. In "Questions of Form

and Interpretation," I argued that the example Partee offered to illustrate how this principle could solve open problems led, rather, to the conclusion that syntactic and semantic rules were not correlated in the way she regarded as crucial for the approach she was outlining. In response, Partee took the position that there is no way (perhaps apart from phonetics) to establish a pretheoretical distinction between what I called "core notions of semantics" such as "synonymous" and "denotes," on the one hand, and syntactic notions such as "precedes" on the other; "Comments on C. J. Fillmore's and N. Chomsky's Papers," in R. Austerlitz, ed., *The Scope of American Linguistics*, (Lisse: Peter de Ridder Press, 1975), where "Questions on Form and Interpretation" originally appeared. Then it would seem to follow that the fundamental and very strong empirical assumption cited above is in fact vacuous. Quite apart from this, it seems an odd conclusion that we cannot make a pretheoretic distinction between semantics and syntax at least clear enough to place "synonymous" and "denotes" on one side and "precedes" on the other.

30. Similarly, consideration of the relation of the representation to other systems (e.g., consideration of articulation, perception, semantic interpretation, etc.) might yield evidence bearing on the choice among representational systems that cannot be empirically distinguished in terms of descriptive power.

31. The point is not that these facts are strictly inconsistent with Montague's theory. In fact, one might incorporate the generalizations in a version of Montague's theory of quantifiers by first converting his notation to the standard quantifier-variable notation, and then applying the rules to the latter. Whether this proposal can be made consistent with Montague grammar I do not know, but even if the answer is positive, it does not really bear on the current point, which is that it is the quantifier-variable notation that is appropriate for LF, and that it can be derived directly from S-structure, without any intermediate steps of the sort required by Montague's "proper theory of quantifiers," which can therefore be eliminated without loss, it appears. The point is of some interest, in that the quantifier theory is really the only basis offered for the belief that semantic and syntactic rules correspond in the way that Montague proposed.

32. See "Questions of Form and Interpretation," in *Essays on Form and Interpretation*, for discussion of proposals of Partee's to this effect. As pointed out in note 29, above, her response seems to me to undercut her original proposal even more completely than the counter-evidence does. Note that her interpretation of Montague grammar is quite different from Thomason's (cf. p. 29, above).

33. See *Essays on Form and Interpretation*, ch. 4, for discussion of FOCUS,

and Michael S. Rochemont, A *Theory of Stylistic Rules in English*, University of Massachusetts, Amherst, Ph.D. dissertation (1978), for a contrary interpretation. I will not explore the issue further here. As in the other cases discussed, I am not attempting here to pursue the empirical issues in detail, but rather to show how empirical evidence may bear on the question of the real nature of rules and representations in a cognitive system.

34. See Howard Lasnik, "Remarks on Coreference," *Linguistic Analysis* (1976), 2:1–22; and from a different point of view, Gareth Evans, "Pronouns, Quantifiers, and Relative Clauses (1)," *Canadian Journal of Philosophy* (September 1977), 7:467–536.

35. See Laverne Jeanne, *Aspects of Hopi Grammar*, MIT Ph.D. dissertation (1978).

36. Cf. Higginbotham.

37. See Tanya Reinhart, *The Syntactic Domain of Anaphora*, MIT Ph.D. dissertation (1976), extending and modifying earlier work referred to there, specifically, Lasnik. This work derives from an important paper by Ronald Langacker, "On Pronominalization and the Chain of Command," in D. Reibel and S. Schane, eds., *Modern Studies in English*, (Englewood Cliffs, N.J.: Prentice-Hall, 1969).

38. For further elaboration, see my paper "On Opacity" in S. Greenbaum, G. Leech, and J. Svartvik, eds., *Studies in English Linguistics: For Randolph Quirk*, (London: Longman Group Ltd., forthcoming); "On Binding."

39. In standard English, though not in all dialects, *for* must delete when it immediately precedes *to*; thus we do not have the expected· "Bill came over for to give bones to the dog." See "Filters and Control."

40. For further discussion see the appendix of "On Binding." Note that the embedded clauses are interpretable as purposives, as in (32) and (33), rather than as infinitival relatives, as we can see, e.g., from "Mary bought Rover to give to John," etc.

41. Similarly, "it is unclear who to visit" (cf. (21), (23)) cannot mean that it is unclear for which person *x*, *x* is to visit someone, as should be possible if the empty NP object of "it is unclear [who [t to visit NP]]" can be moved to the COMP position, filled by *who*.

42. Notice that these considerations interact with the theory of movement, which permits successive cyclic movement from exactly the two positions that are not opaque, namely, the COMP position and position of subject of an infinitive. See "On Binding" for discussion. There are further ramifications and complications that I will not enter into here. Note also that essentially the same configuration that appears in the examples illustrating opacity is found in

cases involving disjoint reference (e.g., "Mary expected her to win," "Mary expected John to visit her," "Mary expected that she would vote for Carter"; only the pronominal subject of the embedded infinitive is necessarily noncoreferential to *Mary*). See "On Binding" for extension of the notion "free" to accommodate these cases.

43. See "On Binding," appendix.

44. For some intriguing discussion of this question, see Lawrence Solan, "On the Interpretation of Missing Complement NP's," mimeographed, University of Massachusetts, Amherst (January 1977).

45. For example, Luigi Rizzi has shown that a rather complex array of facts of Italian, partially distinct from their analogues in English, follow from the choice of S̄ rather than S (as in standard English) as the domain to which movement rules are restricted under the locality (subjacency) principle. See Rizzi, "Violations of the W*h* Island Constraint in Italian and the Subjacency Condition," *Montreal Working Papers in Linguistics*, Colette Dubisson, David Lightfoot, and Yves Charles Morin, eds. (December 1978), 2:155–90. Similar facts have since been observed in a number of other languages, including French, Hebrew, Russian, Norwegian, and certain English dialects, which, however, differ in interesting ways with regard to some of the other relevant parameters.

46. See my paper, "Some Empirical Assumptions in Modern Philosophy of Language" (see chapter 2, note 4). See also David Premack and Guy Woodruff, "Does the Chimpanzee Have a Theory of Mind?" in *The Behaviorial and Brain Sciences*, Special issue on Cognition and Consciousness in nonhuman species (London: Cambridge University Press, 1978), and "Chimpanzee Problem-Solving: A Test for Comprehension," *Science* (November 3, 1978), 202:532–35 for some observations suggesting that apes, while lacking the language faculty, may nevertheless command a conceptual system that enables them to attribute intentions such as "pursuing a goal" to humans in a task situation.

5. On the Biological Basis of Language Capacities

1. This and the following quotations are from Eric H. Lenneberg, *Biological Foundations of Language* (New York: Wiley, 1967), pp. 393–94.

2. The analogy is modeled on an account given by John N. Bahcall and Raymond Davis, Jr., "Solar Neutrinos: A Scientific Puzzle," *Science* (1976), 191:254–57.

3. I think, incidentally, that the explanation outlined is essentially correct,

but that does not matter with respect to the point at issue. For discussion, see my "On Wh-movement," in P. W. Culicover, T. Wasow, and A. Akmajian, eds., *Formal Syntax* (New York: Academic Press, 1977). Note that the sentences identified here as ungrammatical vary somewhat in acceptability and that there are also dialect differences. See also chapter 4, note 45, above.

4. John R. Ross, *Constraints on Variables in Syntax*, MIT Ph.D. dissertation (1967).

5. Assume here a conventional representation of phrase-makers, with a string between paired brackets assigned to the category labelling the bracket. Thus in (10) the phrase *to play sonatas on* is categorized as an S (sentence); *a violin to play sonatas on* as an NP (noun phrase); etc. Other bracketing is omitted here and below for simplicity of exposition.

6. Take *t* to be the "trace" left by movement of *which* from the position where *t* appears in (12), in accordance with the trace theory of movement rules; cf. my *Reflections on Language* (New York: Pantheon, 1975) and "On Cognitive Structures and Their Development," *Proceedings of the Royaumont Conference on Phylogenetic and Ontogenetic Models of Development* (1975), to be published by Harvard University Press, Cambridge, and references cited there. Take PRO to be an abstract "pronominal" form, which can perhaps be regarded as an "uncontrolled trace"; cf. "On Wh-movement" for discussion. See lecture 4, above, for discussion of the status of such "empty NPs."

7. See my *Current Issues in Linguistic Theory* (The Hague: Mouton, 1964), for some comments.

8. Cf. Rudolf P. Botha, *The Justification of Linguistic Hypotheses: A Study of Nondemonstrative Inference in Transformational Grammar* (The Hague: Mouton, 1973), and James W. Ney, "The Decade of Private Knowledge: Linguistics from the Early 60s to the Early 70s," *Historiographia Linguistica* (1975), II.

9. To avoid a possible confusion, recall here that we are considering the problem of discovery of linguistic theory and of particular grammar, two enterprises that go hand in hand. Given a linguistic theory, it should be possible for the grammar to be determined merely from the kind of primary linguistic data available to the child. If linguistic theory (universal grammar) is understood along these lines, as a function mapping experience into the final state attained, then linguistic theory must provide a "discovery procedure" for grammar from a corpus (along with whatever else is essential for the language learner). Each child provides an existence proof. For discussion and an outline of a possible theory of this general sort, see my *The Logical Structure of Linguistic Theory* (1955; published New York: Plenum, 1975). Note that the

"discovery procedure" outlined is radically different in character from the step-by-step analytic procedures proposed as discovery procedures in work of the 1940s and 1950s.

10. See my "On Wh-movement" for discussion.

11. Walter Kintsch, with E. J. Crothers, G. Glass, J. M. Keenan, G. McKoon, and D. Monk, *The Representation of Meaning in Memory* (New York: Wiley, 1974).

12. There are, however, many problems with his account; for example, the discussion of definite and indefinite description on p. 48, or the account of quantificational structure a few pages later. But where the discussion is coherent, it makes use of representations of the sort assumed in one or another competence model, and develops the kinds of arguments that might be used in connection with representation of linguistic competence and the process systems in which they find their place.

13. For detailed discussion of the views of several contemporary philosophers, see my *Language and Mind* (New York: Harcourt Brace Jovanovich 1968; extended edition, 1972) and *Reflections on Language*, and references cited therein.

14. David B. Peizer and David L. Olmsted, "Modules of Grammar Acquisition," *Language* (1969), 45:note 1.

15. Jean Piaget, "La Psychogenèse des connaissances et sa signification epistémologique," *Proceedings of the Royaumont Conference on Phylogenetic and Ontogenetic Models of Development* (1975).

16. B. Inhelder, H. Sinclair, and M. Bovet, *Learning and the Development of Cognition* (Cambridge: Harvard University Press, 1974).

17. Inhelder, et al. attribute to "rationalist psycholinguists" the view that "linguistic competence" and "cognitive structure" are hereditary. Presumably by "linguistic competence" they mean what these psycholinguists call "universal grammar." Surely no one holds "linguistic competence"—for example, knowledge of English—to be hereditary. Similar remarks may be made about cognitive structure. What has been proposed is that specific properties or conditions on cognitive structures attained are hereditary.

18. Inhelder, et al., p. 10.

19. A. R. Luria, "Scientific Perspectives and Philosophical Dead Ends in Modern Linguistics," *Cognition* (1975), 3.

20. Throughout the discussion, Luria mistakenly identifies "universal grammar" and "deep structure." There are other misinterpretations of this sort, but they are easily corrected. The point he is making is clear.

21. See, for example, Jacques Monod, *Le Hasard et la nécessité* (Paris: Edi-

tions du Seuil, 1970). For reference and comment, see my *Problems of Knowledge and Freedom* (New York: Pantheon, 1971), pp. 11f.; François Jacob, *The Logic of Life*, (New York: Pantheon, 1973), p. 322; Salvador E. Luria, *Life: the Unfinished Experiment* (New York: Scribners, 1973), pp. 137f.; Gunther Stent, "Limits to the Scientific Understanding of Man," *Science* (1975), 187:1052–57.

22. P. Grobstein and K. L. Chow, "Receptive Field Development and Individual Experience," *Science* (1975), 190:352–58.

23. Lenneberg, p. 302.

6. Language and Unconscious Knowledge

1. S. Weinberg, "The Forces of Nature," *Bulletin of the American Academy of Arts and Sciences* (January 1976), 28.

2. Karl Marx, *Capital*, (New York: International Publishers, 1967), vol. 1, p. 10.

3. Marx, *Capital*, vol. 3, p. 814.

4. For discussion, see my *Aspects of the Theory of Syntax* (Cambridge: MIT Press, 1965).

5. David Rapaport, "The Theory of Ego Autonomy," in *The Collected Papers of David Rapaport*, M. M. Gill, ed. (New York: Basic Books, 1967). I am indebted to Dr. Joseph Smith for calling my attention to this interesting study. Rapaport contrasts a "Berkeleian view of man," in which "the outside world is the creation of man's imagination," with the "Cartesian Humian world view," which, "admitting no guarantees of man's autonomy from his environment, makes him virtually a slave of it" (pp. 722–23, 726). He notes that the sketch of the opposing positions is oversimplified; but in fact, the actual views of Descartes and Hume, at least, seem very remote from what Rapaport describes, in my opinion.

6. *Ibid.*, pp. 726–27.

7. *Ibid.*, pp. 740–41.

8. For discussion, see L. Wittgenstein, *Philosophical Investigations* (London: Blackwell, 1953); J. Austin, *How to Do Things with Words* (Oxford: Oxford University Press, 1962); J. Searle, *Speech Acts* (London: Cambridge University Press, 1969).

9. For some discussion of Cudworth's perceptive comments on cognitive psychology as related to questions under discussion here, see my *Cartesian Linguistics* (New York: Harper & Row, 1966) and *Reflections on Language* (New York: Pantheon, 1975).

10. For my own views on this subject, see *Reflections on Language* and *Essays on Form and Interpretation* (Amsterdam: Elsevier, 1977). Also chapter 4, above, and references to more recent work cited there.

11. P. Grobstein and K. L. Chow, "Receptive Field Development and Individual Experience," *Science* (1975), 190:356.

12. See Jean Piaget, *Structuralism* (New York: Basic Books, 1970). Also, Piaget's contributions to the *Proceedings of the Royaumont Conference on Phylogenetic and Ontogenetic Models of Development* (1975). Also, B. Inhelder, H. Sinclair, and M. Bovet, *Learning and the Development of Cognition.* (Cambridge; Harvard University Press, 1974).

13. For a discussion of often overlooked complexities in Descartes's views, see G. Buchdahl, *Metaphysics and the Philosophy of Science* (Cambridge: MIT Press, 1969).

14. See Isaiah Berlin, *Vico and Herder* (New York: Viking, 1976), for a very illuminating study.

15. Freud's complex views on accessibility of the unconscious require a far more serious examination than I can attempt here. At some points, he seems to deny accessibility. The clearest example I have found is in the final section of *The Interpretation of Dreams* (vol. 5 of *Standard Edition of the Complete Psychological Works,* London: Hogarth, 1953–64), where he distinguishes the *Ucs.* (unconscious), which is "*inadmissible to consciousness,*" from the *Pcs.* (preconscious), with excitations that "are able to reach consciousness" (pp. 614–15; his italics). Thus there are systems that "can never be accessible to our psychical perception" (p. 611). But the question is whether by "accessible" (or "inadmissible") Freud has in mind accessibility in principle or accessibility in fact, given other contingencies. My impression is that only the latter interpretation is consistent with his general view. Thus in the same work (p. 541), he emphasizes that the *Ucs.* "has no access to consciousness *except via the preconscious,* in passing through which its excitatory process is obliged to submit to modifications" (his italics), which implies accessibility in principle. Elsewhere, Freud discusses ways "in which something that is in itself unconscious becomes preconscious" (*The Ego and the Id,* vol. 19, p. 21), implying again accessibility in principle. In *Moses and Monotheism* (vol. 23), he again defines *Pcs.* as what is "capable of being conscious" (p. 96), so that *Ucs.* is incapable of being conscious; but it is evident from the context that "capable" must mean "capable in fact" or "easy of access," since he goes on at once to argue that "unconscious processes in the id are raised to the level of the preconscious" and that "Thought-processes, and whatever may be analo-

gous to them in the id, are in themselves unconscious and obtain access to consciousness . . ." (pp. 96–97).

The same interpretation seems to me appropriate for the discussion in *An Outline of Psycho-Analysis*, vol. 23. Here *Pcs.* is "preferably described as 'capable of becoming conscious,' " that is, as "Everything unconscious . . . that can thus *easily* exchange the unconscious state for the conscious one" (pp. 159–60; my italics). He reserves "the name of the unconscious proper" for "psychical processes and psychical material which have no such *easy access* to becoming conscious . . ." (p. 160; my italics). His basic principle is this: "What is preconscious becomes conscious . . . without any assistance from us; *what is unconscious can, through our efforts, be made conscious,*" with effort that "varies in magnitude" as "resistance" varies (p. 160; my italics). "The inside of the ego, which comprises above all the thought-processes, has the quality of being preconscious," that is, "having access to consciousness" (p. 162). As for the "contents of the id," a portion thereof can be "raised to the preconscious state" and thus "incorporated into the ego" (*Moses and Monotheism*, pp. 96–97). And more generally, "The core of our being, then, is formed by the obscure id, which has no direct communication with the external world and is accessible even to our own knowledge only through the medium of another agency" (*Outline of Psycho-Analysis*, p. 197). That is, it too is accessible in principle, though generally inaccessible.

It seems to me, then, that a consistent interpretation requires that we take Freud's observations on inaccessibility to be denying "easy access" but not access in principle.

I am again indebted to Joseph Smith for bringing many relevant passages to my attention, but I do not want to imply that he agrees with this interpretation. See his editor's note to *Psychoanalysis and Language*, in *Psychiatry and the Humanities*, vol. 3 (1978), where this article originally appeared, for a detailed discussion of the differences in interpretation.

16. Cited by Berlin, p. 20, from *De Antiquissima*.

17. Cited by Howard C. Warren, *A History of the Association Psychology from Hartley to Lewes*, Johns Hopkins University Ph.D. dissertation, 1917; (New York: Scribner's, 1921), p. 23.

18. *Ibid.*, pp. 54–55.

19. *Ibid.*

20. Cited in glossary, C. G. Jung, *Memories, Dreams and Reflections*, recorded and edited by A. Jaffé (New York: Vintage, 1965).

21. *Ibid.*, p. 348.

22. I. Kant, *Critique of Pure Reason*, transl. by N. K. Smith (London: Macmillan, 1963), p. 142n.

23. David Hartley, cited by Warren, p. 8.

24. D. Hume, *A Treatise of Human Nature* (1738) (New York: Dutton, 1961), vol. 1, p. 156.

25. *Ibid.*, pp. 13–14.

26. *Ibid.*, p. 65.

27. Marshall Edelson, "Language and Dreams: *The Interpretation of Dreams* Revisited." *Psychoanalytic Study of the Child* (1972) 27:249.

28. *Ibid.*

29. *Ibid.*, p. 206. Cf. Edelson's further development of these themes in his *Language and Interpretation in Psychoanalysis* (New Haven: Yale University Press, 1975).

30. For example, Leonard Bernstein, *The Unanswered Question* (Cambridge: Harvard University Press, 1976); Ray Jackendoff and Fred Lerdahl, *The Formal Theory of Tonal Music* (forthcoming). See also Nelson Goodman, *Languages of Art* (Indianapolis: Bobbs-Merrill, 1968).

31. Cf. Dan Sperber, *Rethinking Symbolism* (Cambridge: Cambridge University Press, 1975); Thomas A. Sebeok, "Semiotics: A Survey of the State of the Art," in T. A. Sebeok, ed., *Current Trends in Linguistics*, vol. 12 (The Hague: Mouton, 1974); and his "The Semiotic Web: A Chronicle of Prejudices," mimeographed, (Bloomington: Indiana University Press, 1975); also, Umberto Eco, *A Theory of Semiotics* (Bloomington: Indiana University Press, 1976).

32. For a report on very promising recent research, see David Marr and T. Poggio, "From Understanding Computation to Understanding Neural Circuitry," Artificial Intelligence Laboratory, Memo 357, MIT (May 1976).

Index

298

298